Moving With a Purpose

Developing Programs for Preschoolers of All Abilities

Renée M. McCall, MSEd
Adapted Physical Educator
North Syracuse Early Education Program

Diane H. Craft, PhD
Department of Physical Education
State University of New York, College at Cortland

Human Kinetics

Library of Congress Cataloging-in-Publication Data

McCall, Renee M., 1958-
   Moving with a purpose: developing programs for preschoolers of all abilities / Renee M. McCall, Diane H. Craft.
      p. cm.
   Includes bibliographical references and index.
   ISBN: 0-88011-976-4
   1. Movement education. 2. Education, Preschool–Activity programs. I. Craft, Diane H., 1950- II.Title.

   GV452 .M33 2000

ISBN: 0-88011-976-4

Acquisitions Editor: Scott Wikgren; **Developmental Editor:** Katy M. Patterson; **Assistant Editor:** Amanda S. Ewing; **Copyeditor:** Denelle Eknes; **Proofreader:** Kathy Bennett; **Indexer:** Craig S. Brown; **Permission Manager:** Heather Munson; **Graphic Designer:** Nancy Rasmus; **Graphic Artist:** Kimberly Maxey; **Art Manager:** Craig Newsom; **Cover Designer:** Jack W. Davis; **Photographer (cover and interior):** John Miller; **Illustrator:** Roberto Sabas; **Printer:** Versa Press

Printed in the United States of America   10 9 8 7 6 5 4 3 2

Human Kinetics
Web site: www.HumanKinetics.com

United States: Human Kinetics, P.O. Box 5076, Champaign, IL 61825-5076
800-747-4457
e-mail: humank@hkusa.com

Canada: Human Kinetics, 475 Devonshire Road, Unit 100, Windsor, ON N8Y 2L5
800-465-7301 (in Canada only)
e-mail: orders@hkcanada.com

Europe: Human Kinetics, 107 Bradford Road, Stanningley
Leeds LS28 6AT, United Kingdom
+44 (0) 113 255 5665
e-mail: hk@hkeurope.com

Australia: Human Kinetics, 57A Price Avenue, Lower Mitcham, South Australia 5062
08 8277 1555
e-mail: liahka@senet.com.au

New Zealand: Human Kinetics, P.O. Box 105-231, Auckland Central
09-523-3462
e-mail: hkp@ihug.co.nz

To my daughter Katie.
You are my inspiration and the motivation that
enables me to make dreams a reality. I love you.

—*Renée M. McCall*

To Michele Duca and all preschool teachers like her
everywhere who share their love with young children and
work so very hard to help them learn.

—*Diane H. Craft*

Contents

Game Finder

Curricular Goals

Listing of Learning Experiences	Page number	Body part identification	Cardiovascular endurance	Spatial relationships	Locomotor skills	Motor planning	Muscular strength and endurance	Object, color, shape recognition	Object control	Stability	Recreational equipment	Holiday themes
Balance, Let's	48					✔				✔		
Basketball With Water Balloons	51								✔			
Big on Balloons	53	✔							✔			
Body Bowling	55	✔				✔				✔		
Bubble Fun	57				✔				✔	✔		
Cage Ball Fun	59						✔			✔		
Catching, Throwing, and Kicking; Let's Get	61								✔			
Climbing, Let's Get	64				✔	✔						
Frisbee Toss	66								✔			
Garbage Clean Up	68								✔			
Gutter Ball	70					✔			✔	✔		
Hand-Over-Hand Pull	72						✔					
Heart Power	74	✔	✔									
Jumping, Let's Get	75				✔							
Mat Maze	77				✔	✔						✔
Match the Valentine	79				✔			✔				✔
Mountains and Valleys	81					✔				✔		
Move and Seek	83				✔			✔				✔
Musical Hoops	85		✔		✔	✔						

(continued)

Curricular Goals

Listing of Learning Experiences	Page number	Body part identification	Cardiovascular endurance	Spatial relationships	Locomotor skills	Motor planning	Muscular strength and endurance	Object, color, shape recognition	Object control	Stability	Recreational Equipment	Holiday themes
Stickers on the Body Part	**118**	✔			✔							
Stop and Go to Music	**120**				✔	✔						✔
Striking, Let's Get	**122**								✔			
Superstars Challenge	**124**				✔	✔						
Swings	**126**						✔				✔	
Tag games introduction	**128**											
Tag—Goldilocks and the Three Bears	**128**		✔		✔							
Tag—Imagination	**130**		✔		✔							✔
Tag—I'm the Man From Mars	**131**		✔		✔							
Tag—Match	**132**		✔		✔			✔				✔
Tag—Midnight	**134**		✔		✔							
Tag—Toothbrush	**135**		✔		✔							
Tag—Vegetable Soup	**136**		✔		✔							
Tire Play	**138**			✔			✔					
Tricycle Course	**140**						✔				✔	✔
Tunnel Course	**142**		✔			✔						
Turtle Races	**144**			✔	✔							
Zip Line	**146**						✔					

Preface

Have you ever wondered why young children appear to be always moving? It seems that nature has given them an appetite for large muscle movement that they can scarcely satisfy. Watch a playground full of preschool children. They love to move—to run, jump, twist, reach, slide, turn, and wiggle!

Three- to five-year-old children move so much because movement is vital to their development at this time in their lives. Movement enhances every aspect of the preschool child's growth and development. Through movement, children's brains develop, their bones and muscles develop, and their positive feelings about themselves develop. These active children are busy creating a foundation of fitness and fundamental movement skills that they will build on to become proficient movers throughout the rest of their lives.

It would be easy for teachers if free play on the playground offered every child all the movement experiences needed for optimal growth and development, but children need to have many varied opportunities to experiment and explore through different movements. Simply letting them play on the playground does not provide all these necessary opportunities. Children must have instruction in movement to develop optimally and to be the best movers they can be.

Although preparation in physical education is ideal, it is our belief that preschool teachers, regardless of circumstances, can learn how, when, and where to provide this necessary instruction in movement for young children. Teachers will be able to develop movement programs that give consideration to their experience, class size, space limitations, and time constraints. This book will help teachers design movement programs for all preschool children, including those with special needs.

The purpose of this book is to provide the information teachers with varying prior experiences need to teach movement programs to all preschool children in a variety of settings—because kids gotta move!

We designed this book to assist teachers and parents working in different settings with preschool children of all abilities. We wrote it with three audiences in mind: preschool teachers in child care centers; early childhood educators and physical educators in school-based preschool programs; and teachers and parents in any preschool or home setting that includes young children with special needs. Part I provides straightforward information on why it is important to teach movement, followed by an explanation of how to teach movement to preschool children using a child-centered approach. It concludes with what to teach in the movement program, based on observing the children move. We wrote in a manner that does not require prior experience in teaching movement programs or prior knowledge of physical education.

Part II is the heart of this book. More than 50 games and activities form the movement experiences through which the children learn. We offer suggestions for linking these learning experiences to goals for children. Part III builds on the first two parts, including further information for developing a movement program interesting to early childhood educators and physical educators working in school-based preschool programs. This part explains children's motor development and links this information to curriculum development. It also offers ideas for working with toddlers. It concludes with ideas for promoting movement programs.

Part IV focuses on children with special needs and examines how to meet their physical education needs through implementing comprehensive special education programs. We review special education regulations pertaining to physical education programs. Teachers who understand special education regulations and the implementation process can use their knowledge to obtain needed services for the children they teach. The focus of this part of the book is on situations teachers encounter when working in integrated preschool centers that serve children of all abilities. We introduce special education law and explain the special education process. We offer ideas for writing the gross motor section of an Individualized Education Program (IEP) and explain the team approach to special education. The final chapter emphasizes the importance of developing mutual trust and respect between parents and teachers. With this powerful alliance, wonderful things can happen for children!

Acknowledgments

Thank you to my parents for their never ending support and ability to drop everything and come watch Katie during many periods of writing this book. I can only say how much I love you. Thank you also to my sister whose encouraging phone calls and cards were such a help when the days were getting really long. I also wish to thank my coauthor Diane. You are a great friend and colleague. Thank you to my principal, Kathi Esposito, for her continued support of the adapted physical education department and her leadership in maintaining such a quality early education program. And, thank you to Sookie Kayne and Diane Chermak, two talented people who share some of their knowledge in this book. Thanks for all you do for me and the children. Finally, thank you to all my coworkers at the early education program, who make coming to work each day such a joy.

—Renée McCall

I wish to also thank my coauthor and friend Renée, whose unflagging, positive attitude has made writing this book a joy. I wish to thank my husband Craig Smith, for the countless days you set aside what you were doing to share your thoughts with me, and for caring for our children so many, many evenings and weekends while I was writing. Finally, thank you to my children, Laura and David, for giving me the time to write. I love you, Craig, Laura, and David.

—Diane Craft

We appreciate the skillful help from everyone at Human Kinetics. In particular, we would like to thank Scott Wikgren, acquisitions editor, for his enthusiastic support of this book since its inception; Katy Patterson, developmental editor, for her friendly cooperation and masterful skill in turning the manuscript into a book, assisted by Amanda Ewing and Heather Munson; and Nancy Rasmus who created the book's graphic design. It has been a pleasure to work with each of you. We also wish to thank the following individuals for their thorough and helpful reviews of the manuscript: Karen Paciorek, Sookie Kayne, Kathi Esposito, Cathy Houston-Wilson, Nina Schwartz, Joanne Wickman, along with Elin Pantas and Amber Bonham-DeLarm of the Cortland Child Development Program.

We wish to thank Craig Smith for his editorial insight and continual feedback. Your contribution to this book was invaluable. In addition, thank you to Diane Chermak, for all your special efforts. We also appreciate the assistance of John Miller of North Syracuse, NY, our photographer and friend. You did a great job!

Credits

Figure 4.1 (a-c) – figure 4.6 (a-c) Reprinted, by permission, from B.A. McClenaghan and D.L. Gallahue, 1978, *Fundamental movement: A developmental and remedial approach* (Philadelphia: W.B. Saunders), 88-99.

Figure 7.2 Reprinted, by permission, from S.L. Kasser, 1995, *Inclusive games: Movement fun for everyone!* (Champaign, IL: Human Kinetics), 10-11.

Figure 10.1 Reprinted, by permission, from Diane M. Chermak.

Figure 10.2 Reprinted, by permission, from Diane M. Chermak.

Box 11.1 Adapted, by permission, from Mary I. King and Dale King.

Box 14.2 Reprinted, by permission, from J.G. Coleman, 1999, *The early intervention dictionary*, 2d ed. (Bethesda, MD: Woodbine House).

Box 15.2 Reprinted with permission of author. © 1987 Emily Perl Kingsley. All rights reserved.

Box 15.4 Adapted, by permission, from Lori M. Davis.

Part I
Offering a Preschool Movement Program

Part I is written for everyone interested in offering movement in their preschool program. We wrote it to cover the basics needed to lead children through the learning experiences presented in part II. Part I is designed for easy reading by those without prior experience instructing physical education or early childhood education. It also provides a solid background for those professionals responsible for developing and directing a movement program.

We present why we believe movement instruction is so critical for the optimal development of young children. Next, we recommend what children need to learn in a movement program along with the child-centered approach to instruction. Finally, we offer an easy method of recognizing and recording a child's movement skills.

Why Movement Is So Important for Young Children

Children move to be happy, to express themselves, to develop their bodies, their intellects, and their motor skills. Children learn about themselves and their environment through movement. Children learn to move more skillfully through movement. And they become healthier through movement. Learning gross motor movement skills and activities is a vital part of every young child's developmental process.

McCall and Craft's
Movement Program Mission Statement

Most days Elizabeth is up, moving, and enjoying life as a 12-year-old. She plays basketball—not the best on the team, but she plays well enough to get the thrill of being part of the game. She hikes, invigorated instead of exhausted by the experience. Weekdays after school she will often relax by putting on music and dancing with abandon around the living room. She loves movement and seeks opportunities to move. She thinks it helps her feel better and keeps her alert as she does her schoolwork. Elizabeth is comfortable with how she feels about herself. Today she is sledding, exerting the effort to pull the sled up the hill and experiencing the exhilaration of sledding downhill.

Ann, also 12 and a lifelong friend of Elizabeth, watches the sledding from the car. Most days Ann just sits, watching others move. Even though she is physically able to do the activities, she avoids sports, dancing, hiking, and most other physical activities because she doesn't feel comfortable with herself. When asked to participate in a physical activity, she says, "No, thank you, I don't know how to do that." She doesn't see herself as a person who enjoys movement—she never has.

It seems that Elizabeth has always been moving. Her parents talked about the importance of physical activity but were rarely active themselves. It was her preschool teacher who took an interest in Elizabeth's physical activity. Elizabeth's teacher, though not a physical educator, understood the importance of movement and offered Elizabeth and all the children in the class many joyful experiences moving throughout the preschool years. Elizabeth's love of movement extended through her childhood years, during which she continued to be active because she felt successful.

Unlike Elizabeth, Ann did not experience movement instruction when she was a young child. Her parents and preschool teacher were uncomfortable with physical activity. During her critical formative years, no one in Ann's life did much to get her moving. Now let's go many years into the future. At age 60, Elizabeth is active, walking most mornings to work and biking with her grandchildren on the weekends. Her friend Ann, however, continues the pattern of inactivity she began at a young age. Ann enjoys watching sports, but never participates. She avoids walking at every opportunity. She even drives her car a few hundred yards to the corner convenience store. Over years of chosen inactivity her muscle tone has decreased. She is twice as likely to experience serious chronic diseases as her active friend Elizabeth, but after a lifetime of inactivity, she is unlikely to start moving now.

This chapter presents the case that movement is essential for the best growth and development of the whole child. Although children need free play to develop their movement skills, they also need instruction to become optimum movers (Avery, Boos, Chepko, and Gabbard, 1994). Teachers can help children learn movement by using the information contained throughout this book.

Why Children Need to Move

Research and experience suggest that movement helps children grow intellectually, emotionally, and physically and has an impact on their future health.

Movement helps children's brains develop, as Hannaford explains (Pica, 1998).

"Beginning in infancy and continuing throughout our lives, physical movement plays an essential role in creating nerve cell networks that are the essence of learning," and in studies where children spent extra time in daily physical activity, they showed a higher level of academic success.

In addition to helping brains develop, movement helps children feel good about themselves.

"The improved self-concept that results from a carefully planned progression of successful movement activities may be the greatest contribution that physical education can offer the education process" (Sherrill, 1993).

Movement helps develop children's bones and muscles, balance, agility, reaction time, and overall coordination. Growing children who are successful in movement will use what they learn about movement to learn new movements. So if they don't learn how to balance as young children, they are unlikely to want to take ballet classes as six-year-olds. If they don't learn how to run, they are unlikely to play tag with the neighborhood children after school. If they don't learn how to catch, they are unlikely to want to play ball with friends on the school yard. If they don't learn how to jump, they are unlikely to join their friends jumping rope at recess.

Plus, growing children gradually gain the freedom to choose to be physically active or physically inactive. As teenagers, they will choose whether they want to play sports, or hike, or swim at the town pool, or shoot baskets in the driveway. As mature adults the health consequences of their lifetime choices to be physically active or inactive will have an impact on their health that becomes increasingly pronounced. Those adults who do not feel comfortable moving, perhaps because they never learned the fundamental movement skills as young children, are at much greater risk of developing health problems due to their choice to remain physically inactive.

> **Meaningful movement programs are those that allow children to learn movement skills based on sound physical education principles in an interesting, organized manner.**

Children Need Instruction in Movement

Children need many movement opportunities during the first years of life as they strive to become proficient movers. This period of motor development is so critical in a child's life that one who has not mastered fundamental movement skills during preschool years is at a disadvantage. "The critical time for the development of motor skills is between eighteen and sixty months of age" (Charlesworth, 1992). The child who has not developed most mature patterns by age five needs special help.

Instruction in movement is necessary for preschoolers to become skillful movers. The goal is to have preschool children master a set of fundamental skills that will form a foundation for more complex skills the children will learn as they mature. Free play alone is insufficient for preschoolers to become skillful movers for a variety of reasons:

- Many preschoolers, when left on their own, may not get sufficient opportunities to move. Our culture is evolving away from physical activity toward a sedentary lifestyle. Fifty years ago most children came home from school and spent much of their afternoons outside playing. Now many children stay inside after school, in their own home or in a child care provider's home, for safety and supervision. Watching television and videos, and for older children, playing video and computer games, are seductive alternatives to the physical activities favored by the children of 50 years ago. Research suggests that a slight increase in physical activity contributes to significant improvement in coordination and endurance capability (Krause and Richter, 1998). Therefore, it is very important that children be physically active.

- Preschool children respond to the environments in which they find themselves. On a playground with standard equipment and adult supervision, but little adult educational interaction, children will participate in familiar and fun activities. They will not benefit from the variety and depth of movement experiences a meaningful movement program could bring to them.

Meaningful Movement Programs

Meaningful movement programs are those that allow children to learn movement skills based on sound physical education principles in an interesting, organized manner. They include all children, regardless of their abilities. These programs are not restricted by space or time limitations existing preschool environments impose. You can help children improve their motor skills, using games and activities in this book to develop your own meaningful movement programs.

Meaningful motor programs focus on children *learning* movement skills rather than just keeping them happy, active, and good. Preschoolers learn optimally by exploring and experimenting with movement. Teaching by encouraging children to learn through using their natural instincts to explore and experiment is called a child-centered approach. In theory, the teacher provides environments designed for learning, and children make decisions as to what part of a particular learning environment they want to explore. The teacher's role is to facilitate the child's learning of the task the child has chosen. To facilitate learning among preschoolers, using a child-centered approach is considered very appropriate because it complements young children's natural interest in exploration and experimentation as their preferred methods of learning. A majority of learning experiences found in part II of this book are designed to work well within a child-centered approach.

A prepared teacher who exudes loving, enthusiastic, positive energy while working with children is an essential ingredient to their success. The learning experiences compiled in this book, as well developed as they are, will only succeed for the children when they experience them within the framework of enthusiasm and love that a considerate teacher provides. Such positive energy can go a long way toward compensating for any lack of professional preparation or experience in teaching movement programs, and no amount of preparation can compensate for a teacher's lack of such loving, enthusiastic, positive support.

Types of Movement Experiences Children Need

Preschool children need a wider variety of movements than they typically get during free play on the playground. As one example, preschoolers need to roll to help develop their bodies' vestibular, visual, and kinesthetic systems. The vestibular system is key to balance. People with a keen sense of balance are likely to do gymnastics moves; an inverted dive; snowboard down the mountainside; walk through the woods with ease on the uneven trail; and dribble a basketball down the court, weave around the defense, then jump, and gracefully lay the ball into the basket. However, unless there is a piece of equipment on the playground that specifically stimulates rolling and a ground surface that makes rolling safe, preschoolers will not get this vital experience. So teachers need to provide opportunities that will entice the children to roll.

There are many ways to give children opportunities to roll. Here is one: Create an obstacle course that contains inclined mats for the children to roll down. They'll want to roll over and over. However, rolling is just one of many movement skills and abilities preschool children need to develop. They need to learn to throw, catch, and kick, skills central to many playground games, team sports, and lifetime recreational activities. They need to

develop their balance to ride a bicycle, ski downhill, or walk gracefully. They need to learn climbing to walk up a flight of stairs, get on top of playground equipment, or climb a ladder as an adult making household repairs. Teachers can help children learn these movement skills.

Create Meaningful Movement Programs

The authors believe that every teacher can help preschool children improve their motor skills by following the techniques described in this book and by using the learning experience activities and games in part II. Some readers, however, may have concerns about their lack of formal education or training in teaching movement. Others may feel anxious about equipment and space limitations in their preschool environment, and some may be unsure about what to teach. We address these issues throughout the book. We have taken great care to provide ideas within the games and activities to overcome most obstacles common to preschool environments.

What kind of success can you expect following the suggestions of this book?

Teachers currently offering only an informal playground recess movement program can provide increased movement opportunities for children within the first days. Teachers who choose to consistently implement a movement program based on this book are likely to feel comfortable and confident in their instruction within the first year.

> Children who learn to be successful movers during their childhood are likely to become active movers throughout their lives.

Children who learn to be successful movers during their childhood are likely to become active movers throughout their lives. They develop skills and establish habits in physical activity at a young age. What children learn about movement in preschool today can have an enormous impact on how active they choose to be throughout their lives. It can influence not only how skillfully they move, but also whether they will include movement activities in their lifestyles as they grow older (U.S. Department of Health and Human Services, 1996).

The next generation of Elizabeths and Anns from the scenario opening this chapter are in our preschool programs now. Think of the enormous opportunities their preschool teachers have to influence these children's attitudes about active lifestyles and movement. Their teachers can be the ones to bring movement into the children's lives. They can help children accept physical activity and movement as a normal, healthy part of living. Some children they teach may go on to excel in sports or in active recreational pursuits. Others, perhaps, may simply choose walking over driving at times as a conscious effort to obtain the health benefits of an active lifestyle. Whatever choices these children make as adults, their preschool programs must give them many opportunities now to become the most successful movers they can be. Preschool is where it all starts!

Deciding What to Teach: Goals of a Preschool Movement Program

Experience is the chief architect of the brain.

J. Madeleine Nash,
Fertile Minds

Shawn slowly gets up from circle time and picks up his carpet square to put it away. As he places his carpet square on the pile, he stumbles and laughs as a classmate helps him to his feet. He claps his hands with delight as he sees the teacher bring out a box of Nerf balls. He knows this means they will be throwing today. One classmate comments about Shawn's earlier fall, but Shawn shrugs off the criticism and responds, "My legs just get tired sometimes." During the warm-up, the children try balancing on one leg. Shawn casually asks a nearby child, "May I hold your hand to help me balance?" Shawn is aware that the Let's Get Catching, Throwing, and Kicking learning experiences planned will require him to use both legs. He finds movement awkward as he continues adjusting to the above-the-knee prosthesis, but he knows he will have an enjoyable day. Over time, he has learned that if he concentrates, he can maintain his balance and throw with success! He is proud of his accomplishments.

The teacher is delighted that Shawn has become so much more comfortable with his movements during the past year. She recalls when Shawn would hang back, head down, embarrassed by classmates' comments critical of his awkward movements. His teacher realized that in addition to helping Shawn develop movement skills, she would need to address how Shawn thought and felt about the way he moved. She set two goals for Shawn: (1) learn to move more skillfully, and (2) feel more confident about his movements. In planning lessons she purposely selected games and activities that she could adapt to help Shawn achieve these two goals. She also talked with Shawn about his feelings about himself and his movements. She was straightforward with Shawn, stating, "Yes, you move differently than your classmates. That is not bad—just different." She emphasized respect among everyone in the group, with particular reminders to classmates who made unkind comments. She also helped Shawn understand that avoiding movement would not solve the problem. He needed to accept himself, both his prosthesis and his bright intellect. She explained that only through practice would he move better, and she would be there to guide him. She encouraged Shawn to let his classmates know when they hurt his feelings. Gradually, he is learning about his capabilities in movement. His successes are more frequent, and the days of avoiding movement are long gone. A year later, Shawn has become a confident, skillful mover.

This chapter builds on the concepts that learning to move skillfully is important for preschool children, and their teachers can help them learn to move skillfully. The focus is on the first step in conducting a movement program—deciding what to teach. We discuss the concepts introduced in this chapter in greater depth within chapter 8, Developing a Movement Curriculum.

Children at Play

Children are doing more than just moving when playing games and activities. As they play, they are feeling, thinking, *and* moving all at the same time. Through these movement experiences they are changing their behaviors. They are learning! This is why we call the games and activities in this book learning experiences.

The following applies to all children, including those with special needs, as with Shawn in the previous scenario. Although there may be differences in how they learn movements, children with special needs feel, think, and learn to move more skillfully through movement, as discussed in part IV.

Moving and Feeling

Preschool children are feeling while they are moving. They are deciding

whether they like themselves and if other children like them,

whether they like those around them,

whether they like moving and will want to keep moving when no one is making them move,

whether they *can* do movement and if they will take chances to try new movements,

whether they want to share with others and if they are willing to take turns and cooperate, and

whether play gives them joy and meets their needs.

These feelings and attitudes that children have while they move are part of what we call the affective domain. The affective domain refers to emotions. Through moving, children continually decide how they feel about themselves and others.

When planning movement programs for preschoolers, look to achieve goals in the affective domain, such as accomplishing the following:

- Strengthen the way children feel about themselves.

  Develop positive self-images and self-esteem.

  Develop self-motivation to become independent learners who confidently choose to be active.

- Develop children's social skills.

  Learn to share, cooperate, and take turns.

  Learn to play safely and talk kindly.

- Develop joyful and purposeful play.

Moving and Thinking

Preschool children are thinking while they are moving. They are

learning how to communicate;

learning about rules and game play;

learning how to follow directions;

learning how to recognize and name objects, colors, shapes, and many other things;

learning about their bodies, the parts, and how they move; and

learning movement concepts, such as moving with different kinds of effort, in different shapes, and in different relationships with objects and other people.

All these concepts children experience while moving are part of the cognitive domain. The cognitive domain refers to knowing or perceiving. Through moving, children continually learn about ideas.

When planning the movement program for preschoolers, look to achieve goals in the cognitive domain, such as accomplishing the following:

- Learn how to communicate.
- Learn basic rules and game play.

- Learn to follow directions.
- Learn to recognize objects, colors, and shapes.
- Learn about body awareness.

  Identify body parts.

  Identify movement concepts.

  Effort (time, force, flow)

  Shape (self-space, general space, levels—high, low)

  Relationships (of body parts, to objects and other children—over, under, in front, behind)

Moving and Developing Skills

Preschool children are learning to move more skillfully while they are moving. They are

learning how to walk, run, jump, gallop, hop, skip, leap (locomotor skills);

learning how to throw, catch, kick, strike, and bounce (object control skills);

learning how to balance in one place and while moving around the room (stability);

developing strong heart and lung systems that will sustain vigorous activity for many minutes without needing to rest (cardiovascular endurance);

developing strong muscles that will exert force (muscular strength) repeatedly (muscular endurance);

learning how to organize all the information they get from their senses to plan and do sequences of movements (motor planning); and

learning how to use recreational equipment.

Children are doing more than just moving when playing games and activities. As they play, they are feeling, thinking, and moving all at the same time.

These movements children experience while moving are part of the motor domain. The motor domain refers to movement. Through moving, children continually become more skillful movers.

When planning the movement program for preschoolers, look to meet preschool movement program goals in the motor domain, such as the following:

- Learn rudimentary movement skills, if not already mastered.
- Learn fundamental movement skills.

Learn locomotor skills (walk, run, jump, gallop, hop, skip, leap).

Learn object control (throw, catch, kick, strike, bounce).

Learn stability (static and dynamic balance).

- Develop health-related physical fitness.

Develop cardiovascular endurance.

Develop muscular strength and endurance.

- Develop motor planning (sequencing movements based on sensory input).
- Develop functional and generalizable adaptations of motor skills, as needed.
- Learn to use equipment, such as tricycles, roller racers, and scooters, adapted as needed to increase mobility.

Curriculum Is Necessary

How convenient it would be to teach the same few favorite games and activities such as Midnight and Red Light, Green Light over and over again! Unfortunately, if we adopted this approach to teaching movement to preschoolers, many children would be deprived of the wide range of movement experiences they need to develop optimally. Repeatedly teaching the same few activities strengthens a limited number of skills and ignores many other important skills. Create and use a comprehensive curriculum for the preschool movement program to ensure that preschoolers are getting the variety of movement experiences

> **Create and use a comprehensive curriculum for the preschool movement program to ensure that preschoolers are getting the variety of movement experiences needed for optimum development.**

needed for optimum development.

A curriculum is everything in a course of study. In this case, the curriculum is everything children are taught in the preschool motor program. An important part of the curriculum is the curricular goals set for children to achieve through the curriculum.

Curricular Goals

Curricular goals are the compass of the curriculum, the general direction for what to teach. The curricular goals are broad-based statements of what children are to achieve through participating in the curriculum. We present our recommendations for preschool movement program curricular goals in box 2.1. We have combined the curricular goals for the affective, cognitive, and motor domains into a convenient checklist for your quick reference. Teaching to meet these curricular goals provides the wide range of movement experiences that help children develop optimally. This checklist appears again in chapter 8, along with information about how curricular goals develop.

It is our experience that preschool children who learn these fundamental movements are prepared to learn more complicated movements throughout the rest of their lives. It all starts in preschool, and we can achieve it through helping children meet these curricular goals.

The next chapter explains ideas for teaching toward these curricular goals in a way that focuses on what each child is ready to learn. This is a child-centered approach to conducting a preschool movement program.

Box 2.1 The Preschool Movement Curricular Goals

Preschool Movement Program Goals in the Affective Domain

☑ **Strengthen the way children feel about themselves.**

Develop positive self-images and self-esteem.

Develop self-motivation to become independent learners who confidently choose to be active.

☑ **Develop social skills.**

Learn to share, cooperate, and take turns.

Learn to play safely and talk kindly.

☑ **Develop joyful and purposeful play.**

Preschool Movement Program Goals in the Cognitive Domain

☑ **Learn how to communicate.**

☑ **Learn basic rules and game play.**

☑ **Learn to follow directions.**

☑ **Learn to recognize objects, colors, and shapes.**

☑ **Learn about body awareness.**

Identify body parts.

Identify movement concepts.

 Effort (time, force, flow)

 Space (self-space, general space, levels—high, low)

 Relationships (of body parts, to objects—over, under, in front, behind)

Preschool Movement Program Goals in the Motor Domain

☑ **Learn rudimentary movement skills, if not already mastered.**

☑ **Learn fundamental movement skills.**

Learn locomotor skills (walk, run, jump, gallop, hop, skip, leap).

Learn object control (throw, catch, kick, strike, bounce).

Learn stability (static and dynamic balance).

☑ **Develop health-related physical fitness.**

Develop cardiovascular endurance.

Develop muscular strength and endurance.

☑ **Develop motor planning (sequencing movements based on sensory input).**

☑ **Develop functional and generalizable adaptations of motor skills, as needed.**

☑ **Learn to use recreational equipment—tricycles, roller racers, scooters, swings, adapted as needed to increase mobility.**

Deciding How to Teach: Using a Child-Centered Approach

All children—whether they are infants, preschoolers, or second graders; children with mental retardation, learning disabilities, or above average intelligence—are active learners. They acquire knowledge by actively experiencing the world around them—choosing, exploring, manipulating, practicing, transforming, experimenting.

Principles of the High/Scope Curriculum

It's Monday morning and Mr. Jacob is leading 15 three- and four-year-old children to the activity room. As they enter the room, he walks away from the children, calling over his shoulder, "Please go to the green line and sit quietly. When everyone is silent, I will explain the activity we will do today." Over the next five minutes, Mr. Jacob carefully explains and demonstrates the throwing activity. He stops frequently to remind the children to sit still and listen. Mr. Jacob then directs the children to each pick up a tennis ball and hold it until he signals to throw it at the clown targets 12 feet away. As the activity progresses, Mr. Jacob continually reminds the children to wait for his command to throw and to stay behind the throwing line until he gives the command to retrieve the balls. He finds the children fidgety and not focused on the activity. He reminds three children at the end of the line not to throw the balls at each other. He tries to help some children with their throwing skills, but does not have time for most children because he needs to continually correct their misbehavior. He does, however, manage to point out how much farther Bill, a four-year-old, can throw the ball compared with the rest of the children. Mr. Jacob is glad when the movement lesson is over and wonders why the children were so disruptive today.

Across town on that same Monday morning, Mrs. Baker has also planned a movement lesson for her 15 preschool children. She leads the children to the activity room, then stands by the door, acknowledging each of the children as they enter. The children know they can run into the room and sit on their choice of attractive shapes, carpet squares, or painted figures on the floor. Over the next minute and a half, Mrs. Baker describes and demonstrates the throwing activity of the day. Running the width of the room is a two-foot high rope boundary draped with curtains. She has placed four buckets with 30 to 40 tennis balls in each on one side of the curtain. A large variety of targets, such as smiley faces, large colored shapes, hanging posters, balloons, and bells, are one to seven feet behind the boundary. She tells the children that when the music starts, it is their cue to get up and begin throwing the balls at whatever targets they choose. While the children are throwing, Mrs. Baker walks among the children, facilitating the lesson objective of learning to throw. She prompts a child, "Put your hand by your ear." To another child she says, "Look at the target as you throw." With the children actively engaged in throwing, she has ample time to watch each child and provide corrective feedback in a playful manner. She pretends to bounce the ball off her knee, waiting for the children to laughingly remind her to throw the ball toward the target. When the buckets are empty, Mrs. Baker stops the music and draws the curtain back. The children then take the buckets under the boundary and fill them with the balls. As the children push the full buckets back under the rope, Mrs. Baker draws the curtain, starts the music, and the throwing resumes. After several more repetitions of the throwing and filling, with Mrs. Baker coaching each child, the movement lesson ends. As the children follow Mrs. Baker out of the room, she overhears the children tell each other about all the balls they threw and all the targets they hit. She smiles as she reflects on the successful lesson.

In this scenario, Mrs. Baker is using a child-centered approach in her teaching. Although she is teaching in an activity room, this approach works equally well in a classroom. This chapter will present the concept of the child-centered approach, then address strategies for communicating with children within this approach.

Child-Centered Approach Defined

Lawrence Schweinhart (1988) describes the importance of child initiated activity by stating:

Encouraging children [with disabilities] to initiate their own activities enables them to develop their strengths as well as to strengthen their weaknesses. As children develop their strengths, they learn they can do things that they want to do, so they develop feelings of competence and self-confidence.

The child-centered approach emphasizes learning experiences that are child initiated and teacher facilitated, enabling each child to achieve specific goals and objectives. The child-centered approach consists of the following:

- It is consistent with developmentally appropriate practices. The learning experiences are planned based on what each child is ready to learn.

- It works with young children's natural interest in exploration and experimentation.

- It includes many opportunities for the child, rather than the teacher, to initiate the activity within the environment that the teacher has created. "While the teacher will select some activities and movements, most activities used for intervention are based upon what motivates and interests the child" (Block and Davis, 1996). Child-initiated activities are similar to Walt Davis' Ecological Task Analysis (Davis and Burton, 1991) approach to teaching, in that both use activities that the child has selected within an environment that the teacher has designed. Child-initiated activities are also consistent with Muska Mosston's (Mosston and Ashworth, 1994) guided discovery teaching style, in which children control much of the learning process as the teacher guides them to discover the solution to problems the teacher poses.

- It focuses on children *learning*. The teacher identifies goals and objectives for each child, based on their individual needs and current abilities. All activities are designed to be fun and playful, but the overall goal is for the children to learn (Block and Davis, 1996).

- It encourages the teacher to guide and facilitate learning rather than direct children.

- It is consistent with activity-based intervention that seems appropriate for children with special needs (Bricker and Cripe, 1992).

We designed the learning experiences in this book to use in a child-centered approach. More than half the learning experiences in part II are child-initiated activities. In these learning experiences, all activities and play stations accessible to the children focus on the lesson's goals and objectives. In the learning experiences involving station work, children are allowed to choose the activities they wish to do and how long they wish to do them. In designing the lesson's activities, ask for the children's suggestions. Draw upon their interests. For example, in setting up an ob-

> **The child-centered approach emphasizes learning experiences that are child initiated and teacher facilitated, enabling each child to achieve specific goals and objectives.**

stacle course, seek the children's suggestions in its design. Also, be sure to conduct the movement program in a way that the children feel successful. Feeling successful is an important part of learning to move. Place the emphasis on exploration, experimentation, and problem solving rather than on one correct way of moving that the children must imitate. Instead, there are many solutions to a movement problem. Encourage the children to choose the activities they wish to do and when they want to do them. If you allow the children to choose among activities, and you facilitate learning, the children will get the practice they need to master the lesson's objectives. The remaining learning experiences in part II are teacher-directed activities, including tag games and self-testing activities. In these learning experiences, the teacher selects and initiates the activity, yet the children have choices at every opportunity. The emphasis remains on exploration, experimentation, and problem solving, so the teacher does not demand one response from every child, but accepts a wide range of responses.

Schweinhart (1988) describes child-initiated activities as follows:

Child-initiated activity should be central to an early childhood development curriculum (p. 1).

In child-initiated activity, children choose an activity within a framework created by the teacher. Children then carry out the activity as they see fit unconstrained by the teacher's definition of the "correct" answer or the "correct" use of materials. Child-initiated activity is distinguished from random activity by its purposefulness; it is distinguished from teacher-directed activity by the fact that the child controls what happens (p. 1).

The best early childhood learning activities are child initiated, developmentally appropriate, and open-ended. They are child initiated to take advantage of children's curiosity and motivation to learn from such activities. They are developmentally appropriate, meaning they match the children's interests and abilities, neither too easy nor too difficult. The best learning activities are open-ended in that they allow more than one correct response or way of acting; such opened activities more closely parallel many real life situations (p. 8).

A child-centered approach is supported through the following teaching strategies and classroom routines.

1. Create a learning environment that screams, "Welcome, I am so glad you are here."
2. Let each child know that he or she is important.
3. Create a routine for the beginning of each class.
4. Use music as a signal to start and stop the activity.
5. Create boundaries that clearly indicate where the children are and are not to go.
6. Give brief, concise instructions.
7. Select an activity in which all children are actively engaged and focused.
8. Select an activity that allows the freedom to roam the area and facilitate children's learning.
9. Keep each activity open-ended.
10. Create a friendly atmosphere, accepting of individual differences.
11. Allow the children a feeling of control over the activity.
12. When using multiple stations, plan only one station with equipment that requires constant adult supervision.
13. When using multiple stations, plan only one activity station that involves turn taking.

Child-Centered Teaching Strategies and Large Group Activities

When setting up a large group movement activity, employing the following key strategies will lead to a successful lesson. Let's use Mrs. Baker's throwing lesson from the scenario at the beginning of this chapter to illustrate how one teacher creates a successful learning experience using the child-centered approach.

The activity Mrs. Baker selected in the scenario is an example of a group activity that involves throwing. The curricular goal is object control. She selects the instructional objective: When throwing toward a target, the child will use a mature overhand throw at least once. Mrs. Baker selects an activity in which the children are all throwing at the same time, providing each child with the maximum opportunity for practice. When Mrs. Baker chooses a different movement activity, she will change the setup in the room, but she will

continue to use the child-centered teaching strategies she uses for throwing.

1. Mrs. Baker motivates the children from the moment they see the room by creating a learning environment that screams, "Welcome, I am so glad you are here." Within this enthusiastic environment, the children know they *can* play with most everything they see. She has already stored any equipment that the children are not to touch out of sight and reach. Bright, fun images are on the walls, such as posters of favorite cartoon characters. These further convey the message, "This is a wonderful space for children." Mrs. Baker makes sure that she has all the equipment ready before the children arrive so they don't have to wait to engage in the activity.
2. Mrs. Baker lets each child know that he or she is important. She acknowledges the children at the door, smiling and speaking to each child as he or she enters.
3. As the children enter the room, Mrs. Baker directs them where to go, but allows some flexibility of choice for the child. She has created a routine for the beginning of each class in which the children are to sit on their choice of shapes on the floor. Carpet squares also work well for positioning the children. If she cannot avoid using a painted floor line, she lets the children find their own spaces on the line.
4. Mrs. Baker uses music as a signal to start and stop the activity. She teaches the children that when the music begins they may start throwing the balls, and when the music stops they may retrieve the balls. She has a much easier time directing the group than Mr. Jacob, who shouts each command and waits for all children to respond. Additionally, the music playing in the background provides natural motivation for the children!
5. Mrs. Baker creates boundaries that clearly indicate where the children are and are not to go. She uses chairs, benches, stacked mats, ropes, or cones to create clear boundaries. She has found that using a painted line on the floor as a boundary is too abstract for most preschoolers to understand. In the scenario, Mrs. Baker uses a rope with curtains hung over it to create a single boundary that indicates, "Stand here to throw, but don't go past this rope toward the targets until I pull the curtains aside."

6. Mrs. Baker gives brief, concise instructions so the children are active most of the class time. Through using established class routines for starting, stopping, and changing activities, she spends less than three minutes explaining most learning experiences.

7. Mrs. Baker selects an activity in which all children can be actively engaged and focused. She does not give children opportunities to be distracted while waiting for the next command, as frequently occurs in Mr. Jacob's group. Mrs. Baker's approach allows children the privacy of being in a crowd, a concept Maryanne Torbert of Temple University promoted (Torbert and Schneider, 1993). With everyone active, there is privacy for each child because no other children are standing around, watching, or criticizing classmates.

8. Mrs. Baker selects an activity that allows her the freedom to roam the area, facilitating each child's movements as needed. Unlike Mr. Jacob, who makes himself the focal point of the activity by requiring that the children only throw on his command, Mrs. Baker allows the children to throw continually. She is now free to teach, walking among the children, facilitating their skill learning. The children are motivated to continue in Mrs. Baker's class because they are completely involved in the activity and are receiving specific, positive teacher feedback, such as "Nice job throwing, Katie. You remembered to put your hand by your ear."

9. Mrs. Baker keeps each activity open-ended by allowing more than one way for the children to complete the task. By choosing this approach, she encourages exploration of movement. For example, if a child decides to roll or bounce the ball at the target, Mrs. Baker allows this. Similarly, she encourages a child with limited movement who pushes a ball off her wheelchair tray toward a target.

10. Mrs. Baker creates a friendly atmosphere, accepting of individual differences. Mr. Jacob unwittingly promotes competition by singling out children, such as Bill, for praise in front of the group because of their superior proficiency. In contrast, Mrs. Baker gives attention and recognition to each child during her class.

11. Mrs. Baker allows the children a feeling of control over the activity. She lets children add rules to a game, even if they are silly rules. She will also, during group games, purposely make a mistake that the children are sure to catch, so they can have the fun of correcting the teacher! She *plays* with the children in her class. She finds this motivates both her and the children.

Child-Centered Teaching Strategies and Station Activities

In the scenario, Mrs. Baker selected a single, large group activity. She could have instead designed four or five different stations in the room that each involved throwing. If planned appropriately, there is no problem allowing the children to roam freely from station to station to experience what each offers. It becomes their choice either to remain at a crowded station waiting for a turn or to move on. No matter where the children choose to go, she designs the lesson so the children participate in the skill of throwing. When Mrs. Baker uses multiple stations, she plans to have only one station with equipment that requires constant adult supervision or has many loose pieces of equipment. Equipment suggestions and setup of this type might include the following:

- Targets that she needs to reset. Plastic bottles and foam shapes are motivating targets, but they need to be set up after the children knock them down. If an adult is unavailable to reset the targets, you can tie plastic bottles at intervals along a rope and suspend them. Consider also tying bells along the rope that will make stimulating sounds when the children hit the bottles. The sounds help motivate children to continue throwing. Other ideas for creating stationary targets include throwing beanbags at tires stacked along a wall; throwing fleece balls at balloons tied to suspended ropes; or throwing foam balls at basketball hoops or into the cut out mouth of a face painted on plywood or cardboard.

- Balls that roll all over the place, with the children chasing them! To maximize activity time, position a station that uses many loose pieces of equipment so the children are throwing toward a wall, thus containing the balls and target pieces in a small area. This is preferable to standing against the wall and throwing toward the center of the room, where the balls and target pieces can scatter into other activity areas. At other throwing stations, use foam gator balls, fleece balls, beanbags, and other objects that stay where they land. If using playground balls, deflate them slightly to reduce rolling.

Mrs. Baker recognizes that taking turns is a skill preschoolers are just developing. She plans only one activity station that involves turn taking, and then only if there is an adult available to stay at that station. When children do have to wait, she has created an interesting waiting area with cartoon characters of bright, primary colors.

Communicating With Preschool Children

Communicating effectively with preschoolers in the child-centered teaching model is important because when children clearly understand teachers' expectations, they are more likely to meet them. Communication starts as the children are walking through the door. Always greet the children at the door and direct them where to go. Once the class is settled in the room, let the children know how exciting it is to have them there. As with adults, children read body language. In the scenario, Mr. Jacob did not acknowledge the children and gave the first directions with his back to the children, without eye contact. Mrs. Baker, on the other hand, let the children know she was happy to be with them. She stood at the door, smiling, and making eye contact with each child as they entered. A hallmark of effective teachers—at any grade level—is infectious enthusiasm for what they are teaching.

Once the activities have begun, continually encourage children as they play. Be specific when giving feedback to children so they can completely understand what you mean. Although saying "great job" can be confusing to some children because it is vague, phrases such as "Katie, you did a great job throwing that ball. You remembered to put your hand by your ear" are specific and understandable.

When explaining or making a comment to a child, use more "dos" than "don'ts." Phrase requests positively as in the following examples:

Do Say

Please walk down the stairs.
You can throw the fleece balls at the big target on the wall.
Remember to keep balloons away from your face.

Don't Say

Don't jump on the stairs.
Don't throw the fleece balls around the room.
Don't put balloons near your face.

When stating an important safety rule or behavioral expectation to children, do so in a firm, but not loud, voice. Be lovingly firm. Use a firm tone of voice but one that still has a loving manner, rather than a cold, harsh, or angry edge to it. Most of the time when communicating with children, teachers use warm, friendly, enthusiastic, high-pitched voices. When making these lovingly firm statements, use a more directive, low-pitched voice. At these times it is particularly important to check that the children understand the request. For example, state "Use the climber only when an adult is standing next to it." Then ask the children, "Do you go on the climber if there is not an adult there?" and listen to see if they understand. If they say "Yes!" with big smiles, it is time to reteach this important safety request. Soon after making a request of the entire class, give positive feedback to the children for what a great job they are doing. If you make a request to an individual child, approach the child individually soon after stating the request and express appreciation for how well the child is doing now. Remember to talk with children, not at them.

Avoid asking a question when really seeking to make a direct statement. Preschoolers have favorite activities, so if teachers ask general questions, they may hear a specific answer that they did not anticipate. An example of this idea follows. When introducing a lesson that will focus on jumping, the teacher may casually ask, "Do you want to jump today?" She has left herself open to a preschooler's honest answer, "No, I want to ride a trike!" Now she has to backtrack and explain that the lesson focus today is jumping. What she might have said initially was, "Children, we are going to *jump* today!"

In summary, effective teacher communication that is enthusiastic and clear is an integral component of a child-centered approach. The next chapter focuses on ways to determine what children are learning within the movement program. We share ideas for observing children's movements that can help you plan learning experiences and give feedback that will help children learn to move more skillfully.

> A hallmark of effective teachers—at any grade level—is infectious enthusiasm for what they are teaching.

Observing Children's Movements

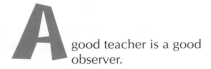

A good teacher is a good observer.

Mrs. Baker provides a movement program for the preschool children she teaches. This morning the children are in the activity room exploring ways to jump. Mrs. Baker is observing the children jump, then recording their current jumping level on a daily progress note. She finds it easy to observe the children jump while still being in control of the class. She accomplishes this by selecting an activity that is safe for the children to do with general supervision and that will entice them to jump. Today she is leading the children in the Let's Get Jumping learning experience. Before the lesson, Mrs. Baker had decided to observe five specific children today. She keeps a pad of yellow sticky notes in the pocket of her pants and writes her observations of one child. She then walks over to the clipboard hanging on a nearby wall. She will add this sticky note to the several others that she has written during the activity. At the end of the day, Mrs. Baker will spend a few minutes reviewing the sticky notes and recording the information on each of the five children's progress sheets.

During her observations, Mrs. Baker notes that one child is not jumping with both feet simultaneously. She now has the knowledge to say to the child, "Lift both feet up at the same time when you jump." If she observes the child does not yet understand the concept of jumping, she now can encourage the child to bounce on a crash mat or bed mattress on the floor.

Mrs. Baker knows she has a principal's meeting at the end of this month and wants to be prepared with documentation that the movement program is effective. With satisfaction she observes how the children are making individual progress. Three months ago, few in the class could coordinate the lift with their arms and the extension of their legs in the jump. Now, most children can jump with a mature pattern, lifting with their arms in nearly every jump, and for the remaining children, the skill is beginning to emerge.

Chapters 1 through 3 discussed why a movement program is important for preschool children, what to teach in a movement program, and how to teach using a child-centered approach. This chapter focuses on how to closely observe (and record) each child's movements. As teachers become skillful observers of children's movements, they can teach movement to children more effectively.

Why Observe Children's Movements?

The essence of teaching is observing and giving feedback. This chapter emphasizes the first part of the process—observing. Through watching, teachers learn what each child can and cannot already do. Only through paying attention to each child can you decide what a specific child is ready to learn. To be a skillful teacher, it is essential to be a skillful observer. Through observing, you can give specific feedback to help children move with a mature pattern.

Observing Three Stages of Movements

In this scenario, Mrs. Baker is observing children's skill in jumping. She is using the sketches of the jump, found in figure 4.1, to help her with observations. Study these sketches, and notice that the initial stage of jumping (shown in the top row of sketches) is the least mature. As the child improves in jumping, he or she progresses through the elementary stage (middle row) and eventually performs at the mature stage (bottom row). Gallahue (1996) identifies three stages of the jump through which typical children progress. Study the sketches in figures 4.2 through 4.7 to observe the three stages of maturity for the run, gallop, throw, catch, kick, and strike. Then teach to only the mature stage, not to the initial or elementary stages. We show the initial and elementary stages only to identify a child's stage. Please note that although figure 4.3 pictures the slide (a sideways movement), we recommend teaching the easier-to-learn gallop (a forward movement). The descriptioins apply to both movements.

4.1a Jumping: Initial Stage

Arm Action	The arms, limited in their swing, do not initiate the jumping action. They move in a sideward–downward or rearward–upward direction to maintain balance during the flight.
Trunk Action	The trunk at takeoff is propelled in a vertical direction with little emphasis on the length of the jump.
Leg-Hip Action	The preparatory crouch is limited and inconsistent with regard to the degree of leg flexion. At takeoff and landing the child has difficulty using both feet simultaneously, and one leg may precede the other. The extension of the hips, legs, and ankles is incomplete at the takeoff of the jump.

4.1b Jumping: Elementary Stage

Arm Action	The arms are utilized more productively in the jumping action. They initiate the pattern at takeoff and then move to the side to maintain balance during the jump.
Trunk Action	No observable change.
Leg-Hip Action	The preparatory crouch is deeper and more consistent. The legs, hips, and ankles extend more at takeoff; however, they remain somewhat bent. During the flight, the thighs are held in a flexed position.

4.1c Jumping: Mature Stage

Arm Action	The arms move high and to the rear and then reach forward during the takeoff. The arms are held high throughout the jumping action.
Trunk Action	The trunk at takeoff is propelled at an angle of approximately 45 degrees. The major emphasis is on the horizontal direction of the jump.
Leg-Hip Action	The preparatory crouch is deep and consistent. The hips, legs, and ankles are completely extended at takeoff. During the flight, the hips flex, bringing the thighs to a position nearly horizontal to the ground. The lower leg hangs in a nearly vertical position. The body weight upon landing continues forward and downward.

4.2a Running: Initial Stage

Leg Action (side view)	The legs appear stiff and the stride is uneven. There is no observable flight phase, and the base of support is wide. The swing of the leg is short and limited.
Leg Action (rear view)	The recovery knee is swung outward, then around and forward to a support position. The swinging foot tends to rotate outward from the hip, which allows the foot to be swung forward without a great deal of body lift and thereby helps the child to maintain balance.
Arm Action	The arms swing stiffly with varying degrees of flexion at the elbow. The range of motion of the arms is short, as the arms tend to swing outward horizontally rather than vertically. This outward rotation counteracts the excessive rotary movement of the swinging leg.

4.2b Running: Elementary Stage

Leg Action (side view)	Stride length, leg swing, and speed increase. There is a definite observable flight phase to the pattern. The support leg begins to extend more completely at takeoff.
Leg Action (rear view)	At the height of recovery to the rear, the recovery foot swings across the midline before it is swung forward to the contact position.
Arm Action	The arms swing for a greater distance vertically, and there is limited horizontal movement on the backswing as the child's stride length increases.

4.2c Running: Mature Stage

Leg Action (side view)	The recovery knee is raised high and swung forward quickly. The support leg bends slightly at contact and then extends completely and quickly through the hip, knee, and ankle. The length of the stride and the duration of flight time are at their maximum.
Leg Action (rear view)	There is very little rotary action of the recovery knee or foot as the length of the stride increases.
Arm Action	The arms swing vertically in a large arc in opposition to the legs. The arms are bent at the elbows in approximate right angles.

4.3a   Gallop/Slide: Initial Stage

Arm Action   Arms are of little use in balance or force production.

Leg-Foot Action   Trailing leg often fails to remain behind and often contacts the surface in front of the lead leg. There is 45-degree flexion of the trailing leg during the flight phase. Contact with the surface is a heel-toe combination.

Tempo   Movements are arrhythmical at a fast pace.

4.3b   Gallop/Slide: Elementary Stage

Arm Action   Arms are slightly out to the side to aid in maintaining balance.

Leg-Foot Action   The trailing leg may lead during flight but lands adjacent to or behind the lead leg. There is an exaggerated vertical lift. Feet contact the surface in a heel-toe or toe-toe combination.

Tempo   Movements are at a moderate tempo with a choppy and stiff action.

4.3c   Gallop/Slide: Mature Stage

Arm Action   Arms are not needed for balance so they may be used for other purposes.

Leg-foot Action   Both legs are flexed at 45-degree angles during flight, with a low flight pattern. Feet contact the surface in a heel-toe combination.

Tempo   Movements are at a moderate tempo with a smooth, rhythmical action.

Text from D. Gallahue, 1997, *Developmental physical education,* 4th ed. (New York: McGraw Hill). Reproduced with permission of the McGraw-Hill Companies.

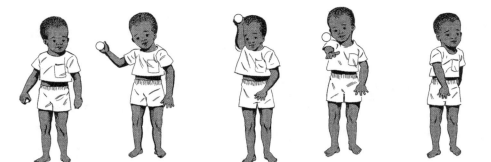

4.4a Throwing: Initial Stage

Arm Action   The throwing motion is performed mainly from the elbow, which remains in front of the body. The throw consists of a pushing action. At the point of release, the fingers are spread. The follow-through is forward and downward.

Trunk Action   The trunk remains perpendicular to the target throughout the throw. There is very little shoulder rotation during the throwing motion. The child tends to move slightly backward as the throw is made.

Leg-Foot Action The feet remain stationary, although there may be some purposeless shifting of the feet during preparation for the throw.

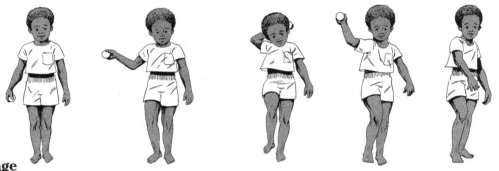

4.4b Throwing: Elementary Stage

Arm Action   The arm is swung in preparation, first sideward-upward and then backward to a position of elbow flexion where the ball is brought to a position behind the head. The arm swings forward in a high over-the-shoulder action. The follow-through is forward and downward. The wrist completes the throw, and the ball is controlled more by the fingers.

Trunk Action   The trunk rotates toward the throwing side during the preparatory phase of the throw. As the arm initiates the throwing action, the trunk rotates back toward the nonthrowing side. The trunk flexes forward with the forward motion of the throwing arm.

Leg-Foot Action The performer steps forward with the leg that is on the same side as the throwing arm. There is a forward shift in the body weight.

4.4c Throwing: Mature Stage

Arm Action   The arm swings backward in preparation for the throw. The throwing elbow moves forward horizontally as it extends. The thumb rotates in and downward and therefore ends up pointing downward. At release the fingers remain close together.

Trunk Action   During the preparatory phase of the throw, the trunk is markedly rotated to the throwing side and the throwing shoulder drops slightly. As the forward motion begins, the trunk rotates through the hips, spine, and shoulders. The throwing shoulder rotates to a position in line with the target.

Leg-Foot Action During the preparatory phase of the throw, the weight is on the rear foot. As the trunk rotates, the weight is completely shifted with a step on the foot that is on the nonthrowing side of the body.

4.5a
Catching:
Initial stage

Head Action	As the ball is thrown, there is a definite avoidance reaction of turning the face away from the thrown ball or protecting the head with the arms and hands.
Arm Action	The arms are held out with the elbows extended in front of the body. There is limited arm movement until contact with the ball is made. The catching pattern resembles a scooping action as the performer attempts to direct the ball to the chest. The catch is poorly timed.
Hand Action	The fingers are extended and held tense. There is very little use of the hands during this stage of the catching pattern.

4.5b
Catching:
Elementary Stage

Head Action	The performer exhibits an avoidance reaction only by closing the eyes when contact with the ball is made.
Arm Action	The arms are held slightly bent in front of the body. The performer attempts initial contact with the hands; however, timing is poor and the ball is then clasped to the body with the arms.
Hand Action	The hands are held in opposition to each other in preparation for the catch. The fingers are extended and begin to point increasingly toward the ball in anticipation of the catch. As contact is made with the ball, the hands close unevenly in a poorly timed motion.

4.5c
Catching:
Mature Stage

Head Action	The avoidance reaction has been completely suppressed. The eyes follow the ball from the point of release to final contact.
Arm Action	The arms are bent at the elbows and held relaxed at the sides or in front of the body in preparation for the catch. The arms give upon contact with the ball to absorb its force. The arms make adjustments to variations (changes in height, for example) in the flight of the ball.
Hand Action	The hands are cupped together with either the thumbs or the little fingers in opposition, depending upon the height of the tossed ball. In a well-timed motion, the hands are clasped together as contact is made.

Reprinted from McClenaghan and Gallahue 1978. **27**

4.6a Kicking: Initial Stage

Arm-Trunk Action	The movement of the arms and trunk is limited during the kicking action. The body remains erect, with the arms held down at the sides or out for stability.
Leg Action	The kicking leg is limited to the backswing during the preparatory phase of the kick. The forward swing is short, and there is no follow-through. Rather than kicking the ball squarely, the leg tends to kick "at" the ball.

4.6b Kicking: Elementary Stage

Arm-Trunk Action	No observable change.
Leg action	The kicking leg is brought backward during the preparatory phase of the kick, which is made from the knee. The kicking leg tends to remain bent until the ball has been contacted.

4.6c Kicking: Mature Stage

Arm-Trunk Action	As contact is made with the ball, the arm on the kicking side tends to swing from a forward to a backward position while the other arm tends to move from a backward or sideward position to a forward one. The trunk bends at the waist during the follow-through.
Leg Action	The movement of the kicking leg is initiated at the hip, and there is limited knee bend. The leg swings through a long arc, and the support leg bends upon contact with the ball. During the follow-through, the support foot raises to its toes. The foot kicks with a complete and high follow-through.

4.7a   Strike: Initial Stage

Arm Action   The elbow(s) are fully flexed. Force comes from extension of flexed joints in a downward plane.
Feet Action   The feet are stationary.
Trunk Action   The trunk faces the direction of the tossed ball. During the strike there is no trunk rotation. The motion is from back to front.

4.7b   Strike: Elementary Stage

Arm Action   The elbow(s) are flexed at a less acute angle.
Feet Action   The weight shifts to the forward foot prior to ball contact.
Trunk Action   The trunk is turned to the side in anticipation of the tossed ball. There is combined trunk and hip rotation. The force comes from the extension of flexed joints. Trunk rotation and forward movement are in an oblique plane.

4.7c   Strike: Mature Stage

Arm Action   Striking occurs in a long, full arc in a horizontal pattern.
Feet Action   The weight shifts to the back foot in anticipation of the tossed ball. The weight shifts to the forward foot while the object is still moving backwards. Weight shifts to the forward foot at contact.
Trunk Action   Trunk turns to the side in anticipation of the tossed ball. Hips rotate and there is a transfer of weight in a contralateral pattern.

Text from D. Gallahue, 1997, *Developmental physical education,* 4th ed. (New York: McGraw Hill). Reproduced with permission of the McGraw-Hill Companies.

Organizing Observations

Observing children's movements can be an easy and natural part of teaching. We organize tasks for observing into those to do before teaching, while teaching, and after teaching.

Before Teaching

Before teaching the activity, plan the following:

- Select the skill to observe. Consider selecting a fundamental movement skill illustrated in figures 4.1 through 4.7.
- Plan a learning experience that will entice the children to perform the skill you will observe. Choose an activity in which the children can safely participate with only general adult supervision. This frees you to observe the children while still controlling the class.
- Study the mature stage of the skill you will observe. Use the sketches in figures 4.1 through 4.7 to guide observations of children's fundamental movements. At first, you may wish to keep the sketches handy for quick reference. Over time, these skills will become familiar.

During Teaching

While teaching, observe and note the following:

- Observe one child as he or she performs the skill.
- Compare the child's performance with the sketches. Decide which stage of the skill the child is demonstrating. It may be necessary to look back and forth between the child and the

sketches several times when first observing. With practice, teachers find they can quickly identify the skill stage after only a brief observation.

- Record the skill stage next to the child's name, as shown in the daily progress note below. Alternatively, record each child's skill stage on a record form that has the children's names in a column on the left side. You can photocopy the form and write the skills you will observe across the top.
- Move on to observe the next child, observing the child's skill stage and recording it on a sticky note or on a record form.

After Teaching

At the end of teaching, review the following:

- Transfer the information on the sticky note with the observation of the child's skill stage to a page with the child's name. Keep the children's papers in a three-ring binder. Refer to the binder for a record of each child's performance level.

- Review the record of each child's skill stage in the binder to make decisions about future instruction. To plan lessons, identify the skill that several children need to learn. Plan learning experiences that will provide children practice in this skill.

The technique for recording observations just described is quick, requires a minimal amount of your time, and permits informal observation without disrupting the flow of the regular class activity.

> **Two primary purposes of assessment are to guide teaching and to evaluate learning.**

Daily Progress Note

Child's name: *Zachary Brown*   **Date:** *0/0/00*

Curricular goal: ✔ locomotor   ____ object control   ____ fitness

____ motor planning   ____ social

Comments: *continuing to work on a two foot take off when jumping*

Skill level observed: ✔ initial   ____ elementary   ____ mature

Comments: *Zachary is bending his knees to initiate a jump. He then attempts to jump by stepping forward.*

Making Accurate Observations

The key to accurately observing children's performance is to remain inconspicuous! If children know you are watching and assessing them, then their behavior may change immediately. Some children may become shy, and others may begin to show off.

Do observations in the natural environment, such as during a movement program class or on the playground. The intent is to capture the children moving in an environment that most stimulates them. Uninhibited children, among their peers and in a comfortable environment, will typically move to their maximum ability level. You can consider observations made under these circumstances to be fairly accurate.

Set a goal to observe and record children's performances on one objective from the lesson plan each day. Although daily observation of every child is ideal, observing each child once a week may be more realistic. With large classes, divide the class into small groups and plan to observe and record a different group each day. As an example, recall that in the scenario Mrs. Baker informally assessed the jumping skills of five children during one lesson.

We based these steps on the notion that there is, for each skill, one optimum way of moving. Although this may be accurate for typical children, it is clearly not accurate for many children with special needs. Physical, motor, or cognitive limitations may require unique forms of movement for some children.

Assessment enables teachers to demonstrate that children are learning, an indication that a movement program is effective.

Assessing Children's Movements

Educators refer to the process of observing children's movements and making decisions based on these observations as informal assessment. The following section discusses formal and informal assessment, and describes assessment principles in general and assessment's role in teaching in detail. This information may be most useful for those educators responsible for documenting student learning and evaluating program effectiveness.

Defining Assessment

"Assessment refers to data collection, interpretation, and decision making" (Sherrill, 1993). It serves as the cornerstone of teaching. It is critical to deciding what to teach a specific child. The assessment process begins with testing or observing the child's motor performance (data collection). It continues with analyzing the test or observation results (interpretation). It concludes with deciding what to teach the child based on the interpretation of the test or observation results (decision making). There are two types of assessment— formal and informal.

Formal Assessment

The first type, formal assessment, uses standardized test instruments to measure performance. You will usually require a formal assessment of gross motor performance when you are writing an Individualized Education Program (IEP) for a preschool child with special needs. An adapted physical education specialist and perhaps a physical therapist usually conduct formal gross motor performance assessment.

Informal Assessment

In contrast to formal assessment, the second method, informal assessment, does not use standardized tests. Instead, it uses teacher observation and anecdotal note taking to assess children as they move in natural environments. Informal assessment enables the teacher to assess children on the specific skills being taught in the curriculum. Informal assessment helps you determine which skills the children can and cannot do. With this information, teachers decide what to teach. Informal assessment offers simple and quick approaches to assessing student learning in their everyday environment.

Informal assessment is also appropriate for some children who are not functioning at the level necessary for formal assessment with standardized tests. For the child with special needs, such as a severe motor impairment, emotional need, or communication disorder, informal assessment may be the only appropriate way to measure the child's abilities.

The preschool teacher who leads a movement program is usually the one who informally assesses each preschool child in the movement program. As noted before, an adapted physical education specialist, and perhaps a physical therapist, assess the movement skills of preschoolers with special needs.

Typically, all children are informally assessed as they begin a movement program. For school-based preschool programs, this usually occurs during the first weeks of the school year or as new children enter the program. Assessment is also done on an ongoing basis throughout the year. Please refer to the first six weeks of the 40-week curriculum plan for ideas on selecting learning experiences that facilitate assessment of a group of children. This plan is in the appendix.

Assessment, Evaluation, and the Teaching-Learning Model

"Evaluation is the continuous process of determining student gain and program effectiveness. Although evaluation should be ongoing, it typically is emphasized the last few days of an instructional unit or school term" (Sherrill, 1993). You will often hear the terms assessment and evaluation used interchangeably. In the teaching-learning model used in this book, however, assessment occurs at the beginning of instruction (before beginning to teach a child), and evaluation occurs during and at the end of instruction. Assessing children's skills helps in identifying what they are ready to learn, and evaluating children's learning indicates whether they have indeed learned what you have taught.

The teaching-learning model is based on curricular goals (see figure 4.9).

Importance of Assessment and Evaluation

Assessment and evaluation are extremely important to teaching. Only through assessment and evaluation can you be sure that you are teaching the children what they need to learn and that they are, in fact, learning. In the preschool movement program, assessment and evaluation provide a means to the following:

- Guide teaching. Assessment through teacher observations is key to making instructional decisions. Information recorded will act as a guide for planning the next lesson.

- Measure student learning. Recording observations enables teachers to show skill progression by the child. Evaluation enables you to demonstrate that children are learning.

- Screen children for any special needs. Teacher observations act as a screening tool to identify those children that appear to have significant delays and may need a formal motor assessment.

- Evaluate the effectiveness of a movement program. Evaluation enables teachers to demonstrate that children are learning, an indication that a movement program is effective.

Informal Assessment and Curricular Goals

Chapter 2 presented some ideas about curriculum and curricular goals. A curriculum is everything in a course of study. In this case, the curriculum is everything you teach children in the preschool motor program. Curricular goals are the heart of the curriculum. They are broad-based statements of what children are to achieve through participating in the curriculum. Curricular goals give general direction for what to teach.

Curricular goals and assessment have an interesting and somewhat symbiotic relationship. Curricular goals, previously selected, indicate what skills and abilities the teacher must assess. The assessment results identify what instructional objectives you need to teach to best meet the preschool children's curricular goals. So from the curriculum, by way of assessment results, you can derive weekly plans and daily lesson plans. You teach the lesson and conduct evaluations to decide if the children are really learning. Then use evaluation information to revise plans for teaching the next lesson.

The following chapter explains the link among curricular goals, assessment, planning, teaching the learning experiences, and evaluation in greater detail.

assess → plan → teach → evaluate

Figure 4.9   The teaching-learning model shows the relationship among assessing, planning, teaching, and evaluating.

Part II

Learning Experiences

The learning experiences in part II are the heart and soul of this book. They are developmentally appropriate games and activities that we have developed and used for many years. They are meaningful to the children who experience them because they give the children multiple opportunities to learn and practice skills based on age-appropriate movement objectives. You can use them in a setting that includes many children with special needs and their typically developing peers. They are also fun for the children because we designed them with the idea that children have a tremendous potential to enjoy themselves while they are learning. These learning experiences, with the techniques for structuring a movement program and other interesting ideas in the book, will give the preschool educator the tools to create an influential movement program for children of all abilities.

5

Movement With a Purpose: Planning Learning Experiences

Everyone has a purpose in life . . . a unique gift or special talent to give to others.

Deepak Chopra,
***The Seven Spiritual Laws
of Success***

Michelle is a loving and kind teacher in the local childcare center. She has always thought it important that children learn to move skillfully but has been unsure how to do this because she has no training in teaching movement. This year she has become more interested in helping her children move because of Angie. Angie is a five-year-old girl with spina bifida who spends each weekday afternoon with Michelle. Angie's parents are interested in their daughter getting as much help with her movement as possible. They realize that because of the spina bifida movement will be more difficult for her, making it important that she gets lots of practice moving each day while at the childcare center. Michelle has decided to use the 40-week curriculum, found in the appendix on page 215, as it is written, until she feels comfortable observing children moving and designing her own curriculum.

In planning for next week's lessons, Michelle reviews the curricular goals and learning experiences listed under week 1 in the 40-week curriculum. She sees that these learning experiences introduce the children to the structure of the movement program and provide her with the opportunity to observe them as they move. Michelle notes the name of each learning experience, then turns to the pages in chapter 6 where they are listed alphabetically. Michelle reads the directions for conducting Big on Balloons and Stickers on the Body Part. She checks the equipment list and has everything on hand. Both activities will work well in the small space available to Michelle, and Angie can participate in both. Michelle is now ready to lead these learning experiences.

Carol has been teaching for many years in a school-based preschool program that is part of a large school system. She is widely respected for her excellent teaching. So when the school district decided to implement a movement program for all preschool children, Carol was the teacher recommended to pilot the program. In planning the learning experiences, Carol reviewed the 40-week curriculum in the appendix to get an idea about how to organize the curriculum. However, she enjoys being creative and bringing her ideas to what she teaches, so she decided to create her own preschool movement program curriculum following the steps discussed in this chapter.

Preschool movement programs help children grow and develop optimally. These programs use movement to help children learn. This chapter instructs teachers in two specific ways to create a preschool movement program: use the 40-week movement program curriculum in the appendix, or develop a unique movement program from the learning experiences in chapter 6. We also include definitions of fitness and motor planning, an explanation of mobility equipment, suggested equipment and music, and ideas for overcoming obstacles to providing movement experiences.

> **The process of selecting learning experiences begins with deciding what the children need to learn.**

Developing Learning Experiences

The title of this book *Moving With a Purpose* underscores the importance we place on conducting games and activities that help preschool children develop new skills and abilities. Playing games and doing activities can and should be fun, but there is a *purpose* for movement in addition to having fun. That purpose is to help children *learn* to become proficient movers. The following information will help you select learning experiences that will help children learn new movement skills, while having fun along the way.

There are at least two ways to use the learning experiences in chapter 6. First, you may turn to the appendix and teach the learning experiences in the order listed, without modification. Teachers who are new to conducting a preschool movement program may wish to start in this way. This is a sound curriculum. Variations of this 40-week curriculum have been developed and used over several years. The second way to use these learning experiences is to select them based on a simple five-step process.

Selecting Learning Experiences: The Five-Step Process

Curricula are best when you modify them to meet the unique needs of the children in the movement program. So as you gain confidence in teaching movement, you may wish to use the alternative approach below.

1. Identify, in general terms, what children need to learn in a preschool movement program. The process of selecting learning experiences begins with deciding what the children need to learn. Use the curricular goals presented in box 2.1 to decide, or you may wish to create your own curricular goals, responsive to the unique needs and interests of the children in your setting, by following the curriculum development process described in chapter 8. For a further understanding of fitness terms and motor planning, refer to boxes 5.1 and 5.2.

2. Assess children's skills and identify what skills each child is ready to learn. Observe children moving and assess their movement skills, using the strategies presented in chapter 4 and the sketches in figures 4.1 through 4.7. Assess which skills children have mastered and which skills they are ready to learn. For a further understanding of how children learn to move, refer to the motor development concepts presented in chapter 7.

3. Select the learning experiences that will help each child learn the skills you identified in the previous step. Find the learning experiences that will help the children achieve each of the curricular goals listed in the game finder at the beginning of the book. From among those listed, select specific learning experiences to teach. Plan the details of the lesson. Organize the equipment, space, and time.

4. Conduct the lesson using a child-centered approach. During the lesson, observe, encourage, and challenge the children to learn. Refer to chapter 3 for further discussion of a child-centered approach to preschool movement programs.

5. During and after the lesson, evaluate the children and the learning experiences. Are the children able to do the learning experience? Is each child successful? Is each child challenged to learn new skills? Modify the learning experience as needed. Take notes on the children's movements. After the lesson, review the notes and recall the lesson. Using this feedback, design the next learning experience.

> During the lesson observe, encourage, and challenge the children to learn.

Mobility Equipment

The remainder of this chapter provides specific ideas for easily creating an appropriate environment for teaching the learning experiences in chapter 6. The first topic we will discuss is mobility equipment.

Some children with special needs will require mobility equipment to participate in many games and activities. Here are some pieces of mobility equipment with which you may need to become familiar.

- Wheelchair. You can propel wheelchairs in a variety of ways, based on individual needs (figure 5.1). Manufacturers can construct motorized wheelchairs to respond to numerous types of touch. Standard wheelchairs can be propelled by the individual or with assistance.

- Walker. As with wheelchairs, there are a large variety of walkers available to children (figures 5.2 a–b). Based on their needs, the walker will be designed to function best when positioned either in front of or behind the child.

- Gait trainer. Use a gait trainer to assist a child to develop a stronger, more mature gait pattern (figures 5.3 a-b). It can also stabilize a child who needs support to stand, leading to independent participation in games involving throwing, catching, or striking.

- Mobile prone stander. A mobile prone stander, also known as a dynamic stander (figure 5.4), allows a child unable to stand independently to assume an upright position. If capable, the child can also propel the wheels.

Recreational Equipment

Learning to use recreational equipment is an excellent way to develop children's motor skills. It's also fun to play with! Adapted swings, tricycles, roller racers, and scooters are readily available.

Box 5.1 Definitions of Fitness Terms

Everyone needs a minimum level of physical fitness to perform physical activities. There are at least three components of fitness that are important to health. These health-related fitness components are cardiovascular endurance, muscular strength, and muscular endurance.

Flexibility is often considered a component of health-related fitness. Although not included as a curricular goal in this book, developing flexibility is especially important for preschool children with spastic cerebral palsy.

Cardiovascular endurance is the ability to sustain large muscle activity for a long time. This sustained large muscle activity requires considerable use of the body's circulatory and respiratory systems. Cardiovascular endurance is important for health-related fitness. We develop cardiovascular endurance through regular participation in activities that use the large muscles of the body over many minutes, such as running for several minutes in an active tag game.

Muscular strength is the maximum force that a person can exert on an object in one all-out effort. Activities in which children lift their own body weight, as when climbing, or lift heavy objects can increase upper-body strength. Activities in which children push or pull heavy objects, run, or cycle against resistance can increase lower-body strength.

Muscular endurance is the ability to exert force on an object repeatedly. We develop muscular endurance through activities such as pedaling a tricycle; climbing a steep incline; or doing pull-ups, sit-ups, or push-ups. Throughout this book muscular strength and muscular endurance are grouped together because you can use similar learning experiences to develop these two fitness components.

Box 5.2 Motor Planning

Motor planning is a process that is developed through the intimate interactions between a child's sensory and motor systems. When children are first developing they initially move and become aware of what these movements feel like using many of their sensory systems. These systems are sight, sound, and touch. They also include proprioception, the awareness of how our joints are positioned, and vestibular sensation, awareness of where our body is in relation to the horizontal plane and gravity and what to do to maintain balance and equilibrium. As the repertoire of sensory-motor experiences increases, a child develops a dynamic body awareness in relation to the environment. This allows a child to understand and create an idea of what body movements are needed to interact in a particular situation, and to retrieve, assemble, plan, and then execute these movements to achieve a desired outcome. Problems in motor planning can occur if, (1) either the sensory or motor systems are not functioning properly; (2) there is a problem integrating information from the various sensory systems; or (3) the feedback from movement is not processed appropriately.

Sookie Kayne, personal communication, October 19, 1999

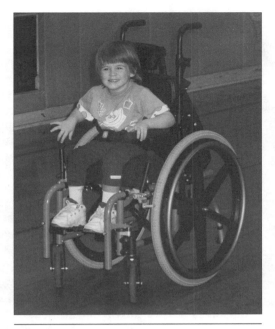

Figure 5.1 Standard wheelchair.

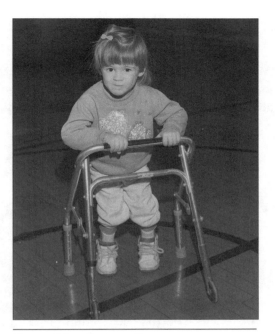

Figure 5.2a Basic walker.

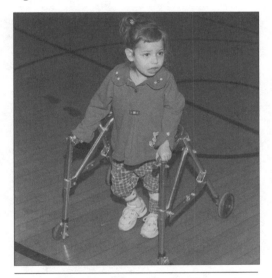

Figure 5.2b Posture control walker.

Photo © Rifton Equipment. Used by permission.

Figure 5.3a Gait trainer.

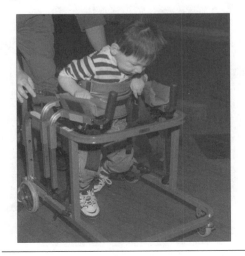

Figure 5.3b Child using a gait trainer.

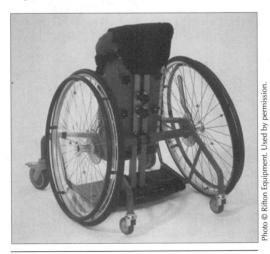

Photo © Rifton Equipment. Used by permission.

Figure 5.4 Mobile prone stander.

Swings

Different types of swings are available to meet different types of needs. Select the swing that will best fit your students' needs.

- Half-bucket and full-bucket swings are good for toddlers and preschool children who have difficulty supporting themselves independently (figure 5.5).
- Strap swings, made from a heavy rubber strip, are for children who can independently support themselves (figure 5.6).
- Bar swings, made from a straight wooden or heavy plastic bar, invite children to hang by their hands from the bar, hang with their knees draped over the bar, or, for a real challenge, sit on the bar. The second and third way require close adult supervision.

- Platform or vestibular swings are made from a large square board, typically three feet square, suspended by ropes at each corner. One to three children can use these swings at one time, either draping their legs off the side or sitting completely on the swing. These swings work on directionality and spatial awareness and are especially helpful for children who have difficulty tolerating movements that send their bodies back and forth, side to side, or in a circular motion. These swings also may be calming to children in temporary need of a consistent rhythmical motion (figure 5.7).
- Net swings envelop children within a net that is cinched closed at the top. These swings are helpful for children who are unable to support themselves in any way. Place the child in a tumble form chair, then place the chair in the net swing. Children of any ability level can also sit in a net swing and let it drape around them, offering a comforting sense of enclosure (figure 5.8).

Figure 5.5   Half bucket swing.

Figure 5.6   Strap swing.

Figure 5.7   Platform swing.

Figure 5.8   Net swing.

Tricycles

Many children with special needs can learn to ride a tricycle independently using a variety of commercially available equipment adaptations.

- Hand and hand-foot propelled tricycles, with a seat and cushioned back, can be propelled using only the hands, only the feet, or both the hands and feet (figure 5.9).

- Hand propelled tricycles, with a platform as a footrest, can be used by children who are nonambulatory (figure 5.10).

- Adapted tricycles are standard tricycles with added sissy bars and foot straps, which secure children's shoes to the pedals (figure 5.11). Not shown are waist straps, which aid children who need additional support to remain upright, and upright handlebars or attached dowels, which provide an easier hand grip for children with difficulty grasping.

Roller Racers

A roller racer (figure 5.12a) is a great piece of equipment for developing reciprocal movements and upper-body strength in a fun way. Children with roller racers at home can continue to practice these skills as they play. Adapted roller racers have easy-to-grip handles and seats that accommodate straps (figure 5.12b).

Figure 5.11   Tricycle with adaptations.

Figure 5.12a   Roller racer.

Figure 5.9   Hand and foot powered tricycle.

Figure 5.10   Hand powered tricycle.

Figure 5.12b   Adapted roller racer.

Scooters

Children with limited mobility can participate in scooter activities using equipment adapted to their needs (figure 5.13). Adaptations include a jettmobile, tumble form chair on a wheeled platform, and a long scooter.

- The jettmobile allows a child to be firmly positioned in either the prone or seated position (figure 5.14).

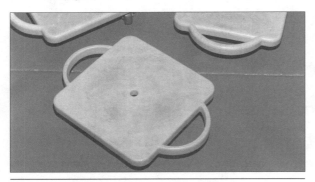

Figure 5.13 Scooters.

Figure 5.14 Jettmobile.

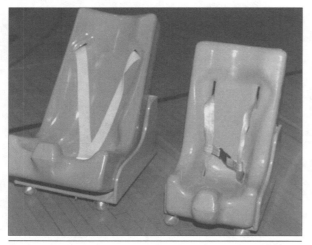

Figure 5.15 Tumble form chair on a wheeled platform.

Figure 5.16 Long scooter.

- A tumble form chair placed on a wheeled platform enables children needing maximum support to still be at floor level with their peers on scooters (figure 5.15).
- Long scooters are convenient to use when you want children to use only their arms to propel themselves (figure 5.16). They are also useful for nonambulatory children who do not need as much support as a jettmobile provides.

Motivating Children Through Music

Music can be a wonderful way to create an environment in which children are focused, active, and learning. Use music to accompany the warm-up, cool-down, and as background during the body of the lesson. Recent research (Miles 1997) indicates that the systematic use of music can be an effective way to consciously manage our mind, mood, and body. If used appropriately, music can help develop an environment that promotes quality engagement while enhancing the neurological superhighway within our brains.

The music we hear can influence the brain wave frequency and thus our state of mind. Play upbeat selections to energize children during tag games. Play slower beat selections to help the children relax and focus during balance activities. So, rather than just grabbing the nearest CD or tape, thoughtfully select the type of music to enhance the lesson's goal. Box 5.3 offers music suggestions suitable for preschool children.

Overcoming Obstacles to Providing Movement Opportunities

It is appropriate, before looking at the learning experiences in chapter 6, to consider some common environmental constraints you may encounter as you begin to develop movement programs for preschool children. We present here suggestions for overcoming common obstacles, such as space limitations, insufficient or inadequate equipment, and lack of time to prepare sufficiently. It is our point of view that most obstacles are challenges that you can overcome satisfactorily, with a little creative thinking and perhaps some extra effort. As one great optimist wrote, "Where there's a will, there's a way." Keeping a positive attitude while learning the games and activities presented in chapter 6 will undoubtedly provide teachers the firmest foundation for building quality movement programs.

Getting Started

Flying a kite is an enjoyable and memorable activity for children of all ages. Watching a kite rise, we're exhilarated by the notion that something as frail as a kite can soar against the wind and connect us so thoroughly with our spirits. However, kites don't just pop up into the air by themselves. First, they must be planned and constructed to be rigid enough to fly, yet flexible enough to withstand gusts of wind. Then we bring them to the field and search for and claim a suitable and safe open space. We must estimate the wind currents, and if required, adjust the weight of the kite with bits of cloth tied to the tail to give it stability as it flies. Perhaps we must tow the kite to get it airborne, the flier running with string in hand, letting out a bit at a time, coaxing the kite up to the air currents that will sustain its flight. In the end, our kite-flying efforts usually provide us with great exercise, uncommon delight, and thorough satisfaction.

Creating and teaching movement programs for children is similar to the process of flying a kite. Whether creating an entire movement program for many or dealing with the special needs of one, teachers translate desires into action by planning and doing, making adjustments and modifications as needed. When learning and teaching the games and activities described in chapter 6, think often of the characteristics of successful kite flying. Follow a plan, yet be flexible. Find the right space and the right time. Adjust your approaches as conditions require. Start a little at a time, then put in all the effort necessary to get up and going, and please enjoy the experience as children happily learn to become proficient movers.

Getting Space

Clearly, many games and activities in chapter 6 had their origins in large gymnasiums where chil-

dren could run unhindered in relative safety. However, running is only one component of physical education covered by these learning experiences. There are many other movements, including locomotor movements, that children can learn and practice in smaller spaces safely. Here are some suggestions.

When an activity requires running through large, open spaces, do the following:

- If the activity also teaches to another goal, such as spatial awareness, eliminate running and substitute a locomotor skill more appropriate to the space available, such as jumping, walking on tiptoes, crawling, or galloping.
- If you can teach outdoors or in a large room, plan to do the activity then.
- Seek to locate a larger space that may be available for your use in another building nearby, such as a church basement, a school yard, or an open field.
- Share a large common area with other teachers. On a cooperative basis, take responsibility for setting up equipment and preparing the area, and let others participate in using the equipment for a few days.

When an activity requires you to make space available in the classroom, do the following:

- Make clearing the floor space part of the activity. Have children push chairs and tables aside as a warm-up and to develop muscular strength.
- Make a game of clearing the space. Put on lively music, supervise with a watchful eye, and let the children push and pull the furniture out of harm's way.

Getting Equipment

Many games and activities in the following chapter require specific pieces of equipment. See box 5.4 for equipment suggestions. Keep in mind that items listed under Equipment for each learning experience are usually suggestions. We encourage substituting less expensive or more available items that are safe and provide the same function.

Repurposing Equipment

Most preschool classrooms have play items that you can repurpose and use to teach movement, providing they have the same functionality and can be safe. For instance, large wooden blocks laid end to end become an instant balance beam.

Sturdy chair backs become supports for bedsheets to make an instant tunnel. Cardboard bricks, milk cartons, or shoe boxes standing on end become bowling pins. When reviewing game and activity equipment lists, keep in mind that substitutes are welcome, as long as you preserve function and do not compromise safety.

Using Strung Ropes

Some activities require that you string a rope across the game area or loop it down from the ceiling. In the classroom, this usually means having sturdy eye hooks attached permanently in the appropriate positions to allow you to string ropes or loop them through. Attaching eye hooks to building walls and ceilings usually requires administrative permission, and the installation is best left to someone who knows the materials in which the eye hooks will be fastened. For safety reasons we advise against attaching ropes to any furniture that can slide or shift, such as bookshelves and tall cabinets. Heavy, immovable, stable furniture may be suitable if you can use it safely.

Getting and Storing Tires

Tires are wonderful to climb on, wiggle through, swing from, and roll over. You can usually get tires for the asking in places where municipalities charge a per-tire recycling fee when they are discarded. Tire stores, garages, and landfills are good sources to obtain tires. Unfortunately, tires may be difficult to store between use. Some suggestions for storing tires are keeping them outside and covered with a tarp to prevent water from accumulating inside them; storing them at the end of a hallway or in an unused space under stairs; asking for them on loan from a junkyard or recycle center, having a parent volunteer haul the tires to the center, use them for a week, then haul them back to be recycled. If you borrow tires, request newspaper coverage for the activities using them and give credit to the person who loaned the tires for making that learning experience possible.

Cage Balls and Omnikin Balls

Some activities require a large diameter, inflatable ball. Cage balls and Omnikin balls are expensive. You can purchase a single ball and share it among all the classes in the preschool program. If purchasing a large ball is not possible, investigate borrowing one for a specific time from a local school. Physical therapists may have access to these balls and might be willing to loan them for a few days at a time.

Tennis Balls

You can often obtain used tennis balls free from parents and friends who play tennis and are willing to donate them. Keep lots of tennis balls in a few large buckets with a lid on each bucket. Grab a bucket of balls from its storage place (perhaps under a cupboard or where the container serves as a small table) when you are ready to lead learning experiences such as Let's Get Catching, Throwing, and Kicking, or Gutter Ball.

Getting Help

Preschool movement program teachers require assistance constructing special equipment, setting up equipment for the equipment-intensive activities, and supervising stations during the involved activities. It is important for the preschool teacher interested in providing a full program of movement learning activities to take the initiative to arrange for assistance when required. Here are some suggestions for recruiting help:

- When appropriate, enlist the help of children to move tables and chairs and to set up less complicated pieces of equipment. Participating in the preparations can provide movement practice as well as help develop a child's sense of worth.

- Seek the talent of parent volunteers to construct targets and other pieces of equipment or to help set up an area with equipment. If you keep parent volunteer work to once a month, parents will be more willing to volunteer. Begin recruiting parent volunteers with a sign-up sheet (or a note home) for specific tasks and dates at the beginning of the year. Plan the movement program curriculum to accommodate the availability of help. Call in a local newspaper reporter to write a story about the efforts of the parent volunteers. The publicity will make it easier to recruit more help in the future.

- Establish a cooperative effort with other teachers, and share the use of the equipment with them after it is set up.

- If you are located near a local college that has students in education courses (physical education, early childhood education, elementary education, developmental psychology, speech and language education, and special education), make some calls to see if there is any interest within the college to offer stu-

Box 5.3 / Music

Music naturally motivates children, and if you use it properly, it can be an invaluable addition to any child's movement experiences. The following list includes three categories of music for use in preschool movement programs: music that includes songs with directed movement or action, upbeat background music children love, and alternative background music with a softer beat.

These titles are suggestions for music you may want to acquire as you establish your music library. Enjoy!

Music That Includes Songs With Directed Movement or Action

Bean Bag Activities & Coordination Skills—Kimbo Records
Children's All Time Rhythm Favorites—Activity Records
Greg & Steve—*Big Fun*—Youngheart Records
Greg & Steve—*Kids in Motion*—Youngheart Records
Greg & Steve—*On the Move*—Youngheart Records
Hap Palmer—*Get a Good Start*—Activity Records
Hap Palmer—*Sally the Swinging Snake*—Activity Records
Hap Palmer—*Walter the Waltzing Worm*—Activity Records
Mousercise—Walt Disney Music Co.
Preschool Action Time—Kimbo Records
Preschool Aerobic Fun—Kimbo Records
Raffi—*One Light, One Sun*—A&M Records
Raffi—*Singable Songs for the Very Young*—A&M Records

Upbeat Background Music Children Love

Best of Disney—Walt Disney Records
Cool Kids & Groovy Grown Ups—Old Navy and Rhino Records
Disney for Our Children—Walt Disney Records
Jock Jams—Tommy Boy Music
Minnie & Me—Walt Disney Records
Reggae for Kids—RAS Records
Rugrats Motion Picture Soundtrack—Interscope Records

Alternative Background Music With a Soft Beat

Deep Forest—Sony Music
Enya—*Paint the Sky With Stars*—Reprise Records
Heart of the Rain Forest—Earthtone Records
Kevin Roth—*Dinosaurs & Dragons*—Sony Music
Mozart Effect: Music for Children—BMG

---

dents the opportunity to volunteer once or twice a week to work with children, or perhaps to have the children visit the campus for an organized movement program. The skill of the college students and their educational background will influence who takes leadership in providing the learning experiences.

By no means are these suggestions a comprehensive list of ideas for teachers with limited space, equipment, or assistance. We are interested in learning from you some ideas for overcoming obstacles to providing movement experiences for preschool children. Please send your success ideas to us at Human Kinetics, Attn: Scott Wikgren, P.O. Box 5076, Champaign, IL 61825-5076.

Box 5.4 **Equipment Lists**

The following equipment is used in the 40-week curriculum located in the appendix.

You may want to use these lists as a guide to inventory the equipment you have and to develop a list of equipment you would like to purchase or make.

Equipment Available Through Commercial Catalogs or Large Toy Stores

Balance beams—aluminum, carpet, foam, high, plastic, tapered, vari, and zigzag

Balls—fleece, foam, koosh, rubber, Velcro

Beanbags

Bike helmets

Climbers—five- step A–frame, large plastic structures

Cones

Foam shapes

Hippity hops

Hula hoops

Mats—crash, folding, incline wedge

Roller racers

Roller skates

Scooters

Stairs—portable

Swings—bar, bucket, net, strap, vestibular

Tricycles

Tunnels

Wagons

Adapted Equipment Available Through Commercial Catalogs

Roller racers

Scooters

Seating

Tricycles

Catalog Suppliers

Flaghouse—601 Flaghouse Drive, Hasbrouck Heights, NJ 07604   800-793-7900

Sportime—One Sportime Way, Atlanta, GA 30340   800-850-8602   Fax: 800-845-1535

Things From Bell—P.O. Box 135, East Troy, WI 53120   800-543-1458

Inexpensive or Homemade Equipment

Balance beams—board, lighted*

Balloons—helium quality

Balls—tennis, yarn

Bells

Bowling pins—plastic

Boxes used in packing large household appliances such as washing machines and refrigerators

Bubble mixture for blowing bubbles

Chairs—child size

Containers—plastic bottles, detergent, and so on (weighted and empty)*

Foam tubes

Fruits and vegetables—plastic or real

Gutters*

Ladders

Paper plates

Pictures—animals, numbers, shapes, and so on

Plastic bags or burlap sacks

Plastic pools

Pulleys*

Rackets—nylon, plastic*

Red Light, Green Light sign*

Rope

Scoops—plastic*

Sheets

Stickers

Stuffed animals

Swimming kickboard

Tape—colored

Targets—wooden*

Tires

Toothbrush—giant*

Wands—plastic

*Directions for constructing each make-it-yourself piece of equipment are located within the learning experience that applies its use.

Learning Experiences: Movement Games and Activities

6

We present more than 50 movement games and activities in alphabetical order on the following pages. Use them to help children learn to move skillfully! In order to select activities that fit certain educational objectives, or to quickly locate a favorite game, refer to the game finder found on page viii. It is an alphabetical listing of the games, supplies, page numbers, and goals for the children for each game.

Let's Balance

Balance is a lifetime ability. Riding a bicycle, skiing down hill and cross country, or just walking across a floor cluttered with children's toys are all activities that require balance. Balance courses and balance stations, constructed from the equipment listed below, provide children with a wide variety of stimulating and enjoyable ways to develop their balance.

OVERVIEW

Place a variety of equipment designed for children to walk on for balance practice throughout the area. Encourage children to choose and experiment—walking, scooting, or crawling on the equipment from one point to another. The number of participants will depend on space availability and adult supervision. You can set up work on balance as a group activity or as station work. Either way the activity concepts will remain the same. A balance obstacle course that requires children to navigate their way over the balance equipment is ideal for a group activity. You can also set up individual stations to give children the option of moving from one balance activity to another, sequencing their way through a variety of activities.

GOALS FOR CHILDREN

- Develop balance while walking on a variety of surfaces—high, low, wide, narrow, zigzag, tapered.
- Develop motor planning through sequencing movements among three or four pieces of equipment.

EQUIPMENT

- Carpeted area or mats to place under beams.
- Balance boards (flat boards, 8-foot lengths of two-by-fours or any length or width, that can rest on the floor).
- Wooden, plastic, or cardboard blocks (can vary in size as long as children can independently step on them).
- Clothesline rope placed on the floor to walk on.
- Foam beams (typically 4 feet long by 4 inches high by 6 inches wide).
- Zigzag beams (typically multicolored plastic pieces, approximately 4 inches high by 6 inches wide, that snap together in a variety of curved patterns).
- Vari-beams (wooden boards approximately 3 feet long with holes at each end that fit into movable connectors, about 4 inches high by 6 inches wide. You can set up vari-beam courses in a variety of shapes).
- Aluminum beams (typically 6 feet long by 10 inches high by 6 inches wide).

- Carpet beams (wooden beam covered in carpet, typically 10 feet long by 4 inches high by 6 inches wide).
- Tapered beams (typically start approximately 2 inches high by 3 inches wide and widen to 6 inches high by 5 inches wide).
- High beams (typically 6 inches wide and 2 to 3 feet high).
- Lighted beam created by Dereck Bigford (to make a lighted beam, place colored lights, preferably blinking, inside a wooden shell approximately 6 feet long by 6 inches wide and cover the top with Plexiglas).
- Walking blocks.

PREPARATION

Set up the balance equipment before the activity begins. Place mats under balance equipment. If the piece of balance equipment is only a few inches from the floor, a carpet underneath will be sufficient.

Important—Safety is a priority when designing balance practice activities for children. When creating stations for balance practice, plan only one station that requires adult supervision and turn taking. Make all other stations children use easily accessible and without the need for continual supervision. Following are examples of five balance stations:

Station 1. The high beam. An adult must supervise this activity closely. One child practices at a time.

Station 2. Four foam beams placed in a row.

Station 3. Zigzag balance beam and vari-beam.

Station 4. A variety of balance boards.

Station 5. Lighted beam.

DIRECTIONS

1. Demonstrate the use of balance equipment so children will know what you expect of them.

2. Discuss safety requirements such as (a) identifying equipment that needs supervision, and (b) emphasizing no pushing others aside when moving on a piece of balance equipment.

3. When practicing balance at stations, it is OK for a short time if all the children seem to be in one area. Crowding typically does not last long, and the children are learning great lessons in problem solving, turn taking, and decision making.

ADAPTATIONS

You can include children who are nonambulatory through providing alternatives, such as allowing the children to scoot or crawl across a beam, with assistance as needed. For children at the beginning stages of developing balance, sitting on a balance beam or standing on the floor with only one foot on the beam may be the first step. The stair climbing or high beam equipment may not be suitable for some children with limited mobility.

You can encourage children with visual impairments to scoot or crawl on their own or be physically guided through the balance obstacle course. Use bright colors

(continued)

to aid those with some vision. Add sounds such as the ring of a bell, repeated beeps, or hand clapping to help with orientation.

VARIATIONS

Set up a balance obstacle course like a maze. Connect the balance beams. The children are then free to roam the room without getting off the balance beams.

IN SMALL SPACES

For practicing balance in small areas, use only one or two different balance beams at a time. When practice time is short, practice balance while moving to and from other activities. As an example, have the children walk along a balance beam or rope on the floor as they make their way to the bathroom, or as they enter or leave the room.

Place blocks and clothesline rope along the floor as an alternative to balance beams.

Incorporate other objects in the room into a balancing maze.

Memories are made when the children walk across the balance beam on the floor for the first time without the teacher's helping hand.

Basketball With Water Balloons

The novelty of throwing water balloons into scaled down basketball nets absolutely delights preschool children! This activity gives them the chance to enthusiastically throw, a skill needed to play sports such as basketball and baseball. Children also enjoy the unique feeling of the jiggly, wiggly water balloons, which are easy to retrieve because they do not roll far when thrown.

OVERVIEW

Spread basketball nets of varying heights and styles over an open area. Place buckets of water balloons in an area all children can easily reach. Children practice throwing water balloons into their choice of nets. Children retrieve the water balloons and repeat the activity. An unlimited number of children can play, depending on the space and number of basketball nets available.

GOAL FOR CHILDREN

Improve throwing.

EQUIPMENT

- Various height basketball nets on stands. Have something as simple as a basket or crate on the floor, a few nets 2 to 4 feet high, and one net 6 feet high.
- Substitute bushel baskets, crates, clean garbage cans, or boxes if basketball nets are not available.
- Have at least 10 helium-quality, 6- to 8-inch water balloons. Helium-quality balloons will withstand a lot of activity if replaced each day after use. They are typically difficult to break.

PREPARATION

Fill water balloons and put them in buckets ahead of time. Thick, helium-quality water balloons usually resist breaking. Have a mop and bucket or several towels handy for mopping up in case a water balloon does break.

Important—Some children are allergic to the latex in balloons. Know who cannot be exposed to latex and cover the balloon with a cloth balzac cover (available at most toy stores) or with a nonlatex protective glove.

(continued)

DIRECTIONS

1. Review the safety rule for playing with balloons: Always keep balloons away from your mouth.
2. Demonstrate how easy it is to hold, throw, and pick up a water balloon because it does not roll far away.
3. Establish any necessary boundaries.
4. Play music to encourage a high activity level.

ADAPTATIONS

To make the game easier for children who need practice grasping and releasing, lower the basket so the children can simply drop the balloons into the basket. Consider using a gait trainer or mobile prone stander for children who rely on mobility support such as a walker. This equipment allows the child's hands to be free while in an upright position. Children with visual impairments may be able to see the target more easily by outlining the rim with brightly colored tape. Attach a bell to a balloon to enable these children to hear the balloon's location.

VARIATIONS

Incorporate a variety of balls, such as nerf and rubber, along with the water balloons and let the children choose.

IN SMALL SPACES

Use only a few water balloons and a few nets to fit the space available.

Water balloons indoors? It really isn't a mess. Sturdy helium balloons seldom break, and if they do, it is only water. A classroom carpet will dry, and a floor can be mopped.

Big on Balloons

- **Body part identification**
- **Object control**

Preschool children in a room with a lot of balloons will naturally practice the object control skills of striking, catching, kicking, and throwing. Balloons don't move fast or far when struck, which makes them ideal for introducing these skills to preschool children. Along with being great fun, this activity is quick to set up and children can enjoy it in small or large spaces.

OVERVIEW

Children hit a balloon with any body part they can. The goal is to keep the balloon in the air as long as possible.

GOALS FOR CHILDREN

- Improve throwing, catching, striking, or kicking.
- Name body parts.

EQUIPMENT

- Balloons—10-inch or larger helium-quality balloons in various colors.

  Important—If a child cannot be exposed to latex, cover the balloon with a nonlatex protective glove or a cloth balzac cover (available at most toy stores).
- Soft rackets or homemade rackets constructed from hangers covered with stockings are optional.
- Music.

PREPARATION

Inflate many balloons in advance, and keep them in large bags or boxes.

DIRECTIONS

1. With children seated, demonstrate hitting balloons with different body parts to keep them in the air. Stress safety: Keep the balloons *away* from your mouth. If a balloon breaks, let an adult pick up the pieces.
2. Hand each child a balloon or dump the balloons out of the boxes or bags. Turn on an upbeat music tape. Music provides natural motivation!
3. Encourage the children to shout out what body part they are using when hitting balloons.

ADAPTATIONS

For children unable to grasp standard size balloons, partially inflate a balloon and place it inside a nonlatex protective glove. The child can now experience the feeling of playing with a balloon while controlling it easily by grasping any empty finger slot of the glove. For children with visual impairments, attach a bell to brightly colored balloons.

(continued)

VARIATIONS

- Use a small foam racket or one made with a hanger and stocking to keep the balloon in the air. This helps to simplify this activity for children who are learning the rudimentary skills of reaching and touching an object.
- Drop the balloons from a higher elevation than the children and have them reach up to catch the balloon, then place it in a big box. This is most successful when you do it with three to four children at a time. This activity is great for children with IEP goals involving extension!
- Tie balloons to a rope extended across an open space. Have children hit the balloons with either body parts or soft rackets. Vary the height of the balloons to accommodate all children, including those seated in wheelchairs.
- Tie balloons to a rope, suspended at floor level, and allow students to practice kicking.
- Set up a low net, two or three feet high, and let several children practice hitting many balloons over the net at the same time. Have the net reach to the floor, otherwise the children will inevitably try to go under it!
- Scatter balloons around the floor. Have the children pick them up with a rolled magazine or a wooden dowel in each hand and place the balloons in a box.

IN SMALL SPACES

Many children can be playing together with balloons in a room. Use discretion in determining how many children can play safely at one time. For a small area, use just a few balloons and have groups of children take turns.

Balloons in a small space? Jimmy can hit the balloon up as high and hard as he wants and the balloon won't hurt the furniture, the walls, or another child.

Body Bowling

- **Body part identification**   - **Stability**
- **Motor planning**

Body Bowling is a stimulating and motivating activity for preschool children. It's more novel than Simon Says for helping them learn the names of their body parts, and they love to roll, twist, bend, stretch, and reach in this activity.

OVERVIEW

Children logroll across mats or carpeted areas, attempting to knock over bowling pins with designated body parts.

GOALS FOR CHILDREN

- Improve rolling, twisting, bending, stretching, and reaching.
- Move identified body parts.
- Follow game directions.

EQUIPMENT

- Mats or carpeted area.
- Twelve plastic bowling pins for every one or two children.
- Masking tape for marking carpet.
- Clear, 2-liter plastic bottles filled with colored paper as a substitute for bowling pins.

PREPARATION

Space the 12 plastic bowling pins along the four sides of each mat, with one or two children per mat, or mark with masking tape an 8- to 10-foot area on the carpet.

DIRECTIONS

1. Children lie in the middle of a designated area on either their stomachs or backs. You can be near the children, ready to give directions.
2. Ask each student to logroll and knock over one pin with a designated body part. For example, "Knock over a bowling pin with your hand."
3. Children then logroll toward a pin and knock it over with a hand.
4. Continue with, "Knock over a bowling pin with your knee."
5. Children roll to a different pin and knock it over with a knee.
6. The game continues until the children knock over all the pins.
7. Ask children to reset pins, and repeat the activity.

(continued)

ADAPTATIONS

This activity can work well with children who have limited mobility, especially those who need opportunities to extend and move while out of wheelchairs. With the child lying on a mat, prompt him or her to move a limb normally kept immobile by placing pins very near the child's limb to assure success. To assist children with visual impairments, clap or place a beeper next to the bowling pin the child is to knock down.

VARIATIONS

- Use bowling pins in a variety of colors. Designate a body part and color. For example, "Knock over the blue pin with your elbow."
- Use numbered bowling pins. Ask children to knock over the pins in numerical order.
- Ask children to crawl on elbows and knees or all fours to each bowling pin.

IN SMALL SPACES

Limit the number of pins set up on a carpeted area or mat and have the children take turns.

Brie is nonambulatory, yet she enjoys rolling and giggling through this activity with her classmates.

Bubble Fun

- **Locomotor skills**
- **Stability**
- **Object control**

Catching soap bubbles is an activity preschoolers love doing over and over. Fill the room with bubbles, and children will jump with delight trying to pop them by clapping their hands together. The practice they get jumping, balancing, catching, and following objects with their eyes in this activity will help build the skills they'll use one day for quality athletic performances in softball, baseball, or basketball. Bubble Fun is also great for helping children who don't like touching (tactually sensitive) to accept the touch of something sticky.

OVERVIEW

Stand by a fan with a bowl full of bubble mix. Continually dip a bubble wand into the bubble mix and place it in front of the fan so it emits a spray of bubbles. The bubbles float in many directions so children will have the fun of tracking different bubbles and trying to pop them before they hit the floor. Bubble Fun works best with up to 20 children.

GOALS FOR CHILDREN

- Improve jumping, catching, and following objects with eyes.
- Improve walking forward, backward, and sideways while reaching up, out, or down to clap a bubble.

EQUIPMENT

- One gallon of bubble mix (always have a gallon on reserve) or homemade bubble mix. If you'd like to make your own bubble mix, combine 1/4 cup glycerin (available at pharmacies), 1 cup dish detergent (Dawn or Joy works best), and 10 cups of cold water.
- A large bowl to pour bubble mix into.
- A circular bubble wand with at least 10 holes in it.
- A standard size oscillating fan placed on a table.
- Objects to create a barrier in front of fan, such as 4 large cones.

PREPARATION

Locate the fan against a wall near an electrical outlet. Place a barrier in front of the fan to prevent a child from accidentally getting too close. Place an old carpet or blanket directly in front of the fan to absorb bubble mix coming off the wand. This prevents the floor from becoming slippery.

(continued)

DIRECTIONS

1. Review safety rules: Stay away from the barrier and keep your hands far from the fan.
2. Demonstrate how to pop a bubble and have the children practice by clapping their hands. Children unable to clap can point at the bubble with their finger or grab at it with one hand.
3. Turn on the fan and fill the room with bubbles!

ADAPTATIONS

Give nonambulatory children the freedom to use their hands by placing them in one of several types of mobility equipment listed in chapter 5. Position the children so the bubbles will drift to them. Encourage children with visual impairments to reach and feel the bubbles as they pop against their hands.

VARIATIONS

Add music! Put on upbeat, fast tempo music and watch the children react. They will be popping bubbles faster than you can make them.

IN SMALL SPACES

This activity works equally well in large or small spaces. Limit the number of children to fit the available space.

The room will fill with bubbles and laughter as children jump, tap, stomp, and clap their way through this thoroughly enjoyable activity.

Cage Ball Fun

- **Muscular strength and endurance**
- **Stability**

A cage ball is about the largest inflatable ball with which children can play. Children moving atop a cage ball develop balance and defensive reactions that may prevent a serious injury during a fall.

OVERVIEW

Place one child at a time on a cage ball and tip the child, with your support, gently front to back, then side to side. Roll a cage ball over a row of children lying on the floor to provide them with unique sensory input, or, while seated in chairs, have children kick or push the ball to each other. There are a variety of ways to have fun with a cage ball!

GOALS FOR CHILDREN

- Stimulate vestibular system.
- Strengthen upper body.
- Improve balance.
- Problem solve.

EQUIPMENT

- One cage ball per teacher.
- A chair for each child.
- Mats or carpeted area, if children will be lying on the floor.

PREPARATION

Clear an area large enough for the activity. Inflate the cage ball inside the activity area, because it may be too large to bring through a doorway.

DIRECTIONS

Here is a suggested list of simple activities to get started using a cage ball:

1. Allow one child at a time to sit or lie on top of the cage ball, with your support.
2. Gently roll the cage ball back and forth, and side to side. Hint—If a child is lying stomach down on the ball with you holding the legs, the ball will move easily as you begin a rocking motion.

ADAPTATIONS

A child of any ability can participate independently in the stationary activities. Mobility equipment may be necessary for those activities in which children move across the room. Add a sound effect to accompany the movement of the ball, such as the ring of a bell or repeated beeps, for children with visual impairments.

(continued)

VARIATIONS

- Have the children lie down in a row on a mat or carpeted area. Roll the cage ball over the top of them. They'll love it!
- Vary the activity by using an Omnikin ball. These balls are much lighter than cage balls, inflate quickly, and are available in three sizes.
- Let children push the Omnikin or cage ball across the room into walls and corners. When the ball goes into a corner or up against a wall, let the children problem solve by figuring out where to stand to get the ball moving again.

IN SMALL SPACES

Have the children sit in chairs placed in a large circle. Put the Omnikin or cage ball in the middle of the circle, and tell the children when the ball comes toward them they can either kick or push the ball, but they must stay in their chairs. Watch their excited anticipation as they wait for the ball to come toward them!

Reduce the number of children playing to fit the space available. With preschool children, these activities work best in small groups of four to six children at a time. However, you can use an Omnikin or cage ball with a large group of children, if the supervised activity is one of several station options.

Cage balls can work well in small spaces. If you choose the variation in which the children roll the ball, there is no waiting time and it's nonstop action. Anticipating the large ball approaching is just as exciting as touching it.

Let's Get Catching, Throwing, and Kicking

Catching, throwing, and kicking are skills central to many playground games, team sports, and lifetime recreation activities. Preschool children need to practice these skills often to become proficient.

OVERVIEW

Children will either throw or kick an object to a partner or at a target. You can set up catching, throwing, and kicking as a group activity or as station work. As a group activity, provide enough equipment for every child to participate at the same time. As station work, provide enough equipment, at all the stations combined, to accommodate all the children at one time. Let the children decide whether to wait at a particular station or move to one where equipment is available.

GOALS FOR CHILDREN
- Improve grasping and releasing.
- Improve catching, throwing, and kicking.
- Learn to take turns.
- Improve color and size identification.

EQUIPMENT
Objects:
- Balls—fleece, koosh, tennis (dyed various colors), Velcro, gator (a squishy ball that expands back to its normal size), foam, and yarn (various sizes and colors).
- Beanbags (various sizes, shapes, and colors).
- Water balloons (use helium quality to avoid breakage).
- Large marshmallows, apples, lemons, and small potatoes.

Targets:
- Clear plastic bottles with different colored paper, sand, or cloth material inside.
- Foam shapes of varied sizes, shapes, and colors.
- Wooden creations, such as large figures cut from plywood, with holes cut in a variety of shapes and sizes.
- Pictures, such as brightly colored smiley faces, animals, shapes, and favorite cartoon characters.
- Tires.
- Bells, balloons, balls, plastic containers, and streamers hung from a safe, strong ceiling suspension.

(continued)

PREPARATION

- Always place targets close to a wall, with clear stop boundaries on either side of the target. The stop boundaries can be ropes, cones, benches, or anything that clearly communicates stop. These boundaries help avoid unsafe situations such as a child running behind a target when someone else is throwing a ball.
- Teach children to put objects in the proper containers when they have completed their turn. Children may need repeated opportunities to learn this responsibility, but it is worth the time.
- Set up targets and objects before the activity starts.
- Designate markers on the floor where children are to stand. Use tape, rope, or carpet squares. Markers facilitate cueing children to stand in the proper area. For example, "Remember to stand on the carpet when throwing at the bottles." Markers also predetermine the distance from which children will be throwing, catching, or kicking.
- Plastic bottles with caps must have the caps taped after you screw them on the bottle. Preschool children are naturally curious and could quickly unscrew caps and put them in their mouths.
- Take time at the beginning of the school year to install eye hooks in handy locations throughout the classroom so it is easy to string the ropes from which to suspend the balls.

DIRECTIONS

Specific directions will vary with the combination of objects and target equipment you chose.

1. Demonstrate the activity for the children.
2. Discuss safety requirements such as stop boundaries and where to stand when engaged in the activity.
3. When doing station work, it is OK for a short time if all the children seem to be in one area. This crowding typically does not last long, and the children are learning great lessons in problem solving, turn taking, and decision making.

ADAPTATIONS

Give nonambulatory children the freedom to use their hands by placing them in one of several types of mobility equipment listed in chapter 5. Position the children so they can reach the targets. Either place a container filled with balls next to the child, or pair the child with an ambulatory classmate who can hand over balls as needed. Children who are just learning to grasp or release have better success with small objects in their hands. Let them drop objects into a stimulating container or target. Gradually progress to releasing objects onto targets placed at eye level with the child. Consider placing a ramp below the child's hand to guide the object down and into the target. A homemade scoop, cut from a gallon plastic jug, will function as an aid for children with difficulties grasping. Select brightly colored objects for children with visual impairments to throw. Consider asking the child to drop the object on a cookie sheet or another container that makes noise. Place a noisemaker, such as a beeper, bell, or tape player, next to the target to help children with visual impairments know where to throw or kick the ball.

VARIATIONS

Preschoolers love to be silly! Throw a marshmallow or toss a lemon. The children will be grinning ear to ear when asked to catch an apple or kick a balloon!

IN SMALL SPACES

Set up one or two stations in which the children have their backs to each other and are throwing or kicking away from each other.

Jimmy is getting the practice he needs grasping and releasing a ball while still playing alongside his classmates. He enjoys the thrill of releasing the ball at the top of the ramp and watching it roll down and knock over the plastic bottles—the same bottles his friends are throwing at.

Let's Get Climbing

- Locomotor skills
- Motor planning

Humans are constantly climbing! We climb flights of stairs at home and at work. We climb ladders to paint and repair our homes. We climb walls and mountains for sport and recreation. We integrate climbing so thoroughly into our daily lives that it's sometimes hard to remember that in our preschool years we needed to practice climbing to become proficient at it!

OVERVIEW

Set up a climbing obstacle course for a group activity or create individual climbing stations. Build the obstacle course and stations from the following equipment suggestions. The number of participants depends on space availability and adult supervision.

GOALS FOR CHILDREN

- Develop climbing skills.
- Develop motor planning.

EQUIPMENT

- Always have a mat, mattress, or other sufficient cushioning as a landing platform.
- Ladders (vary length, size, and angle at which they climb).
- Mats stacked like wide stairs.
- Mats stacked like a mountain.
- Stairs (typically either in 3-step blocks or 3 steps up, platform, 3 steps down).
- Tires.
- A-frame climbing apparatus (2 ladders joined at the top to make an A-frame children can climb).
- Plastic climbing structures (such as those manufactured by Little Tikes or Fisher Price).
- Ask for equipment donations for climbing through sending home a note requesting old tires, ladders, wooden boxes, or pieces of wood from which to construct climbing equipment. Repair any loose parts or splintered edges before using the equipment.

PREPARATION

Set up equipment in advance. Safety is the first priority when creating climbing stations and courses. Preschool children climbing on high structures require close adult supervision and must be able to take turns. Climbing stations ideally have only one station requiring close adult supervision, with the others made easily accessible to children without the need for continual supervision. We present tips for setting up obstacle courses in the Obstacle Course Introduction found on page 87.

EXAMPLES OF CLIMBING STATIONS

Station 1. A large, five-step A-frame climbing apparatus that requires children to climb up, over the top, and down the other side. This is a closely supervised activity, in which one child goes at a time.

Station 2. Two ladders placed flat on the floor for children to freely step through.

Station 3. Tires stacked loosely in a mat area, where children can stack and climb over them.

Station 4. A pile of mats or mattresses stacked like stairs that children can climb up and down.

Station 5. A low, plastic climbing structure on which children can freely climb.

DIRECTIONS

1. Demonstrate the use of climbing equipment, so children will know what you expect from them.

2. Discuss safety requirements such as (a) identifying equipment that needs supervision, and (b) emphasizing no pushing others aside when climbing.

3. When practicing climbing at stations, it is OK for a short time if all the children seem to be in one area. Crowding typically does not last long, and the children are learning great lessons in problem solving, turn taking, and decision making.

ADAPTATIONS

With children who are nonambulatory or fearful of heights, begin by letting them sit at the base of a climbing structure, or coax them to independently hold the bottom rung of a vertically placed ladder, leaning against it in a prone position. Follow by offering adult assistance in facilitating movement. Encourage crawling over tires, scooting up stairs, or rolling over stacked mats or mattresses as independently as possible. Physically guide children with visual impairments through the climbing course. Use colored tape to highlight steps or climbing obstacles for children with partial sight.

VARIATIONS

• Develop a motivating color or animal theme for each climbing station, such as climb over the mountain like a tiger.

• Conduct this activity on a playground if it contains equipment designed for climbing.

IN SMALL SPACES

Create a low-level climbing course in a classroom that reduces the danger of falling, while providing the opportunity to use upper-body muscles. Fill your classroom with free or inexpensive smaller sized items from the equipment list on the previous page. Create a climbing paradise such that whichever direction a child moves they must step or climb over an obstacle. Furthur create a fun atmosphere by giving your classroom a silly title. For instance, tell the children they are entering The Climbing Zone!

Climbing does not have to involve heights. A classroom can become a climbing zone by challenging the children to climb over boxes, blocks, plastic crates, or tires.

Frisbee Toss

Throwing and catching a Frisbee is an acquired skill that provides many children and adults with a noncompetitive, high-quality physical activity that you can enjoy almost anywhere there is open space. Frisbee Toss is a basic way to introduce this activity to preschool children.

OVERVIEW
Children throw and retrieve paper plates, using the Frisbee throwing movement.

GOAL FOR CHILDREN
Throw a Frisbee.

EQUIPMENT
- Paper plates, one for each child (small paper plates may be easier to manipulate than large ones).
- Plastic bottle or foam shape targets.

PREPARATION
Place a sticker or stamp on each paper plate to increase their visual appeal for children.

DIRECTIONS
1. Position children in an open area.
2. Demonstrate how to throw a Frisbee using a flick of the wrist.
3. Instruct the children to throw, retrieve, and continue throwing their Frisbee until you ask them to stop.
4. Distribute plates, observe the children throwing, and facilitate their throwing movements.

ADAPTATIONS

Simplify the activity for children who are not yet ready to throw objects but instead need additional practice grasping and releasing objects. In place of a standard-size paper plate, substitute a small paper plate or container top and place the target directly below or in front of the child to allow easier manipulation of the object and provide a more successful experience while still interacting with peers.

Enable nonambulatory children to use their hands by placing them in a piece of mobility equipment listed in chapter 5. To add auditory cues for children with visual impairments, tie bells to holes punched around the edge of a plastic container top.

VARIATIONS

- Play lively music. When the music stops, have the children sit where they are.
- Restart the music and continue the activity.
- Use theme paper plates. Buy plates with novelty themes on them, such as holidays, birthdays, and cartoon characters.
- Use real Frisbees, instead of paper plates, with small groups or when using the Frisbee Toss as one of several stations. Have the children toss the Frisbee only in an area that has been clearly marked.
- Set up a variety of targets, such as plastic bottles and foam shapes, for the children to knock down with Frisbees.
- Throw the Frisbees through hula hoops and tires standing on end.

IN SMALL SPACES

Use only a few paper plates in small areas.

Chaotic? No! Many children can safely throw paper plates simultaneously. The paper plates don't hurt, sail only short distances, and the children can pick them up and fling them over and over.

Garbage Clean Up

Garbage Clean Up is an easily organized, fast-paced, ball-handling game that gives children a lot of freedom to throw repeatedly.

OVERVIEW

Create a barrier by hanging sheets over a rope dividing the area. An equal number of children stand on each side of the divider. Each side has a bucket of soft balls. You will tip each ball bucket over. Children pick up balls and throw them from their side of the room to the other. The game ends when all the balls are on one side of the room or once you decide they've played long enough. Children then help you pick up the balls, divide them equally, and begin the game again.

GOALS FOR CHILDREN

- Develop a child's ability to follow game directions.
- Enhance development of object control.
- Enhance development of eye-hand coordination.

EQUIPMENT

- A barrier, made from rope and sheets, strung about 2 feet high, to divide an open space.
- Two large buckets of soft objects to throw, such as fleece balls or foam shapes. Make fleece balls by cutting cardboard to the desired diameter of the fleece ball. Wrap yarn around the cardboard many times. Slip a strand of yarn between the wrapped yarn and cardboard, then tie tightly around yarn. Cut the yarn off the back of the cardboard and fluff to complete the yarn ball.

PREPARATION

Have the balls ready in buckets. Design an easy method to hook or tie the fence, if you have to remove it between classes.

DIRECTIONS

1. Explain to the children that the area on their side of the room is their backyard. When you empty the bucket of balls, their yard becomes messy and they need to clean it up.
2. Children on each side throw balls over the barrier to clean up their yard.
3. When one yard no longer has any balls in it, announce that yard is clean instead of introducing competition by announcing a winner.
4. Have children help put the balls back in the two buckets. Make sure the balls are evenly divided between the two buckets, then begin the game again.

ADAPTATIONS

Consider using a gait trainer or mobile prone stander for children who rely on mobility support such as a walker. This equipment allows the children's hands to be free while in an upright position. Place a bucket of soft objects within reach. Arrange for a teacher or other children to hand soft objects to those children with special needs who are unable to reach. In this way, children at the rudimentary movement stage obtain needed practice grasping and releasing objects. Add sound devices such as bells or beepers to the balls for children with visual impairments.

VARIATIONS

Change the theme by changing the name of the game to Clean Up Your Room or Clean Up the Yard.

IN SMALL SPACES

Drape a sheet over a rope stretched across the middle of any size room, limit the number of children playing to fit the space available, and use only soft objects for throwing. To create a barrier, install eye hooks on opposite walls and string a rope between the two hooks across the room. Adjust the rope so it hangs about two feet above the floor across most of the room. Alternatively, tie a rope around the upper part of heavy table legs and string across the room, or drape a row of chairs with sheets. Any safe, convenient way of creating a boundary dividing the room in half will work.

This activity isn't just for the gymnasium. Try it in the classroom. Garbage Clean Up is a high-energy game that involves several children and takes only a minute or two to set up. Enlist the children's help in pushing furniture and equipment aside and draping the sheet while you tie the rope.

Gutter Ball

• **Motor planning** • **Object control**
• **Stability**

Before children learn to catch tossed balls, they need practice grasping and releasing balls rolled toward them. Gutter Ball is a great way for children to independently stop, grasp, or catch a rolling ball. Children with limited upper-body control or limited mobility can participate enthusiastically alongside their more skilled classmates.

OVERVIEW
Connect and support various lengths of vinyl gutters to create a continuous, sloping chute through which tennis balls roll. Children place tennis balls in the top of the gutter chute and let them roll, attempting to stop and grab them before they reach the collection box at the bottom. The number of participants depends on the number of gutters. A rule of thumb is four children to every six feet of gutter.

GOALS FOR CHILDREN
• Develop skill in grasping, releasing, and catching.
• Develop a sense of timing as children anticipate when the rolling ball will reach their hands.

EQUIPMENT
• Vinyl gutters of various lengths. Start with two 6-foot gutters joined to two 3-foot gutters.
• Corner pieces and gutter connectors to join gutters in your choice of patterns.
• Stands to support gutters. Be creative and resourceful. Use sawhorses, boxes, or blocks. You can also use supports made from PVC tubing.
• Tennis balls, 25 to 50.
• Two boxes to hold tennis balls—one at the top of the gutter chute, one at the bottom for collecting the balls.

This learning experience involves special equipment. It might be an ideal project for a parent who is handy and wishes to help the program. Gutters require little storage space, as you can disassemble them and place them on the floor along a wall or store them vertically in a closet. Once the gutters and supports are constructed, you can use them again, requiring about 10 minutes for assembly.

PREPARATION
Assemble gutters, corner pieces, and gutter supports to configure a chute before the activity begins.

DIRECTIONS
An adult needs to periodically empty the collection box of tennis balls at the end of the chute back into the dispensing box at the beginning of the chute. This activity tends to run itself, freeing you to help individual children learn to grasp and release.

ADAPTATIONS
Children with limited mobility can independently participate, using a piece of mobility equipment listed in chapter 5. Position children within easy reach of the gutter.

Stimulate the participation of children who have visual impairments. Add bells or beepers inside the balls to make noise when rolled.

VARIATIONS
- Add more gutters and change the direction of the corner pieces to make more involved chutes.
- If gutters are unavailable, substitute any long, cardboard tubing, such as a carpet tube, cut in half along its length.

IN SMALL SPACES
You can do this activity in a confined space with a few children by setting up a single gutter for as many as four children to use, or set up the gutters in a compressed zigzag pattern.

Kayla is not yet able to grasp a ball, but she enjoys placing her hand midway along the sloping chute to stop the balls her classmates roll down the gutter. When many balls become lined up behind her hand, she lifts her hand and squeals with delight as the balls continue on their way.

Hand-Over-Hand Pull

• Muscular strength and endurance

Today's children—girls in particular—are notoriously weak in upper-body strength. Hand-Over-Hand Pull teaches the motions of climbing a rope or a ladder and is a great activity to enhance upper-body strength. Preschoolers will pull and pull until their arms can't pull anymore!

OVERVIEW

A child, seated in a chair, raises a large plastic bottle or cone attached to a rope and pulley by pulling the rope hand over hand. The child then releases the rope and watches the cone fall to the ground. The child repeats raising and releasing the cone until finished with the turn. The number of children participating at one time will depend on how many pull stations are available. This activity needs to be supervised, so it is best for small groups of children or set up as an individual station. Children who are waiting for a turn must stay out of the way of the falling cone, so designate a waiting area for them, or provide an alternate station activity for them.

GOAL FOR CHILDREN

Develop upper-body strength.

EQUIPMENT

- Sturdy eye hooks or other ways of securing a rope to the wall at least 6 feet above the floor.
- Thin clothesline rope, cut into one long length to stretch across the room and several 15-foot lengths to loop through the pulleys.
- Pulleys.
- Chairs.
- Cones (with a hole at the top side to tie the rope through) or plastic bottles weighted with water or sand (remember to keep the weight limit of the container safe for use by young children).
- Plastic pools, tires, laundry baskets, or other containers into which the cones will fall.

PREPARATION

Tie small pulleys spaced at 2-foot intervals along a 20-foot rope suspended horizontally 6 feet above the floor. Make sure the suspended rope is taut. Run individual 15-foot ropes through each pulley. Tie one end of each 15-foot rope through a cone. Tie the other end to a chair leg to keep the rope from slipping all the way through the suspended pulley. Place a small plastic pool, laundry basket, or tire under each cone as a target into which to drop the cone. Consider requesting assistance from the custodial staff or parent volunteers in installing the required eye hooks and stringing the ropes and pulleys. Little space is required to store the equipment when not in use.

DIRECTIONS

1. Demonstrate a hand-over-hand pull and how to release your grip on the rope.
2. Review these safety rules: (a) children stay away from all cones, and (b) children must wait for their turn in a designated area.
3. Tell children what direction to go when leaving their chairs. Consider placing a stop border around the area where the cones will be falling and instruct the children not to cross it.
4. Use music to cue children into and out of the activity.

ADAPTATIONS

This activity is great for children with limited mobility because it does not depend on mobility for participation. Place children who need support while seated either in a chair or their personal wheelchair. For children who are just learning to grasp and release, tie a knot in the pull rope every few inches to make it easier to grasp when pulling. For children with visual impairments, tie bells along the rope so they will hear sounds as they raise and drop the cones.

VARIATIONS

- Place stuffed toys, plastic animals, or other objects in the pools or on the floor if pools are not available. Children try to make the cones land on the objects.
- Tie different objects, heavier or lighter in weight than cones, on the ropes.
- Tie bells to the ropes so they jingle as the children pull them.
- If outside, fill the plastic pools with water to create a splash when objects drop into the pools.

IN SMALL SPACES

Set up only a few pulley stations to fit the space available.

Bei Linh is an extremely active child who typically moves nonstop. Yet when participating in the Hand-Over-Hand Pull she will remain focused for up to 25 minutes. Bei Linh loves the repetitive pull and release movement of this game.

Heart Power

- **Cardiovascular endurance**
- **Body part identification**

This is an excellent curriculum unit on the heart distributed by the American Heart Association (AHA). The Heart Power Kit includes the following:

- A big book story titled "Big News" accompanied by a narrative tape.
- Large posters depicting healthy food and ways preschool children can be physically active.
- A stethoscope.
- A teacher's curriculum guide.
- Movement activities to promote cardiovascular fitness. The games involve many locomotor movements including running, jumping, galloping, and skipping.

OBJECTIVE

- Explain why cardiovascular fitness is important to health.
- Develop cardiovascular fitness.

Heart Power can be an exciting addition to a movement program. For more information on how to purchase a curriculum kit, contact your local chapter of the AHA at 800-AHA-USA1 or check their Web site **http://www.amhrt.org.**

Parent feedback from this curriculum is positive. Most parents do not realize their children are capable of learning about healthy eating habits and the importance of cardiovascular fitness at this young age.

Let's Get Jumping

The little leapers you teach today will be jumping mud puddles, climbing mountains, and slam dunking basketballs in just a few years! Help them learn to jump the best they can with the activities you develop from the following suggestions.

OVERVIEW

You can set up work on jumping skills as a group activity, with a jumping obstacle course, or as station work. Either way the activity concepts remain the same. In an obstacle course, children can jump their way around a predetermined course picked from the equipment list. If you choose to set up stations, children will have the option of moving from one skill station to another, jumping their way through a variety of activities.

GOAL FOR CHILDREN

Learn to jump over, off, and across a variety of objects.

EQUIPMENT

The following equipment is for jumping down (remember to always have a mat as a landing platform):

- Wooden boxes.
- Plastic cubes.
- Mats stacked at various heights.
- Tires.

The following equipment is for jumping over:

- Foam tubes (cylinder shaped noodles).
- Plastic wands.
- Hurdles made from plastic cones or foam blocks, with plastic wands as crossbars, adjusted to various heights.
- Small objects such as balloons taped to the floor, stuffed animals, imaginary river with fish in it.

The following equipment is for jumping forward:

- Bright floor tape spaced every 6 inches.
- Specifically measured shapes on the floor (square, rectangle, circle, etc.).
- Hippity hops. (Hippity hops, also called hoppity hops, are inflated rubber balls with handles. A child sits on the ball, holds the handle, and pushes off the floor with the feet. The child establishes a bouncing motion that enables him or her to maneuver the ball around the room.)
- Foot stompers, which can be purchased or homemade. Using a wooden dowel and a board (18-24 inches long by 6-12 inches wide), create a miniature seesaw. Glue the dowel across the width in the middle of the board. Place a fleece ball

(continued)

or other lightweight object on one end of the board. As the child jumps forward onto the opposite end, the object is propelled into the air. Add to the challenge by having the child attempt to catch the object.

PREPARATION

Arrange the equipment in advance. We review things to remember when setting up an obstacle course under the preparation section of the obstacle course introduction. When setting up station work for jumping, safety is the first priority. If one station has a high platform from which children jump, requiring adult supervision and turn taking, then make the other stations easily accessible to the children without the need for continual supervision.

Here are some suggestions:

Station 1. A platform 24 to 36 inches high from which children jump into a pile of pillows. This is a heavily supervised activity, in which one child goes at a time.

Station 2. Children freely jump over a pretend river with fish in it.

Station 3. Children freely jump or step over a line of hurdles ranging from 1 inch to 12 inches off the floor.

Station 4. Children freely jump over a variety of brightly colored shapes on the floor.

DIRECTIONS

1. Demonstrate the obstacle course or stations so the children know what you expect.
2. Teach safety rules, such as (a) look forward when jumping so you do not hit a friend, and (b) know which equipment needs adult supervision.
3. In station work, remember it is okay if for a short time all the children seem to be at one area. The crowding typically does not last long, and the children are learning great lessons in problem solving, turn taking, and decision making.

ADAPTATIONS

Assist children who are not yet able to jump by helping them learn to bend and straighten their legs, either while standing or sitting. Encourage them to participate in the jumping activities, substituting other movements for jumping as needed. Encourage rolling (instead of jumping) in a pile of pillows, or stepping or standing (instead of jumping over) in the river. Encourage crawling, scooting, or otherwise maneuvering under instead of jumping over the hurdles. For children with visual impairments, use brightly colored tape to mark jumping blocks and landing platforms. Also use sound effects such as mats that squeak when children jump on them.

VARIATIONS

Set up foam shapes, pillows, and shredded paper into which children can jump. They will love it!

IN SMALL SPACES

In smaller spaces, limit the number of jumping stations.

Juan's teacher has set up a variety of obstacles that the children can jump at their own pace. She enjoys providing Juan the freedom to repeatedly jump his favorite obstacles—the hurdles.

Mat Maze

An attractive maze made from folding mats standing on end and obstacles placed within keeps preschool children moving nonstop. Mazes allow children to plan their movements and focus on spatial awareness, skills necessary for remembering how to get home and, as they become adults, for negotiating highway lane changes.

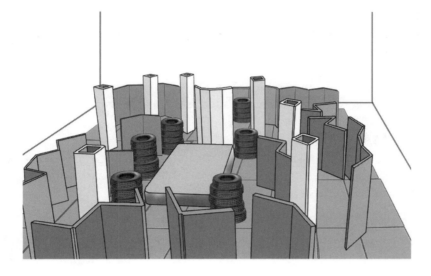

OVERVIEW
Children will walk, run, gallop, and jump their way through the maze trying to find the way out.

GOALS FOR CHILDREN
• Develop a sense of directionality.
• Improve locomotor skills.

EQUIPMENT
• Folding mats positioned on edge to stand upright.
• Large crash mats and other equipment as partitions.
• Substitute chairs, tires, or draped sheets as barriers if mats are not available.

PREPARATION
Construct the maze walls with equipment that will remain upright. If the equipment does happen to tip, be sure it will not harm anyone.

DIRECTIONS
The children will all enter the maze at the same opening. Depending on the size of the maze and the number of children involved, provide one, two, or several ways to exit. Either way, let the children have fun exploring the different paths and learning how to redirect themselves when they come upon a dead end. Play upbeat background music!

(continued)

ADAPTATIONS

Create a maze with pathways that are wide enough so that children using mobility equipment can fit through the aisles. Children with visual impairments can feel their way through the maze, or use adult assistance or verbal cues to orient themselves.

VARIATIONS

- Create tunnels and slides within the mat maze.
- Place surprises along the way, such as stuffed animals sitting in chairs or silly pictures hanging on the wall.
- Challenge the children to find specific destinations within the maze. Give children stickers and ask them to find the pictures within the maze that go with the stickers.

IN SMALL SPACES

Set up a small maze and select equipment to fit the space available. Consider draping sheets over chairs and tables and have children crawl through the maze.

Set up the maze in an area where everyone can use it over several days. Once set up, the mat maze runs itself. Children have fun exploring the endless ways of moving over, around, and through the maze.

Match the Valentine

- **Locomotor skills**
- **Object, color, and shape recognition**

Match the Valentine is a visually motivating and stimulating way to include running, jumping, hopping, and walking backward while learning to match two items.

OVERVIEW

In this teacher-directed activity, the children stand on a line or against a wall, holding one-half of the picture they are to locate. On your cue, the children walk, run, or gallop across the room, tape their half next to its match on the wall, then return to the starting point.

GOALS FOR CHILDREN

- Develop locomotor skills and cardiovascular fitness.
- Develop color and size identification.

EQUIPMENT

- Valentine hearts in a variety of sizes and colors, each cut in half. You may want to laminate or cover the heart sections with contact paper.
- Duct tape for sticking the valentines to the wall.

PREPARATION

Cut a variety of valentines from construction paper and then cut each valentine in half. Laminate each piece for durability. Cut large and small valentines, along with valentines in a variety of colors. Before the children arrive, tape all the valentines, with matching halves together, on one wall of the room.

DIRECTIONS

1. With the children in front of the wall with the taped valentines, review the differences in size and color among the valentines. Some valentines are big, others little, some red, others pink, others blue. Next, have the children line up against the opposite wall. As the children watch, take down one-half of each valentine. Give each child one of the valentine halves.

2. In one small group at a time, ask the children to find the match for their valentines. First, identify the group that will be moving by saying, "If you have a pink (red, blue) valentine" or "If you have a big (little) valentine." Second, identify the locomotor movement this group will use, such as walk, gallop, or jump. Together, the instructions sound like this. "If you have half of a big, red valentine, gallop down and find a match. When you find a matching half, tape yours on the wall next to it and gallop back." Assist children as necessary.

(continued)

3. Continue this format until everyone has had a turn and matched all the valentines. If you made more valentines than children, allow a second turn. Let the children marvel at the wall they have recreated, then start the game again in reverse. The instructions now sound like this, "If you are a boy, run down to the wall, take one-half of any valentine, and run back." You may need to demonstrate.

4. Continue this format until the wall has only halves of all the valentines. At this time ask the children to trade the valentine half they have in their hand with a friend. When everyone has a new valentine half, repeat from step 2.

5. During the game, emphasize the following.
   • Continually review size and color identification. Have a visual reference close by to illustrate.
   • If children make incorrect matches, encourage them for trying. Guide them toward the correct match and ask them, "How about this match?" You are sure to get a smile and a willingness to try next time!
   • Let the children feel the sticky tape on the back of the valentine. Use duct tape because it still sticks when used again and again. This is great sensory input for children with tactile defensiveness.

ADAPTATIONS

Children with limited mobility can participate with the assistance of an adult or a piece of mobility equipment described in chapter 5. Children with visual impairments can participate with more independence if you place a sound device, such as a beeper, on the valentine wall. Ask them to place the valentine on the wall, without regard for exact placement, next to the valentine's other half.

VARIATIONS

To change the theme of this game simply change the objects used. Theme ideas include holiday objects (shamrocks, pumpkins, decorated eggs), foods (cucumbers, apples, carrots), and transportation vehicles (cars, tractors, airplanes).

IN SMALL SPACES

Substitute crawling, tip toeing, or walking backwards for running and galloping.

Making the valentines or other shapes takes time. Consider recruiting parent volunteers to create and laminate shapes that you can use for years to come.

Mountains and Valleys

- Motor planning
- Stability

Use old tires and mats to create a mountain-and-valley landscape on which children can clamber. Mountains and Valleys is a great activity for highly active preschool children in a controlled space.

OVERVIEW

Children of all ability levels will spend as much time as you allow, climbing, jumping, rolling, balancing, slithering, crawling, and sliding over the mats.

GOALS FOR CHILDREN

- Enhance development of motor planning.
- Develop body strength.
- Enhance development of directionality and spatial awareness.

EQUIPMENT

- A minimum of 12 tires. (You can store tires vertically when not in use. Stack them so high that they become a wall barrier that preschool children cannot reach to knock over.)
- Four large, flexible mats, such as wrestling mat sections.

PREPARATION

Make two rows of tires about five feet apart. Make each row four tires long and two tires high. Create mountains and valleys by draping the mats over the tires.

(continued)

DIRECTIONS

1. First explain the rule "No pushing friends while playing on the mountain-and-valley mats."
2. Then let the children start climbing!

ADAPTATIONS

Children with limited mobility can easily participate by rolling or crawling over the mats, with adult assistance as needed. Children with visual impairments may wish to crawl over the mats initially, then switch to walking as they become familiar with the terrain.

VARIATIONS

- Play music with varying tempos and watch the activity level change. Play slow music as a cool-down and encourage rolling over the mountains down into the valleys.
- If space is available, keep adding rows of mats and tires.
- To minimize any waiting for a turn, add stuffed animals or pictures on the other side of the mountains and valleys. Ask the children to climb over and get the animals then bring them back to you.

IN SMALL SPACES

This activity needs a space large enough to safely accommodate mats over tires, with extra room for climbing, rolling, and sliding. For safety, limit the number of children participating based on the size of the mats. If storage space is at a premium, consider borrowing tires and mats once a year for this special week-long activity. This activity requires a space that you can devote to the activity for these days, so it is not suitable for use in a classroom for a single lesson.

Maheeb, who is nonambulatory, enjoys crawling up and down the mountains and valleys alongside his classmates. This activity successfully accommodates children of varying motor abilities. When shown a video of Maheeb participating in this activity with his classmates, viewers are unable to identify the child with special needs.

Move and Seek

- **Locomotor skills**
- **Object, color, and shape recognition**

Move and Seek is a captivating game that allows preschool children to develop memorization skills and practice locomotion at the same time. It is delightful to see how focused even the most distractible preschool children become trying to find hidden objects.

OVERVIEW
The children will move down to the plastic containers or cones in a designated way (walk, run, gallop), look under them until they find the object you have told (shown) them to retrieve, then return. The teacher-directed activity works best when played with two to six children. More players may result in too much waiting time.

GOALS FOR CHILDREN
- Develop locomotor skills.
- Develop matching ability.
- Develop the ability to recall information.

EQUIPMENT
- Use 12 to 15 small cones. Substitute 22-ounce cups, ice cream, cottage cheese, whipped topping, or similar plastic containers, if cones are unavailable.
- Objects that relate to the chosen theme such as plastic replicates of food for a fruit theme or stuffed animals for an animal theme.
- A picture of each object for you to show children.

PREPARATION
Select a theme for the activity, such as fruit. Gather objects that are within the theme, such as an apple, orange, banana, pineapple. Make a card with a picture to match each object, such as a picture of an apple to match the actual apple. Distribute throughout the room one cone for every object you will hide.

DIRECTIONS
1. Explain the activity while the children sit across the room from the cones. Show the children each object you will place under the cones and its matching picture.

(continued)

2. Then place the objects under the cones. Have the children watch or not watch, depending on their ability level.

3. Next, hold up a picture and ask the children what it is. Ask one child at a time to run, hop, jump, or gallop to the cones and find the object that matches the picture, for example, "Zak, can you jump to the cones and find an apple?"

4. The child jumps across the room to the cones and begins lifting cones to find the apple. When successful, the child runs back to the group and places the apple in an imaginary fruit basket or fruit salad.

5. Repeat with each child taking a turn until they find all the fruit.

ADAPTATIONS

Children with limited mobility can participate by crawling, moving in a tumble form chair on a wheeled platform, or moving in any way that allows them to be close to the floor and lift the cones. Use sound such as a beeper or tape player to guide children with visual impairments to the hidden objects.

VARIATIONS

- Hold up a few pictures and have more than one child go at a time.
- Be silly! Hold up a picture that has nothing to do with the theme and see if the children notice. Hold up a picture of a car and ask what fruit it is.
- Instead of hiding objects under cones, scatter objects around the room or tape pictures all over the walls. Play the activity using the same format, except now the children are scanning the walls to find objects or pictures.

IN SMALL SPACES

To keep the children physically active in small areas, ask them to hop rather than run or gallop to the cones.

Maria needs many opportunities to practice the concept of matching. In Move and Seek she gets the opportunity to repeatedly attempt making matches while also practicing her locomotor skills. The teacher finds it rewarding to see Maria's excitement following each successful match.

Musical Hoops

- Cardiovascular endurance
- Locomotor skills
- Motor planning

This fast-paced, nonelimination variation of musical chairs provides children with opportunities to run, hop, gallop, skip, and crawl, and as the hoops dwindle, it requires all the children to fit into the space of one hoop!

OVERVIEW

Spread hoops around an open space. When music plays, the children will move around the room. When the music stops, the children find a hoop to stand in. Slowly eliminate hoops until there is only one left.

GOALS FOR CHILDREN

- Develop locomotor skills.
- Develop cardiovascular fitness.
- Develop balance.

EQUIPMENT

Hula hoops, one for each child in the group.

PREPARATION

While the children are gathered in one area, place the hoops around the floor. Be sure to have the children sprinkle imaginary magic glue over the hoops so they will not move from the floor.

DIRECTIONS

1. Designate how everyone will move around the room when the music starts. Select movements such as running, galloping, jumping, or crawling.
2. Stop the music. All children are to find and stand inside a hoop.

(continued)

3. Dramatically remove two or three hoops, explaining that next time some children may have to share a hoop.

4. Designate a new way to move, and restart the music.

5. Continually reinforce the idea of sharing space throughout the activity. This is a new concept to many children. Have the children count how many hoops are left on the floor or how many you have removed.

6. Continue the activity until you have eliminated all but one or two hoops. Coach the children on ways to cooperatively fit in a single hoop. Congratulate the children on a great job!

ADAPTATIONS

Use oversized hula hoops to accommodate children using wheelchairs or other bulky mobility equipment. Children using wheelchairs can carry a hoop. When the music stops other children grab their hoops.

VARIATIONS

Use decorated mats or large cardboard pads that depict a theme, as a substitute for the hoops in which the children stand.

IN SMALL SPACES

Play with a few children and crawl or jump instead of run or gallop.

Music adds the magic to movement activities. Rachael, who has autism, often needs the teacher's verbal and physical cues to participate in activities, but in Musical Hoops she participates with more independence because she responds well to the music's rhythm.

Obstacle Course Introduction

- **Locomotor skills**
- **Stability**
- **Cardiovascular endurance**
- **Motor planning**
- **Spatial relationships**

Obstacle courses are direct imitations of the wonderful challenges children encounter when scampering through woods and over creeks. Sequencing movements is a necessary skill in everyday living. What better time to start the learning sequencing than the preschool years? This introduction offers information applicable to each of the seven obstacle courses.

OVERVIEW

The obstacle course, as with most learning experiences in this chapter, can incorporate practice of a variety of skills into one activity. The following seven obstacle courses can each incorporate practice of locomotor skills and balance along with developing cardiovascular endurance, motor planning, spatial awareness, and sequencing. Generally, a maximum of 16 children can participate in an obstacle course at one time, if sufficient space and adult supervision are available.

GOALS FOR CHILDREN

- Develop motor planning.
- Develop muscular strength.
- Develop locomotor skills.

EQUIPMENT

Please refer to equipment listed with each of the seven obstacle courses.

PREPARATION

Design and construct an obstacle course that most suits the lesson's objective. Safety is always the primary concern. Create an obstacle course that allows the children to safely go to the equipment of their choice and participate freely without fear of injury. Use the seven obstacle courses presented here as guides.

You can include children in constructing an obstacle course in the classroom. The following list is based on Obstacle Course 7.

1. Designate an area in the room that you will use for the obstacle course and have the children help prepare the space. Picking up toys or moving chairs, children like to help!

2. Sit the children down in the center of this now open area and introduce a theme that correlates with that week's unit. For instance, if you are working on shapes that week, suggest to the children that they will be creating an obstacle course using only equipment with circles in them.

3. Get the suggestions rolling by first offering some choices. Show the children a stack of cut paper squares and circles, and ask which is the correct stack to place on the floor. Then give some children the circles to position on a designated area of the floor.

4. Hold up the rope to walk across, and ask a child to form the rope in the shape of a circle.

(continued)

5. Hold up a square pillow and a circular pillow. When they make the correct choice, have two children position the pillows in another designated area of the floor.

6. Using a standard tunnel will make it easier to point out the circular opening, but if you are draping a sheet, use one with circles in the pattern and ask the children to identify the circles as they crawl through.

7. Remember when calling on children to help set up the obstacle course, make sure you give every child the opportunity to set up something. Children at this age do not understand, "Maybe next time."

DIRECTIONS

When introducing an obstacle course, it is important to maintain a child-centered learning environment. Put away the whistle. Control the urge to group children at each piece of equipment with movement dictated solely by your command. To make preschool children go to a piece of equipment you have chosen, to make children wait until you call their names, then to make them wait for your permission before moving on is a formula for failure, because preschool children learn through moving! This teacher-directed approach typically results in children actively moving only a small portion of the total class time. Boredom with an activity frequently leads to behavior problems, which become contagious, with chaos in the classroom as the result. To create a successful, high-energy obstacle course, allow the children to chose when and where they wish to go on the course. Even better, allow them to contribute their ideas (that are safe) to the construction of the obstacle course. Give them freedom!

1. Gather the children so they can sit and listen to a brief explanation of the obstacle course. Name each piece of equipment. With a child demonstrating, show how to use it safely. Explain that there may be times during the class that they have to wait briefly for a turn on a piece of equipment. Create waiting areas, perhaps on a mat or carpet square, labeled with a silly picture or a funny name. Help the short wait become a fun part of the activity.

2. Let the children pick their own starting points in the obstacle course. At first, the children may all crowd around one piece of equipment. Though it may seem chaotic at first, stick with the plan, and calmly suggest that they go to another piece for a few minutes, then return to this piece. The result is a roomful of active children learning through self-exploration and choice rather than merely following commands in a teacher-directed environment. Also remember that it is all right if a child attempts a skill variation on a piece of equipment, such as sliding across rather than walking on a balance beam. The idea that the child is independently attempting to get across the beam is great! Praise the effort, and on the child's next time around offer assistance to enable the child to work on the skill of walking across the beam.

Independent initiation is a confidence builder.

ADAPTATIONS

Children who are nonambulatory can participate in locomotor activities with adult assistance or crawl and scoot through the obstacle course on their own. Provide children needing continual adult assistance the freedom of choice to explore at a level that is functionally appropriate for them. Let them have fun!

VARIATIONS

- Add decorations, banners, or posters to depict a theme. Play music that fits with the theme.
- Use your own and the children's creativity, with our courses as a guide.

IN SMALL SPACES

Set up only a few pieces of equipment. Obstacle course seven is specifically designed for use in a classroom. Look for other equipment ideas under the balance and climbing learning experiences presented elsewhere in this chapter.

Jared and his classmates love obstacle courses. They give them opportunities to solve problems about working their way through obstacles while refining their motor skills.

Obstacle Course 1

EQUIPMENT

- Four mats or carpeted area.
- One crash mat or thick mattress.
- Six wooden blocks.
- One balance beam.
- Six pillows in a plastic pool.
- Six hanging balloons.
- Six tires.
- Six hurdles, 2, 4, and 6 inches high.
- One platform, 3 steps high.

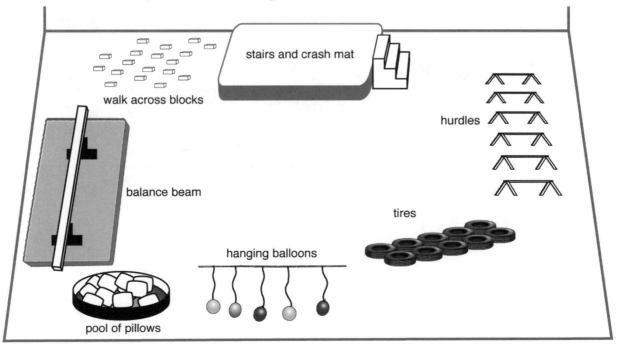

Obstacle Course 2

EQUIPMENT

- Nine mats or carpeted area.
- Five wooden boards.
- Two foam beams.
- One A-frame climbing apparatus.
- Ten tires.
- One tunnel.
- One set of stairs.
- One tapered balance beam (or 8-foot length of a 2-by-8-inch board, cut to create a taper toward one end and placed on the floor).
- One ladder.
- One rainbow barrel.

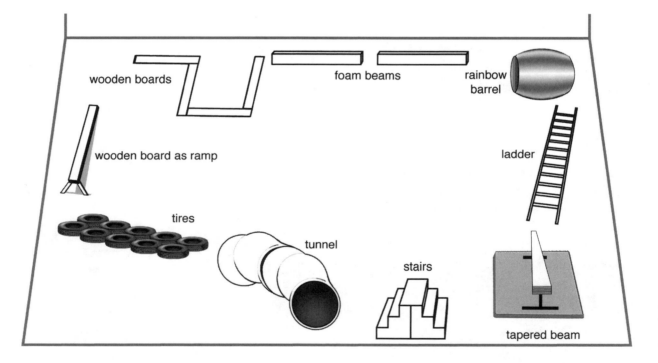

Obstacle Course 3

EQUIPMENT

- Eight mats or carpeted area.
- Two foam wedges.
- Four balance boards.
- One set of stairs.
- One high balance beam.
- One zigzag balance beam.

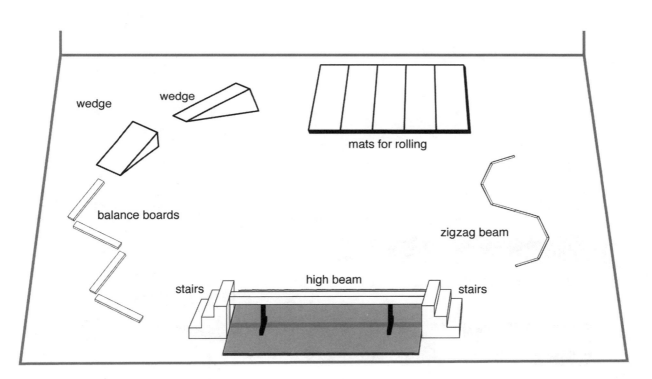

(continued)

Obstacle Course 4

EQUIPMENT

- Four mats or carpeted area.
- One A-frame climbing apparatus.
- One wedge.
- Six scooters.
- Eight tires.
- Two tunnels.
- Eight hula hoops taped together.
- Three boards with sawhorse supports.

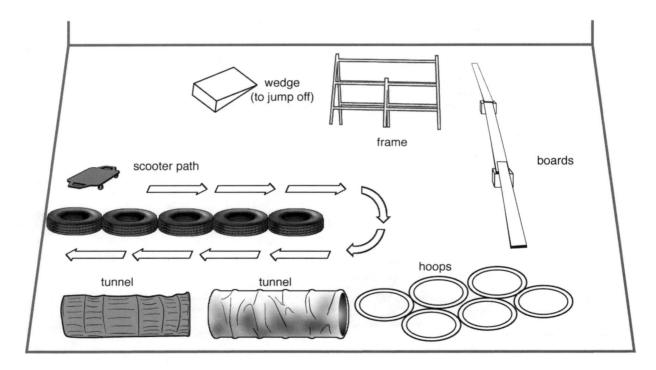

Obstacle Course 5

EQUIPMENT

- Six mats or carpeted area.
- One crash mat or thick mattress.
- Ten pillows.
- One three-step platform.
- One rainbow barrel.
- Ten tires.
- One tunnel.
- One A-frame climbing apparatus.
- Six hurdles, 2, 4, and 6 inches high.
- One balance beam.

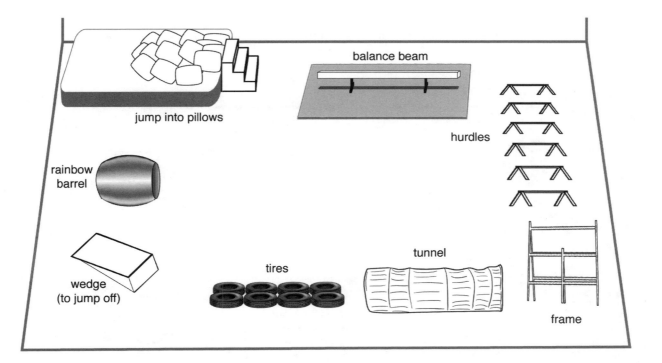

jump into pillows

balance beam

hurdles

rainbow barrel

wedge (to jump off)

tires

tunnel

frame

(continued)

Obstacle Course 6

PREPARATION

Label each piece of equipment with pictures of the animal the children will imitate.

Tunnel—squirrel crawl (crawl through the tunnel)

Ladder—bear walk (bear walk across ladder)

Stacked mats—snake slither (combat crawl between mats)

Rubber pads—lily pad for frog leap (squat and jump to each pad)

Hula hoop lion jump (jump over hurdles)

EQUIPMENT

- Six mats or carpeted area.
- Twelve tires.
- One tunnel.
- Three hurdles, 2, 4, and 6 inches high.
- One ladder.
- Six rubber pads or paper circles.
- Three hula hoops with foam hoop holders to keep hoops vertical.

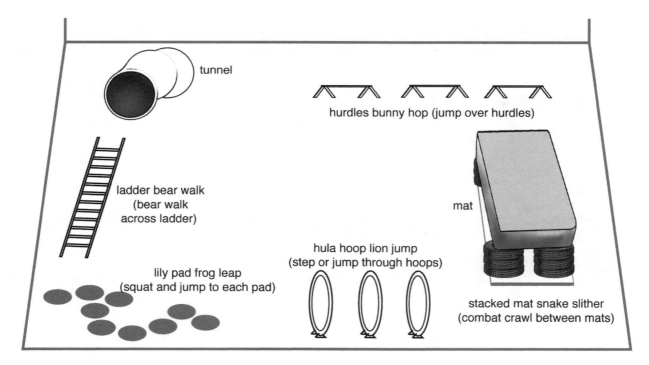

tunnel

hurdles bunny hop (jump over hurdles)

ladder bear walk
(bear walk
across ladder)

mat

hula hoop lion jump
(step or jump through hoops)

lily pad frog leap
(squat and jump to each pad)

stacked mat snake slither
(combat crawl between mats)

Obstacle Course 7

This obstacle course requires limited equipment and a small space, such as a classroom.

EQUIPMENT

- Six 12-inch paper circles, in various colors.
- Thick rope, 5 feet long.
- Tunnel (fabric-covered coil or plastic) or substitute a sheet draped over a table.
- Pillows.

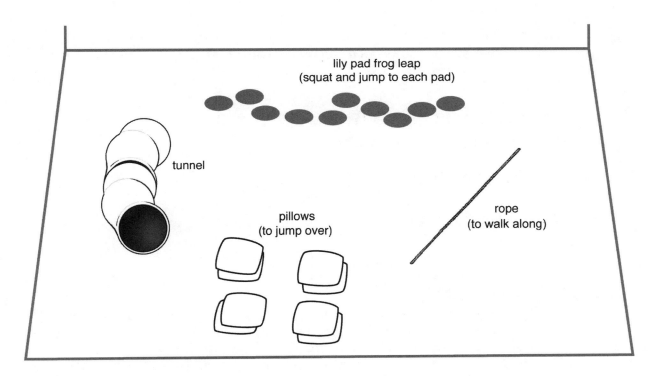

Pendulum Bowling

Pendulum Bowling is a great way to introduce a ball-handling skill in an independent, stimulating environment, where preschool children can feel in control of the ball rather than chasing it!

OVERVIEW
Children swing a suspended ball into bowling pins set up on the floor in an effort to knock them over. Set up three or four bowling stations at a time to accommodate several children.

GOAL FOR CHILDREN
Develop skill in directing a ball at a target.

EQUIPMENT
- Playground ball.
- Plastic grocery bag.
- Rope.
- Three plastic bowling pins or plastic bottles.

PREPARATION
Create the suspended ball by placing a playground ball inside a plastic grocery bag. Tie the bag's handles together, then tie a rope through the handles. Loop the other end of the rope over something that will allow suspension several feet above the floor, such as through a hook in the ceiling or over basketball backboard supports. Tie the rope so the ball touches the floor. Next, tape four x's on the floor as described here. Place the first x about two feet behind the ball. This marks where the child will stand. Tape three more x's about three or four feet in front of the ball. Arrange these three x's to make a triangle with two in the back and one in the front. Place one bowling pin on each of these three x's.

DIRECTIONS

1. Demonstrate to the children how to pick up the ball, return to the *x*, and push the ball forward with two hands to knock over the bowling pins.

2. Demonstrate how to walk over and reset the pins on the *x*'s. Resetting pins can be a challenging, time-consuming, yet worthwhile task that you shouldn't rush.

3. For preschool children ready to work in pairs and take turns, encourage one child to set up the pins while the other pushes the ball and visa versa.

ADAPTATIONS

Children with limited mobility can easily participate in this game by using mobility equipment that allows their hands to be free. Children who are just learning to grasp and release can push a ball that you place in front of them. Place bells on the bowling pins so children with visual impairments can enjoy the sound of knocking over the pins.

VARIATIONS

Substitute foam cylinders, soda cans, or plastic bottles for bowling pins. Create motivating targets by placing strips of colored paper inside the two-liter, clear, plastic bottles.

IN SMALL SPACES

Calculate the number of children who can participate based on the space available. Clear all obstacles within the radius of the rope and provide one ball for every one or two children.

What a joy to be able to swing a ball in a classroom without having to worry where the ball may land. Even the most aggressive child can push the ball forward, and it will travel only the radius of the rope.

Push and Pull

Children love to push and pull objects. This activity helps them develop strong leg and arm muscles, in a fun way!

OVERVIEW

Children push and pull weighted objects to designated spots across the room. As many children can participate as weighted objects are available.

GOAL FOR CHILDREN

Increase body strength.

EQUIPMENT

This list is to choose items from, as well as stimulate your ideas.

- Large boxes.
- Laundry baskets.
- Toddler-size grocery carts.
- Wagons.
- Tires (used loose or with rope attached).
- Chairs.

Here are suggestions for objects to use as weights.

- Sand or kitty litter in 5- or 10-pound bags.
- One-gallon plastic containers filled with water or sand.
- Weights of 5 or 10 pounds.
- Wagon with a child sitting inside.

PREPARATION

Based on the objects you will use, have the weight already placed in or on the piece of equipment. Maintain uniformity with all children pushing or pulling the same type of object simultaneously, whether it be boxes, laundry baskets, tires, grocery carts, chairs, or wagons.

DIRECTIONS

Gather all the children to the designated starting point, whether a floor line or a mat. Identify the spot across the room, such as a wall covered with stimulating pictures, to which the children will travel. Start music to signal the beginning of the activity and help the children push or pull objects to the finish spot.

ADAPTATIONS

Attach weighted objects to a rope that children with limited mobility pull toward themselves. Use sounds such as verbal cues, a beeper, or music from a radio or tape player to guide children with visual impairments to the designated area.

VARIATIONS

- Select a theme, then create a setting that matches it. Use pumpkins as weights in autumn or bricks wrapped as presents for the holidays.
- Create a grocery shopping theme in which children push grocery carts through equipment positioned to make aisles. Place plastic food along the aisles for shoppers to select as they push their weighted carts to the checkout area.

IN SMALL SPACES

This activity works well in small spaces. Children simply go back and forth more times over the short distance.

The teacher adds fun to this activity through her playful teasing. She makes exaggerated straining sounds while pushing a box, then flexes her arm muscle in a show of strength. Once across the room, all the children pretend to wipe their brows, then give each other high fives for a job well done.

Puzzle Pieces

- **Body part identification**   • **Locomotor skills**
- **Object, color, and shape recognition**

Children love to play games that give them the opportunity to successfully complete a task and enjoy moving at the same time. Here is such a game.

OVERVIEW

Children enjoy choosing an oversized puzzle piece, moving across the floor, and assembling the picture again, piece by piece. This game is best played in a group of up to eight children. To play with larger groups, have two or three children take a turn at the same time.

GOALS FOR CHILDREN

- Develop locomotor skills.
- Develop recognition of colors, shapes, and picture identification.
- Develop object control.

EQUIPMENT

Create a puzzle picture that will have at least twice as many pieces as children in the group. This assures each child two turns.

PREPARATION

Select a theme and create a large paper image that fits it. As an example, create a snowman for a winter theme. Cut three large, white paper circles, each at least one and one-half feet in diameter. Add pieces made in proportion to the body, such as a top hat, eyes, carrot nose, mouth, scarf, mittens, three buttons, and boots, totaling 12 pieces, which allows 12 turns. Laminate each piece for durability. Place duct tape on the back.

DIRECTIONS

1. Ask the children to sit along a wall or a line at least 20 feet from the puzzle taped to the wall. The farther the children are from the puzzle, the more practice they get in locomotor movements.

2. Show the assembled puzzle picture to the children, creating excitement about the picture in an animated way.

3. Animate your movements as you take the puzzle apart and place the pieces about 10 feet in front of the children.

4. Call a child to select a puzzle piece from among those on the floor. For some children, learning to bend over and pick up an object while balancing is a lesson in itself.

5. State how the child is to move across the floor, such as walk, run, or gallop; then send them on their way.

6. Let the children place the pieces where they wish, making sure the first child places the puzzle piece low enough that others can reach. Unless a child truly needs assistance, don't correct the work. Let them be creative, rather than requiring that they place the nose perfectly.

7. When the children are done, give a big round of applause! They will surely want to try it again.

ADAPTATIONS

Children with limited mobility can participate using a piece of mobility equipment described in chapter 5. This game is not well suited to children with visual impairments that prevent them from seeing the puzzle pieces.

VARIATIONS

The list is endless. Here are some ideas to get you started.

- Lights on the holiday tree. Hold up a paper light and ask the child to find the matching color, then run down to place it on the tree.
- Eggs in the bunny basket, following the same idea as the lights on the holiday tree.
- Feathers on a turkey.
- Face on a pumpkin.
- Leaves or apples on tree.
- Hearts in a valentine.
- Groceries in the cart.

IN SMALL SPACES

The activity is easily done in small spaces, with you selecting jumping or crawling instead of running or galloping.

Kusum's excitement builds as the children place each puzzle piece on the wall. She giggles when Johnny puts the snowman's eye where its mouth belongs. The teacher has learned to keep the emphasis on creativity rather than perfection. Their snowman will be a favorite no matter how it turns out.

Red Light, Green Light

- Locomotor skills
- Object, color, and shape recognition

Red Light, Green Light helps children learn to associate the color red with stop and green with go, concepts fundamental to crossing a busy street safely. It is also an old favorite that you can get ready quickly, is simple to instruct, gives children plenty of opportunities to move, and easily includes children of all ability levels.

OVERVIEW

Children begin standing in a line, facing the leader. When you show the green side of the sign, the children are to go forward. When you show the red side of the sign, they are to stop. The game continues until the children reach the opposite side of the room.

GOALS FOR CHILDREN

- Develop locomotor skills.
- Follow game directions of starting and stopping on cue.

EQUIPMENT

Red Light, Green Light sign.

PREPARATION

Make the traffic sign using a racket, such a child's toy racket or a badminton, racquetball, or similar racket. Fasten a laminated red paper circle with the word "stop" to one side of the racket face and a laminated green paper circle with the word "go" to the other side. Tape both circles together along the racket edges.

DIRECTIONS

1. Ask the children to line up along a wall or on a line. Their destination is to reach a wall or line directly across the room from them. Stand about five feet in front of the children, holding the stop and go sign.

2. Review what each color of the sign means and have the children repeat it together.

3. Tell the children how you would like them to move, such as walk, run, gallop, or slide.

4. Begin the game. When you hold up the green side of the sign the children go, and when you hold up the red sign the children stop.

5. Focus on who is able to stop and go on cue. Minimize competition by not acknowledging who crosses the finish line first. If children seek to make the game into a race, it may become difficult to keep them focused on using the prescribed locomotor movement. They will all want to run.

ADAPTATIONS

To enhance communication for children who process information slowly, both sign and say the words "stop" and "go." Some children may understand the sign more easily than the spoken word. With children who are just learning the meaning of walk or run, consider chanting these words with each step as they move, such as "You are walking, walking, walking." Nina helps Damon learn to walk as she plays Red Light, Green Light with the entire class. She tells him what he is going to do, "Now walk." Then she tells him what he is doing, "You are walking, walking, walking." Then she tells him what he did, "You just walked." Children with limited mobility can participate through using a piece of mobility equipment described in chapter 5. Encourage children with visual impairments to use your voice to orient themselves during the game.

VARIATIONS

- Children love to be fooled. Spin the sign around from stop to stop and see who notices.
- Place the sign in a variety of positions around your body, such as to the side, overhead, and near the ground.
- Provide each child with a turn holding the sign. Do this only if you are sure there is enough time for every child to have a turn.

IN SMALL SPACES

This activity works best in large indoor or outdoor spaces where the children have at least 40 feet to travel.

Even the most physically involved child can participate in this game. Christopher strives to hold his head upright so he can see the stop and go sign while his classmate pushes his wheelchair.

Roll the Ball Name Game

- **Object, color, and shape recognition**
- **Object control**

Children typically play this game the first week of school to learn each other's names. They also learn how to roll a ball as they practice remembering information.

OVERVIEW

Sit in a circle with the children, rolling a ball from one person to the next, using each other's names in the chant found in step one of the Directions. This activity works best in a group of six to eight children.

GOALS FOR CHILDREN

- Follow game directions and take turns.
- Recall names of classmates and teachers.
- Roll a ball.

EQUIPMENT

- Playground ball.
- Special seating for students requiring such.

PREPARATION

Have the objects to roll ready to go!

DIRECTIONS

1. You begin by rolling the ball to another person around the circle while repeating this simple chant set to the music above: (Name) rolls the ball around. (He or she) rolls the ball to (pick a person). (Name new person) rolls the ball around. (He or she) rolls the ball to (pick a person).

2. Repeat the chant until each child has had several turns. You will probably be doing most of the chanting at first as the children learn it.

When first attending preschool, some children may appear intimidated or apprehensive. Allow them to roll the ball back to you each time. You become responsible for calling out the children's names, allowing the children to focus first on remembering your name.

This activity is a great way to help children feel welcome. Emphasize saying each child's name, adding a friendly "Hello" or "I'm glad you're here."

ADAPTATIONS

Children needing special chairs or other positioning equipment can participate by placing an incline, such as a board or wedge, in front or to the side of them, allowing them to roll the ball independently. Using a beeper ball instead of a playground ball enables children with visual impairments to locate the ball through sound.

VARIATIONS

Put a name tag or picture symbol on each child. Even though most preschool children can't read, some are ready to identify letters or symbols that represent other children's names. Some preschools give every child a symbol, such as Charley—boat, Alan—horse, and so on.

IN SMALL SPACES

Children can easily play this activity in small spaces.

Tina is totally blind but she is able to participate in Roll the Ball Name Game through using a beeper ball. Her teacher had thought that the beeping sound would distract the children. Instead, she has found the continuous sound helps keep all the children focused on following the direction of the ball.

Roll the Pumpkin

Rolling an object is fundamental to learning to throw and catch. Rolling a pumpkin, a potato, or an apple stimulates children's interest because it's difficult for them to know exactly where the object will roll! This game is a variation of the preceding Roll the Ball Name Game activity, without the emphasis on learning names. This is great game to play if you want to slow the pace of the lesson but still have all children participating.

OVERVIEW

Six to eight children sit in a circle rolling a pumpkin, or other objects, to each other, while singing the following song.

GOAL FOR CHILDREN

Develop skill in rolling various objects.

EQUIPMENT

One large pumpkin for each circle of children.

PREPARATION

Gather and place various objects to roll in close proximity to the circle.

DIRECTIONS

1. Have six to eight children form a circle, sitting with their legs spread. The circle should be about 10 feet in diameter.

2. Place a large pumpkin in front of one of the children with directions to roll it in the direction of another child, using two hands, while the group sings the following chant:

> I have an orange pumpkin
> As round as it can be
> I'll roll it over to you
> And you roll it over to me

3. Continue rolling the pumpkin from child to child until everyone has had many turns.

While you are playing, use the following suggestions:

- Use descriptor words for what is happening (push the pumpkin, use your strong arms, look at it roll, describe the size, shape, weight, etc.).
- Because of the weight, size, and shape of a pumpkin, it will not always roll in the intended direction. Have fun animating the movement of the pumpkin as it changes direction, rolling and wobbling around the circle, on its way to the next child.

ADAPTATIONS

Children needing special chairs or other positioning equipment can participate by placing an incline, such as a board or wedge, in front of or to the side of them allowing them to roll the pumpkin independently. Use bright objects to assist children with limited vision in tracking the ball. If feasible, attach a noisemaker to objects, allowing children without sight to locate the rolling objects through sound.

VARIATIONS

Substitute other objects that can and cannot roll. Let the children decide which ones can roll. Use a potato, an apple, a square wooden block, a balloon, and a variety of other objects. When substituting objects, change the words in the song to name the new object.

IN SMALL SPACES

Children can easily play this activity in small spaces. You need only an area as large as the circle of children.

The fun of this game is experimenting with rolling a variety of objects. Leslie Ann laughs as she watches the potato wiggle side to side across the floor. When her teacher tries to roll a wooden block she howls with delight, but she gasps as she rolls the egg, not knowing her teacher has hard boiled it.

Roller Racer Course

- **Muscular strength and endurance**
- **Use of recreational equipment**

A roller racer is a piece of mobility equipment that moves when the rider twists the handlebars from side to side. Most children easily learn to propel roller racers, which also come in adapted models. Children can have a great time in active play with roller racers at school and home!

OVERVIEW

Children maneuver roller racers around the area, learning to steer around the various obstacles in their paths. The number of children participating is limited to the number of roller racers.

GOALS FOR CHILDREN

- Develop the reciprocal movements needed to move a roller racer.
- Develop upper-body strength needed to power roller racers.

EQUIPMENT

- Standard roller racers, one per child.
- Adapted roller racers. Please refer to chapter 5 for information on roller racer adaptations.
- Cones or tires to use as obstacles.

PREPARATION

Place boxes, laundry baskets, cones, or tires randomly around a large open space. Line up the roller racers along one wall.

DIRECTIONS

1. Demonstrate how to use a roller racer.
2. Let the children get on and start moving. This is where the instruction begins!

ADAPTATIONS

Some children may have difficulty learning how to propel a roller racer. Others may have physical limitations that prevent them from propelling it independently. For these children, attach a rope to the front of the roller racer and pull them around the area, simulating the back and forth motion of the roller racer. For children with visual impairments, provide guided assistance locating and getting on the roller racers. Provide open spaces for riding, cautioning other children to avoid collisions. Help these children orient themselves in the room by placing a speaker along one wall and playing music during the activity as a reference point. This helps children know where they are in the room.

VARIATIONS

- Ask the children to maneuver the roller racer straight across the large open space.
- Place a plastic grocery bag or similar carrying pouch on the handle of each roller racer. As the children maneuver in a line or around a course, have designated items sitting on low benches or folded mats for the children to pick up. These items could be plastic food, pictures, small toys, and the like. This adds the challenge of repetitive starting and stopping independently!
- Ask the children to maneuver around obstacles such as boxes, cones, or mats.
- Use the roller racers outside.

IN SMALL SPACES

This activity requires a large open space.

Ajay's mother loves the fact that he can ride his adapted roller racer at home with his playmates, now that he has learned how to ride it through participating in this activity at school.

Roller Skating

Roller skating is a great way for children of all ability levels to learn balance, but it can be difficult and frustrating for preschool children. Make the experience fun by enabling children to learn to skate at their own comfort levels.

OVERVIEW

Children of all ability levels will be able to participate in a roller skating activity with the assistance of mats, walkers, and mobility equipment. The number of children participating at one time will depend on the number of skates available.

GOALS FOR CHILDREN

- Develop balance.
- Develop motor planning.

EQUIPMENT

- Adjustable roller skates that fit over sneakers.
- Mat or carpet, a minimum of 10 square feet in size.
- Child-size walkers.
- Bike helmets (highly recommended, if available).

PREPARATION

You need several pairs of roller skates for this activity. Two inexpensive ways of obtaining roller skates are buying them at garage sales and seeking donations through sending home fliers asking families and coworkers to donate used skates. You may be surprised at how many you eventually get! Also, ask for donations of old child-size walkers from schools' physical therapy departments or medical supply stores.

DIRECTIONS

1. Give children the option of skating on mats or the floor, with mats recommended for beginners. Explain the difference between skating on the mat, which is slower and offers more grip, and skating on the floor, which is faster and more slippery. The give of the mat prevents the roller skates from gliding. Simply walking while wearing roller skates may be enough of a challenge for beginners.

2. Explain that some children may have to wait for assistance in getting on their skates while you are helping others.

3. If the skates are equipped with brakes, use them so the skate wheels only turn forward.

4. Show the children how to skate using a walker for stability. Children love the independence, and it frees you to help others.

ADAPTATIONS

Provide walkers for children new to skating who are having difficulty balancing. Put nonambulatory children in tumble form chairs on wheeled platforms or other seating available and strap roller skates on their feet. They will love feeling the vibration of their skates rolling on the floor as you, or other children, push them around the room. It is common that children and adolescents with visual impairments are never introduced to roller skating. Don't let these children be excluded from the fun. Provide a walker if needed for stability. Help children orient themselves in the room by placing a speaker along one wall and playing music during the activity as a reference point. This helps children know where they are in the room.

VARIATIONS

- Play upbeat music and have a skating party!
- Skate around obstacles placed in the room.
- Skate to pictures posted on the walls.
- Use half-gallon cardboard milk cartons with one side cut out instead of roller skates. A child's shoe fits inside.
- In place of roller skates, use cut off panty hose. Children can slip one end of the hose over each sneaker and hold the other end in each hand, then slide across the floor using a cross-country ski motion.

IN SMALL SPACES

Limit the number of children skating at one time.

This activity is an easy one to do in a carpeted classroom. Simply push the furniture aside and bring out the skates. The carpet or mat limits the glide of the skates, making it easier for beginners to keep their balance.

Sack Races

Sack racing is a stimulating, wonderful activity for preschool children to develop balance and learn the skill of jumping at the same time.

OVERVIEW

Students put either one or both legs in a sack and jump toward a designated target spot. The number of participants is limited to the number of sacks available.

GOALS FOR CHILDREN

- Develop balance.
- Develop motor planning.
- Develop leg strength.

EQUIPMENT

- Burlap sacks, pillow cases, or plastic bags. Plastic bags are an inexpensive and available alternative to burlap bags, but require sufficient supervision to be sure the children put the bags over their legs and not their heads.
- Pictures or signs on the wall toward which the children move.

PREPARATION

Have burlap sacks, pillow cases, or plastic bags ready to use.

DIRECTIONS

1. With the children gathered along a wall or on a marked line, demonstrate how to jump in a burlap sack.

2. Give each child a sack and ask everyone to try it!
3. Have the children step into the bags, hold onto the handles or sides, and first jump in place.
4. Once they appear comfortable with this, point to the destination where the children will jump. Ask them to jump forward across the room to touch a picture, ring a bell, or go around a cone.
5. Once back to the starting point, they rest, then begin again.

ADAPTATIONS

Children with limited mobility can participate by placing a burlap or plastic bag over their legs as they sit in a tumble form chair. To make the bag move, they can wiggle it with their hands, or, if able, they can move the bag by swinging their legs.

This may be a frustrating activity for children with visual impairments, as it reduces their stable base of support. If the child is willing to try the activity, begin with him or her holding your hand.

VARIATIONS

Use music! Challenge the children to jump freely around an open space while the music is playing, then to stop and maintain their balance while standing in their sack when the music stops.

IN SMALL SPACES

This activity works well in small spaces. Just have the children jump back and forth across the room several times.

Heidi uses a walker to ambulate, but this difference doesn't exclude her from enjoying sack races. Instead of placing the sack over her legs, something that would severely compromise her mobility, a sack is placed over Heidi's hands and arms, still permitting her to grasp the walker comfortably. The excitement for Heidi comes from keeping the sack over her hands as she races with the walker.

Scooter Play

• Motor planning • Muscular strength and endurance
• Use of recreational equipment

Children love using scooters. While moving on the scooters, they are simultaneously building their endurance, strength, and ability to coordinate arm and leg muscle movements.

OVERVIEW
Children learn to maneuver scooters, while either sitting or lying down, propelling themselves in a variety of manners.

GOALS FOR CHILDREN
• Develop fitness.
• Develop motor planning.

EQUIPMENT
• Standard scooters.
• Adapted scooters as needed. Possible suggestions include a padded scooter, long scooter, a jettmobile, or a tumble form chair on a wheeled platform, as illustrated in chapter 5.

You may need additional equipment depending on the activity you choose.
• Hula hoops (one for every two children).
• Clothesline rope.
• A small ramp, wide enough to accommodate a scooter.
• Rigid plastic tunnel.
• Tires, clothes baskets, or other obstacles to make a zigzag path.

PREPARATION
Provide one scooter for each child, along with hula hoops, clothesline rope, or equipment to make an obstacle course, according to which activity you select.

DIRECTIONS
Following are general directions that apply to each of the three scooter activities.
1. With the children sitting in a group, away from the scooters, briefly explain and demonstrate the scooter activity of the day.
2. Identify the boundaries for the activity. Review safety rules including: Never stand on a scooter or put your fingers under the wheels. To minimize pinched fingers, show how to hang onto the side handles of the scooter, or, if the scooter is handle free, show how you would place your hands away from the wheels, such as resting your hands on your knees.

3. Distribute the scooters or let the children go to where the scooters are parked and begin the activity.

4. At the end of the activity, have the children return the scooters to where they were parked.

ADAPTATIONS

Children with limited mobility can easily participate when provided with scooters suited for their needs. Children with visual impairments can easily participate in scooter activities because the hoops and ropes guide them around the room.

VARIATIONS

- Substitute the use of scooters for locomotor movements in other activities such as Match Tag, Move and Seek, Match the Valentine, Puzzle Pieces, and Stop and Go to Music.

- Play music during the Scooter Course. It provides natural motivation to move!

- Scooters and Hula Hoops—One child lies or sits on the scooter, hanging onto a hula hoop, while a second child pulls the first child around the room. On a given cue, the two children switch places.

- Scooter Pull—Tie one or more clotheslines across a room at a height that children using a scooter can reach. The children lie down on their scooters and pull themselves hand over hand along the ropes. Table legs or other heavy furniture can anchor the clothesline ropes in a classroom.

- Scooter Course—Set up a scooter obstacle course with tunnels to maneuver under, small ramps to glide down, and zigzag paths to follow. Include a Scooter Pull. Create a course that challenges the children to shift positions on the scooter from sitting to lying on their stomachs and to propel the scooter using their hands and their feet.

IN SMALL SPACES

Children need lots of space in which to use the scooters safely without running into each other, making all but Scooter Pull unsuitable for small spaces.

Initially it might seem impossible to include children with limited movement in a scooter activity. However, with the variety of adapted scooters now available, it becomes entirely possible to find one that will meet the need of each child.

Scrambled Eggs

- **Cardiovascular endurance**
- **Locomotor skills**

This is a great, high-energy game that requires no equipment, just an enthusiastic attitude.

OVERVIEW

Pretend the room or outdoor playing area is a giant frying pan and all the children are the eggs. When you call "scrambled eggs," the children move as directed, running, galloping, or jumping around the open space. When you call a new ingredient to mix with the eggs, this is the signal to stop and sit down. Continue adding new ingredients, alternately moving and stopping, until the scrambled eggs are done. Then everyone pretends to eat the scrambled eggs.

GOAL FOR CHILDREN

Develop locomotor skills.

EQUIPMENT

You will need no equipment.

PREPARATION

You need no preparation, making this an ideal activity for when there has been an unexpected change in plans and you need an activity on the spur of the moment.

DIRECTIONS

1. Ask the children to pick the first ingredient to add to the scrambled eggs, such as bacon. This becomes the first signal to stop.
2. The leader, either the teacher or a child, next designates how everyone will move. As an example, say "Gallop when you hear the word 'scrambled eggs.' Stop and sit down when you hear the word 'bacon'."
3. Play the game, selecting new ingredients and new movements every round. Continue the repetitions as long as you'd like.
4. While playing the game, do the following:
   - Check the eggs (touch the children's heads) to see if they are done.
   - Have the children recall all the ingredients they have added up to a certain point.
   - Continually review rules about moving safely.
   - Be silly! If children want to add peanut butter to the eggs, let them.
5. The game ends when the scrambled eggs are done. Now all pretend to eat them!

ADAPTATIONS

Children with limited mobility can participate using the mobility equipment described in chapter 5. For safety, pair an adult with a child with visual impairments to provide verbal cues and physical guidance.

VARIATIONS

- Try different food themes such as ice cream, spaghetti, or sandwich ingredients.
- Make imaginary spoons from ribbon streamers. The children wave the streamers while they move around the playing area as directed. On the signal to stop, children pretend to stir the eggs, using the streamers as their spoons. Make the streamers from four two-foot lengths of colorful silk or curling ribbon. Place a pipe cleaner in the middle of the ribbons. Tie the ribbons around the pipe cleaner, binding all four together in the middle. Wind the ends of the pipe cleaner together, creating a loop handle for the children to hold.
- Add color identification to the previous variation. Hold up one ribbon and ask the children to name its color. Then challenge the children to name a food that is the same color as the ribbon. Pretend to add this food to the scrambled eggs. You'll likely end up with fun ingredients for your scrambled eggs—like grapes when you hold up a purple ribbon!

IN SMALL SPACES

This game is not suitable for small spaces. You will need a large open space to play this game.

Joey laughs hysterically after he selects hot dogs as the next ingredient in the scrambled eggs. The teacher chuckles as she reviews the imaginary scrambled eggs ingredients that now include chocolate ice cream, mustard, pickles, and hot dogs.

Stickers on the Body Part

- **Body part identification**
- **Locomotor skills**

This matching game gives children the opportunity to use locomotor skills while developing a foundation of self-knowledge.

OVERVIEW

Tape the paper outline of a child's body to the wall. Children travel across an open area to the figure, place a sticker on the designated body part, then travel back to the starting point. This activity works best with groups of four to six children.

Children stand at a designated starting point. The teacher faces the children, ready to give them each a sticker.

GOALS FOR CHILDREN

- Develop locomotor skills.
- Develop the tactile sense through touching the sticky sticker.
- Identify body parts.

EQUIPMENT

- Paper outline of a child's body.
- Book of self-adhering stickers.

PREPARATION

Trace the body of a child onto sturdy paper. Make sure the arms are extended to the sides and the legs are apart. Cut out the body outline. For those children ready to begin reading, use a marker to label each body part—head, arm, hand, and so forth. Tape the figure to the wall. Have plenty of decorative, self-adhering stickers on hand.

DIRECTIONS

1. Seat the children in front of the paper figure. Review the body parts by pointing to the figure, then asking the children to identify the part on their own bodies.

2. Ask the children to move to the starting point (a mat, line, or wall) opposite the figure. Demonstrate how the children are to move back and forth across the room, between the figure and the starting point.

3. Individually hand each child a sticker, name how to move across the room, and where to place the sticker on the figure. One example is "Sally, jump across the room and place your sticker on the leg body part."

4. Once the children start traveling back and forth, the activity goes quickly with no waiting time.

5. Continue the activity until the figure becomes covered with stickers.

6. At the end the game, ask the children to look at the silly body they have created!

ADAPTATIONS

Children with limited mobility can participate by using a piece of mobility equipment described in chapter 5. For children with limited sight, cut the figure from paper that contrasts in color with the wall and use brightly colored, contrasting stickers. Children with no sight can still practice identifying body parts by placing the stickers on their own body parts or on those of the teacher or another child (with guidance to respect the privacy of another's body).

VARIATIONS

- Instead of a child's body, trace a favorite character or an imaginary giant animal with arms and legs. The children love it!
- Use stickers in a variety of sizes and shapes. Include scented stickers.
- Let the children peel their own stickers off the paper.

IN SMALL SPACES

Use movements such as crawling, rolling, and walking on tiptoes to move between the starting point and the figure.

Teachers can enjoy playing the activity in their classroom and outside on the playground. Typically tape does not adhere well to the outside of buildings. Bring out a large inflated or stuffed animal as the object to which the children adhere the stickers.

Stop and Go to Music

Preschool children need to learn to listen. Stop and Go to Music helps children develop this skill as they listen to music cues to stop and start moving. It also gives preschool children the opportunity to practice hopping, walking on tiptoes, galloping, and other locomotor movements!

OVERVIEW

Children move, using the specified locomotor skill, while the music is playing. They stop in the specified pose when the music stops.

GOALS FOR CHILDREN

- Develop locomotor skills.
- Develop listening skills and the ability to recall information.

EQUIPMENT

- An audio tape or CD player.
- Upbeat music.

PREPARATION

Set up the audio tape or CD player and have upbeat music ready to play.

DIRECTIONS

1. With the children sitting together, explain the activity. When the music plays, the children are to move. When the music stops, the children are to stop. Ask the children to repeat the directions as you emphasize the word "go" with movement and "stop" with an exaggerated stop.

2. Select the directional pattern of the game (same direction versus any direction). Clearly explain and show the children how it looks when everyone is running in the same direction (or when everyone is running in different directions).

3. Choose the movement and the stop position. An example direction is "When the music plays, run, and when the music stops, sit down right where you are."

4. Start the music. An adult needs to be near the music box. If more adults are available, they can intermingle among the children during the movement.

5. Stop the music, acknowledging children who stopped quickly.

6. Continue the activity, giving new directions for moving and stopping each time before the music begins. Maintain interest by continually changing the way the children are to move (walk backward, gallop, hop, slide) and stop (lie down on your tummy or back, kneel, stop with your hands touching a wall).

ADAPTATIONS

Children with limited mobility can participate by using a piece of mobility equipment described in chapter 5. For safety, pair an adult with a child with visual impairments to provide verbal cues and physical guidance.

VARIATIONS

- When teaching small groups of children, help the children learn to scan their surroundings while moving. Put several large pictures of animals or favorite characters on the walls. When the music stops, ask the children to locate and run to a predetermined picture.
- Give the children things they can wave around as they are moving, such as scarves, short ribbons, or crepe paper streamers. The children will tend to watch what they are waving. To avoid collisions, provide lots of open space and slow their movement speed by asking them to march, jump, or tiptoe instead of run.

IN SMALL SPACES

You can do this activity safely in small areas with few children and some modification. Select only slow movements such as crawling and walking on tiptoes, instead of running and galloping.

This is a favorite at the beginning of the year when children need lots of practice listening and following directions. It is easy to play and quick to set up.

Let's Get Striking

Swinging a tennis racket, a golf club, or a bat are popular recreational activities. Teachers can create many opportunities for preschool children to practice this lifelong skill of striking.

OVERVIEW

Preschool children lack the skill and judgment to participate in large group activities involving a striking implement. Preschool children will be safe and successful at striking when you set up the activities as stations or as small group activities with three or four children participating at a time. Once you have chosen the activity, the children practice the striking skill independently. Make sure there is at least one striking implement and target to hit for each child.

GOAL FOR CHILDREN

Develop the skill of striking.

EQUIPMENT

Important—Do not use hard objects, such as those made of wood or metal, in striking activities with preschool children.

Objects to use for striking include the following:

- Large plastic bat.
- Plastic tennis racket.
- Nylon racket made from a wire clothes hanger reshaped into an oval. Cover any sharp ends with tape, then insert the wire racket into the leg of an old stocking.
- Foam wand (noodle).
- Swimming kickboard.
- Small plastic golf club or plastic field hockey stick. Make similar striking implements by taping a stuffed sock to the end of a plastic rod.

Objects to strike include the following:

- Suspended balloons. Adjust the height of the suspended balloons, depending on the striking goal (higher for overhead strike, lower for golf swing).
- Foam ball placed on a batting tee.
- Foam or fleece ball on the floor.
- Loose balloons and beach balls.
- Newspaper scrunched into a ball with tape around it.
- Beach balls, placed in plastic bags and suspended.

Targets to strike include the following:

- Plastic bottles of various shapes, sizes, and colors.
- Pictures such as brightly colored smiley faces, animals, shapes, favorite characters.

- A net goal.
- Hanging bells or other objects that make noise when struck.

Spot markers include the following:

- Plastic nonskid place mats, carpet squares, or tape on the floor designate where children are to stand while striking.

PREPARATION

Set up selected targets and striking implements in advance. Whether practicing striking as station work or a small group activity, here are a few things to remember that will make the activities more enjoyable for all.

- Always place targets near a wall, with clear stop boundaries on either side of the target. These stop boundaries can be ropes, cones, laundry baskets, benches, or other pieces of equipment that clearly convey to the children "Do not go past this point." These stop boundaries will alert children not to run into the path of someone who is swinging a bat.
- Have a designated mark on the floor where children are to stand. You can mark this with tape, a rope, or a carpet square. This way if you are currently occupied with one child, you can easily direct another child with a simple cue such as "Remember to swing the bat only when you are standing on the carpet square." This also allows you to predetermine the distance from which the children will be striking.
- Space children and their target at least two bat lengths away from other children.

DIRECTIONS

1. Start with a quick demonstration so the children will know the expectation.
2. Teach safety rules such as (a) stand on the designated spot while striking, and (b) remember not to cross stop boundaries.
3. Specific directions vary with the equipment chosen.

ADAPTATIONS

Consider using a gait trainer or mobile prone stander for children who rely on mobility support such as a walker. This equipment allows their hands to be free for striking while in an upright position. Use brightly colored targets to help children with visual impairments see the targets.

VARIATIONS

Mix and match the ideas from the equipment list to create new variations.

IN SMALL SPACES

Only one or two children can participate in a small area at a time to assure a safe distance between children swinging bats.

Striking games in a classroom? Yes, it can be safe and fun using foam striking implements and soft balls. Colorful place mats can mark where each child is to stand while striking.

Superstars Challenge

- **Locomotor skills**
- **Motor planning**

Superstars Challenge introduces the concept of racing in a nonthreatening way. Children race through a challenging obstacle course against a clock, not each other. As children learn to cheer for each other, the teacher makes sure each child always beats the clock.

OVERVIEW

One child at a time approaches the starting line. At the signal to go, the clock starts, and the child rallies through the Superstars Challenge course, rings the bell, and runs back to the starting point before the clock buzzer goes off. This activity works best in small groups of three to four children and one adult per course.

GOAL FOR CHILDREN

Develop motor skills such as walking across, climbing and jumping over, and crawling through.

EQUIPMENT

- Large, inclined wedge.
- Climbing blocks.
- Two-by-four board placed on the floor.
- Foam balance beam.
- Two-inch high hurdle.
- Four tires or hula hoops in a line flat on the floor.
- Tunnel.
- Wrestling stop clock, photo developing clock, or other countdown clocks with moveable hands and a buzzer.
- Bells suspended from a rope or string, or placed on a table.
- Mats or carpeted area under equipment, as needed.

PREPARATION

Create the Superstars Challenge obstacle course by setting up a line of equipment through which the child is to maneuver. Use a mat or a colored line on the floor for the starting line. In an excited tone, call "Ready—set—go!" At the end of the line of equipment have a bell, either suspended or sitting on a table, that the child must ring at the completion of the course. Provide a pathway, parallel to the course and free of equipment, for the child to follow back to the starting point after completing the course. Prominently display a large clock with a buzzer set to sound when the clock has counted down to zero, just after the child has completed the course.

DIRECTIONS

1. Give a brief explanation and demonstration before starting the activity. You can set up the equipment in any order. The following is one possibility.

   - Stand behind the starting line. On "Ready—set—go," the clock starts.
   - First, run up and jump off an object such as a block or an incline wedge.
   - Next, walk across a two-by-four board or a balance beam on the floor.
   - Climb over a stack of tires or walk through hula hoops.
   - Jump over a hurdle.
   - Then crawl through the tunnel, the last obstacle.
   - Once out of the tunnel, ring the bell!
   - After ringing the bell, run down the side of the course, back to the starting line.

2. As the first child approaches the starting line, set the clock for a designated time. When the time is up the clock buzzer sounds. Always set the clock so it will buzz shortly after the child has finished. (The clock hands move easily so the teacher can change the time to create a close race.) The excitement will escalate as all children now try to beat the clock!

ADAPTATIONS

Involve children who are nonambulatory in an active way, such as crawling or scooting through the course. When this is not feasible and mobility equipment will work best, have the children move down the aisle free of equipment to ring the bell and return before the buzzer sounds. Use adult assistance as needed.

VARIATIONS

- Vary the equipment used.
- Vary the order of the equipment used.
- If there is sufficient equipment and space, set up more than one Superstars Challenge course at a time.
- Instead of ringing a bell, ask the children to bring back a motivating sticker taped to the wall or card placed on a table.

IN SMALL SPACES

Create a compressed Superstars Challenge course. If there is insufficient space for children to run back to the finish line in the aisle parallel to the course, ask each child to go up and back through the obstacles to complete the course.

The children love hearing the buzzer two seconds after they have sped across the finish line.

Swings

Swinging independently at the playground is an important and highly visible activity for young children. Swings provide preschool children with plenty of opportunities to balance, grasp with their hands, and pump with their legs.

OVERVIEW

Indoors, this activity typically works best with three to four children in a group at a time. Set up one or two swings per adult to supervise. Consider using one or two swings as one of several stations in a large room, selecting other stations that require minimal adult supervision. If there is a larger swing platform outdoors, you may be able to set up more swings at one time, as long there is appropriate supervision. The number of participants depends on the number of swings available.

GOALS FOR CHILDREN

- Develop the skill of swinging independently.
- Increase body strength and coordination.

EQUIPMENT

Please refer to chapter 5 for illustrations of these swings.

- Bucket swing.
- Strap swing.
- Bar swing.
- Platform or vestibular swing.
- Net swing.
- Tumble form chair in a net swing.

PREPARATION

Outdoors, conventional swings may already be in place. Indoors, hang swings from either a strong portable suspension system or a permanent suspension system, such as the sturdy, permanent poles behind a stationary basketball backboard. A few simple modifications will usually accommodate an adapted swing, if you need one. A variety of swings are presented in chapter 5 on page 40. Base the type of swing you choose on what the children are to accomplish.

DIRECTIONS

Two skills that preschool children are typically learning while swinging are holding themselves on the swing by grasping the ropes from which the swing is suspended and pumping with their legs to make the swing move independently. Help children learn these skills by giving verbal cues:

1. Hang on tight!

2. Legs out straight!

3. Bend your knees!

Then provide children the opportunity to practice, practice, practice.

ADAPTATIONS

If adapted swings are available, you can include children with special needs in swinging activities. Select from among the variety of swings we have described to find the design that provides the needed support. Swing platforms onto which you can roll wheelchairs are commercially available. These expensive swings are typically unnecessary with preschool children who you can easily lift from their wheelchairs into the swings. Some children with limited mobility can swing independently if you provide a rope with which they can pull themselves forward. Once guided to the swings, children with visual impairments can also participate independently.

VARIATIONS

Add a swinging theme to the lesson, such as monkeys swinging or birds flying. Post pictures or sing songs that depict the theme.

IN SMALL SPACES

Set up one swing and allow the children to take turns.

Preschool children love adults to push them while swinging. Coach children on the pumping technique so they also learn to swing independently.

Tag Games Introduction:
- Cardiovascular endurance
- Locomotor skills

Tag games are a great way to get children moving quickly and easily. There is little equipment involved, and tag games can accommodate a large or small class size. A large outdoor or indoor area, such as a playground or a gymnasium, allows more space for children to move, but with small numbers of children, they can play tag games in an average sized room. Tag games, at the preschool level, are an introduction to the concept of getting caught. The children should not be put in a position of being tagged out nor should they have to wait against a wall, somewhere in the room, while other children remain active. Play the games with a win-win situation in mind. In each tag game offered in this book, getting tagged either never actually occurs or is a part of the game that leads to another exciting aspect. As you refer to each game, the overview will explain this more clearly.

Tag games are a teacher-directed activity. Directions on how to move, where to move, and possibly what to match are commonplace. You are introducing a variety of educational concepts when playing a tag game, so it is necessary for you to take a lead role in the activity. With this in mind, it is important to repeatedly give the children in the game a feeling of control. Let the children make up an additional rule, let them decide how to move next, or purposely make a mistake so the children have the opportunity to correct you. They will love it!

Each tag game has at least two objectives. One objective is developing locomotor skills. Each game gives you the option of asking the children to move in whatever way you wish. You can observe children's performance while they work on skills such as galloping, jumping, and walking backward in a nonthreatening environment.

A second objective is in the cognitive domain. Each game has directions that the children must remember and concepts such as color, shape, and picture identification the children need to recall. In Imagination Tag, you might ask children to remember animals in the zoo or things that fly in the sky. In I'm the Man From Mars, you may ask children to remember concepts related to color and clothing. In Match Tag, you challenge the children to match pictures of flowers, food, colors, or shapes. In Toothbrush Tag, children learn terms related to tooth care in a fun way. Vegetable Soup identifies food, and Midnight introduces terms related to time.

Use the suggested variations listed under each game, and decorate the room to match the theme of the game. In playing each tag game, remember that the more playful you act the more the preschool children are likely to enjoy the game!

Tag—Goldilocks and the Three Bears[1]

This is a great introductory tag game. The children remain stimulated because it is a theme familiar to most, and all players remain involved in some capacity through the duration of the game.

128   [1]From *Ready to Use P.E. Activities for Grades K-2* by Joanne Landy and Maxwell Landy copyright © 1992. Reprinted with permission of Prentice Hall Direct.

OVERVIEW

Children walk across an open space, toward three children who are seated facing them, chanting, "Who's in the house?" Depending on the response from those sitting in the three chairs, the advancing children take one, two, or three steps forward. When they hear the word "Goldilocks," they turn around and flee back to the starting point.

GOAL FOR CHILDREN

Develop locomotor skills such as running, jumping, and galloping.

EQUIPMENT

3 chairs, one in each size (small, medium, and large).

PREPARATION

Place three chairs, ranging in size from small to large, side by side. Clearly mark a starting line across the open space from the chairs.

DIRECTIONS

1. Select three children to sit in the chairs and act the roles of Baby, Momma, and Papa Bear.
2. All other children stand on the starting line, opposite the chairs, and call, "Who's in the house?"
3. The three children sitting in the chairs respond by calling back one of the following names, "Baby," "Momma," or "Papa." (You determine how they take turns calling one of the bears' names.)
4. The children on the starting line take the corresponding number of steps forward—one step for Baby, two steps for Momma, and three steps for Papa.
5. Continue in this way, with the advancing children asking, "Who's in the house?" and the bears responding.
6. When the advancing children get close to the chairs, the children in the chairs can chose to respond, "Goldilocks!"
7. "Goldilocks" is the signal for the children in the line to flee back to the starting line, with the three bears chasing them. Emphasize the fun of chasing children back to the starting line, de-emphasize trying to tag them.
8. Select three different children to sit in the chairs and begin the game anew.

ADAPTATIONS

Children with limited mobility can participate by using a piece of mobility equipment described in chapter 5. Children with visual impairments can participate by holding hands with a partner or following your verbal cues.

VARIATIONS

- Encourage the children to use voice variations for Baby, Momma, and Papa Bear.
- Accentuate the difference in the size among Baby, Momma, and Papa Bear steps.
- Vary the locomotor movement used (gallop, jump, hop) as the children flee back to the starting line.

IN SMALL SPACES

This tag game works best when played in a large open area.

(continued)

Tag—Imagination

This game is a great way to let children use their imaginations. It's also fun, involves no equipment, can include a large number of children, and can make the teacher look silly—which children love!

OVERVIEW

Face the class in a large open area. You or the children think of a theme. From that theme, each child thinks of an object that relates to the theme, but doesn't tell their objects to you. (It is helpful if another adult is available to assist the children in thinking of objects that relate to the theme.) Then, you try to guess each object the children might have in mind that relates to the theme. Every time you correctly guess an object one or more children have in mind, the child(ren) must run across the room to a designated spot. You pretend to chase these children, but never actually tag anyone. The game continues until you have called all children's objects and all children have run to the other side.

GOAL FOR CHILDREN

Develop locomotor skills such as running, jumping, and galloping.

EQUIPMENT

You will need no equipment.

PREPARATION

To begin the game, choose a theme from the following list or write your own.

- Things you see in the sky
- Animals you see at the zoo
- Television show characters
- Colors, shapes, or numbers
- Days of the week
- Breakfast cereals

DIRECTIONS

The children begin by standing in one line, such as along the wall of a playground or large room. When you correctly guess their object, they run past you to the opposite side.

1. If the theme is animals you see at the zoo, each child thinks of an appropriate animal, but keeps it a secret. (Keeping a secret is difficult for young children, so if they say their animals aloud, just pretend to not hear it.)

2. When the children are ready, or the adult assistant says they are ready, designate how the children are to move across the room. Instead of always running, sometimes ask the children to jump, hop, slide, walk backward, or do a silly walk from one side to the other. Also, clearly designate the line or area to which the children are to run.

3. Begin guessing animals seen at the zoo. Guess, "Is anyone a tiger?" Remind the children, "If you are a tiger, run!"

4. After a few guesses, start making silly mistakes the children can catch. "Is anyone a television?" Children love reminding the teacher that a television is not an animal.

5. Keep guessing until all the children have made it to the other side. If a child has stumped the teacher with an uncommon animal, ask questions such as "Does your animal swim?"

6. Once the children have all made it to the other side, pick a new theme and start the game again, now moving in the opposite direction.

ADAPTATIONS

Children with limited mobility can participate by using a piece of mobility equipment described in chapter 5. Children with visual impairments can participate with verbal cues or a partner guiding them by the hand.

VARIATIONS

- Even though the children are listening and a part of the fun, once they have taken their turn running across the room, they have to wait while you guess the other children's objects. So create a silly or stimulating waiting spot at each side. This could be on a mat, under a large picture on the wall, or in plastic swimming pools.

- For children unable to communicate ideas, have pictures ready from which they may choose. When using the animals in the zoo theme, hold up pictures of lions, tigers, bears, and monkeys for the children to see.

- Prepare a poster board full of pictures that correlate with each theme. To help the children think of ideas, hold up the board as you introduce each theme.

IN SMALL SPACES

This activity is best played in large outdoor or indoor areas.

Tag—I'm the Man From Mars[2]

This is another fun way to play a tag game while promoting a variety of preschool educational concepts.

OVERVIEW

Face the class and say, "I'm the man from Mars and I'll take you to the stars if . . . (then give a descriptor such as) you are wearing shorts." The children who have the descriptor run across to the opposite side, as you try to tag them. Tagged children go to the spaceship and wait. When all the children are in the spaceship, lead them in pretending that the spaceship takes off, and all the children return to the starting line.

GOAL FOR CHILDREN

Develop locomotor skills such as running, jumping, and galloping.

EQUIPMENT

A wait area decorated with a space or spaceship theme.

(continued)

[2]From *Ready to Use P.E. Activities for Grades K-2* by Joanne Landy and Maxwell Landy copyright © 1992. Reprinted with permission of Prentice Hall Direct.

PREPARATION

Select and mark two lines in front of opposite sides of the room or playground. Create the spaceship waiting area complete with decorations, so it becomes a special place to be. This makes being tagged *no big deal*.

DIRECTIONS

1. Direct the children to stand on the starting line, showing them the line to which they will run and the spaceship where they go when tagged.

2. Stand several feet in front of and facing the children. Begin the game with the chant, "I'm the man from Mars and I'll take you to the stars if . . . (then give a descriptor such as) you are wearing something blue."

3. The children who have the descriptor then run to the line in front of the opposite wall, as you try to tag them. Children who make it without being tagged wait there for another turn. Those who you tag go to the spaceship.

4. Continue repeating the chant, changing the direction each time, until you have tagged all the children and they are waiting in the spaceship. Minimize the elimination aspect of this game by tagging all the children within only two or three turns. This assures that no child is waiting at the space ship more than two minutes.

5. Pretend to make the spaceship blast off. Count down (5-4-3-2-1) or count up (1-2-3-4-5), depending on what the children may understand. At the end, say "Blast off," and let the children run from the spaceship back to their starting line.

6. Begin the game again.

ADAPTATIONS

Children with limited mobility can participate by using a piece of mobility equipment described in chapter 5. Children with visual impairments can participate with verbal cues or a partner guiding them by the hand.

VARIATIONS

Substitute galloping, jumping or walking backward, or skipping for running.

IN SMALL SPACES

This activity is best played in large indoor or outdoor areas.

Tag—Match

This active, vigorous game brings squeals of delight from the children while they are learning to match objects.

OVERVIEW

The children stand in a line in front of one wall. From here they will run to the line in front of the opposite wall. Give each child a card that fits today's theme of the game. You also hold a match for each different card distributed. When you hold up a card, all the children with a match for that card try to run (hop, jump, scoot) to the opposite wall of the room without you catching them.

GOAL FOR CHILDREN

Develop locomotor skills such as running, jumping, and galloping.

EQUIPMENT

Match cards, one set of cards for each game theme.

PREPARATION

Make the match cards to use in the game. For each theme chosen, make several cards for each symbol within the theme. Examples of pictures to match include numbers; shapes; foods; colors; animals; familiar characters; cars, trucks, planes; or holiday visuals. If the theme is shapes, there may be four cards with squares on them, four with circles, four with triangles, and so on. Under each shape, place the word for the shape, such as square, to promote reading readiness. Make enough card symbols for each child in the class plus an extra card of each symbol for you to hold. Laminate the cards to protect them. To make necklaces from the cards, punch two holes in the upper corners and loop yarn through the holes. Necklace cards may work better in classes that include children who have difficulty holding onto things or who need to use their hands for mobility.

DIRECTIONS

1. Review the theme for the day and describe each match card picture or symbol you will use. If the theme is shapes, show a square with the word square written underneath. Repeat for circle, triangle, and so on.

2. Direct the children to stand in a line along one wall of the room. Demonstrate how they are to run from that line to the line in front of the opposite wall. Check for understanding by asking them to point to where they will be running.

3. Hold up one shape at a time. Children holding match cards with the shape that matches the one shown are to run, without getting caught, to the opposite wall. Be patient and positive. Children will make mistakes.

4. Continue holding up match cards until all the children have made it to the other side. You may choose to intentionally never catch a child, instead letting him or her enjoy running back and forth. If you will tag children, set up a silly place to go when caught. This might be a shape cave decorated with large shapes. After a minute, let the children escape from the shape cave and go back to join the fun. Do not make getting caught an elimination, make it part of the fun!

5. Repeat the game, running in the opposite direction.

ADAPTATIONS

Children with limited mobility can participate by using a piece of mobility equipment described in chapter 5. Wearing the cards on necklaces frees hands for mobility. Children with visual impairments can participate with verbal cues or a partner guiding them by the hand.

VARIATIONS

- There are limitless numbers of things that you can use for matching in this game. It's a great game to modify for holiday themes.

(continued)

- Ask children to move using a variety of locomotor movements.
- After a few turns, ask children to trade cards with a friend.

IN SMALL SPACES
This activity is best played in large indoor or outdoor areas.

Tag—Midnight

This is another great introductory tag game, simplified from its original version. Have fun while introducing preschoolers to terms related to time.

OVERVIEW
Most children take the role of chickens, but a few children play foxes. The chickens walk across an open space, repeating the chant, "What time is it, Mr. Fox?" Depending on the response from the few children pretending to be the fox, the chickens take a designated number of steps forward. When the chickens hear the fox say the word "Midnight," they turn around and run back to their original starting point, while pursued by the fox.

GOAL FOR CHILDREN
Develop locomotor skills such as running, galloping, and jumping.

EQUIPMENT
You will need no equipment.

PREPARATION
You need no preparation. This is an ideal activity for when, despite the best laid plans, you need an activity on the spur of the moment.

DIRECTIONS
It is helpful to have an adult assisting each group of children: one prompting the foxes with the time to call and one prompting the chickens to take the specified number of steps.

1. In a large open space, ask the children to line up along one wall. They are called the chickens. Have four or five children leave the line and go to the opposite wall. They are called the fox.
2. The children in the chicken line call out, "What time is it, Mr. Fox?"
3. The children in the fox line respond with a time, "One o'clock."
4. The students in the chicken line then take one step.
5. The children in the chicken line again ask, "What time is it, Mr. Fox?"
6. The children in the fox line respond with a time. The number of steps the chicken line may take is based on the time the fox calls out. If it is four o'clock, the chicken line may take four steps.
7. This interplay continues until the chicken line gets close to the fox line. The next time the children ask the fox line, "What time is it Mr. Fox?" they respond, "Midnight!"

8. "Midnight" is the cue for the children in the chicken line to run back to their starting point while the children in the fox line chase them. Emphasize the fun of the chase back to the line, rather than tagging others.

9. You then pick a new set of children to be in the fox line and repeat the game.

ADAPTATIONS

Children with limited mobility can participate by using a piece of mobility equipment described in chapter 5. Children with visual impairments can participate with verbal cues or a partner guiding them by the hand.

VARIATIONS

Vary the way children move back to the line, such as galloping, jumping, or walking backward.

IN SMALL SPACES

This activity is best played in large indoor or outdoor areas.

Tag—Toothbrush

This is a silly, fun way for children to play a basic tag game while learning an introductory concept of why you brush your teeth.

OVERVIEW

Three children stand along one line, each holding a toothbrush. They are the teeth. The rest of the children stand along a line opposite them. They are the germs. The germs slowly walk in a line toward the teeth chanting, "The germs are coming." When the germs get close to the teeth, they say, "The germs are here!" When the teeth hear this, they chase after the germs with their toothbrushes.

GOAL FOR CHILDREN

Develop locomotor skills such as running, jumping, and galloping.

EQUIPMENT

- Three giant toothbrushes.
- Giant toothpaste container.

PREPARATION

To make a toothbrush, take a clear, plastic, two-liter soda bottle. Slit the bottle lengthwise. Insert foam padding inside the bottle for stability, but also have the foam protrude from the slit like bristles on a toothbrush. Duct tape a thin, round, plastic handle about two feet long to the top of the bottle. To make a tube of toothpaste, stuff a white pillowcase or sheet of folded white plastic. Gather it at the end by wrapping it with duct tape to simulate a tube of toothpaste. Label the container with any brand you would like!

(continued)

DIRECTIONS

1. Start with the entire class along one wall. They are the germs.

2. Pick three children (or however many toothbrushes you have made) to be the teeth. They go to the opposite wall and pretend to put toothpaste on their toothbrushes. Have fun exaggerating the imaginary squeezing of toothpaste onto the toothbrushes. These children designated as teeth stand in a line, with their brushes, waiting for the germs to come.

3. The germs, in line at the opposite end, start walking toward the teeth chanting, "The germs are coming, the germs are coming."

4. When the germs are within reach of the teeth, prompt the teeth to say, "The germs are here!"

5. At that point, the teeth chase the germs back to the starting line.

6. The intention is to chase, not to tag.

7. The teacher assigns three other students to be the teeth and the game begins again.

ADAPTATIONS

Children with limited mobility can participate by using a piece of mobility equipment described in chapter 5. Children with visual impairments can participate with verbal cues or a partner guiding them by the hand.

VARIATIONS

Consider letting the germs run freely around the room as the teeth try to tag them with a toothbrush. When tagged, the germs switch and become the teeth holding the toothbrush. This variation is suited for kindergarten children and advanced preschool children.

IN SMALL SPACES

It is best to play this activity in large areas.

Tag—Vegetable Soup[3]

This is a great tag game that incorporates labeling food names with locomotor movements.

OVERVIEW

In this activity the children are vegetables and the circle is a pot in which vegetable soup is made. The children in each group think of a vegetable. You begin guessing vegetable names. When you correctly guess a group's vegetable, the group approaches the circle and walks around it chanting, "The soup is boiling." As you guess other groups' vegetables, those around the circle continue to chant. When all the children are walking around the circle, you unexpectedly announce, "The soup is burning!" On this cue the children run back to their starting point as fast as they can.

136 [3]From *Ready to Use P.E. Activities for Grades K-2* by Joanne Landy and Maxwell Landy copyright © 1992. Reprinted with permission of Prentice Hall Direct.

GOALS FOR CHILDREN

- Develop a child's ability to follow game directions.
- Develop locomotor movements.

EQUIPMENT

- A mat, cone, or picture for each group of children.
- A circle in the center of the area, marked on the floor with paint or tape.

PREPARATION

Distribute mats around the floor and designate a circle. If mats are not available, designate a meeting spot with masking tape, cone, or picture hanging on the wall.

DIRECTIONS

1. Begin the activity with an equal number of children in each group. If possible, have one adult helping each group. Stand in the middle of the area, in full view of all the children.

2. Explain to the children that they will be making pretend soup, with the circle as the pot and them as the vegetables. Ask the children at each mat to think of the name of a vegetable, but not to tell it to you. It is helpful if another adult is available to assist the children in thinking of vegetables and guiding the activity.

3. Guess the name of the vegetables. You may ask, "Are there any tomatoes?" Each group responds, "Yes" or "No."

4. If a group responds, "Yes," they walk to the circle and begin chanting, "The soup is boiling."

5. If a group responds, "No," make a big deal over the fact they are stumping you, and guess again.

6. Continue until all the groups are around the circle chanting. Then say, "The soup is burning!"

7. The children flee back to their starting point, with you pretending to chase but never actually catching any children.

8. Repeat the game, selecting new vegetable names.

ADAPTATIONS

Children with limited mobility can participate by using a piece of mobility equipment described in chapter 5. Children with visual impairments can participate with verbal cues or a partner guiding them by the hand.

VARIATIONS

- Tape pictures of vegetables on the walls for children to use as a visual cue.
- Change the theme and modify the chant. If the children think of flavors of ice cream, change the chant to "The ice cream is melting," then "The ice cream is all gone."

IN SMALL SPACES

It is best to play this activity in large indoor or outdoor areas.

Tire Play

Tire Play gives preschool children plenty of opportunities to balance, jump, roll, crawl, pull themselves along, and learn directional relationships to objects such as over, under, in front, and behind.

OVERVIEW

Ask questions that teach spatial relations, such as "Can you balance on, walk around, climb over, or jump on your tire?" Add strength activities by challenging the children to pull, push, roll, swing, or stack the tires. Conclude with free play activities on the tires. Provide one tire for each child.

GOALS FOR CHILDREN

- Develop muscular strength and endurance through pushing and pulling tires.
- Develop balance and spatial awareness through moving over, under, around, and through tires.

EQUIPMENT

- Tires.
- Mats for activities that involve climbing on stacked tires.

PREPARATION

Collect tires. Garages are usually happy to give away used automobile tires. Clean each tire thoroughly with soap and water. Check to be sure there are no sharp wires protruding or stones caught in treads. Place the tires in a formation such as in a line, circle, or scattered.

DIRECTIONS

1. Ask each child to sit in a tire, facing the teacher. Turn on the music and give some informal suggestions about ways to balance and jump on the tire. Use guided exploration questions such as "Who can jump on the tire, walk around the edge of the tire, balance across the tire?" The children do not have to precisely imitate your movements.

2. After exploring their own tires, ask the children to independently roll the tires to a designated spot.

3. Next, ask the children to pull the tires across the floor to another designated spot, where you have placed mats on the floor.

4. Conclude the activity by encouraging the children to stack all the tires on the mats, then climb in, over, and through them. Automobile tires can be heavy for preschool children to move. Give lots of verbal encouragement during the activities. The children are likely to feel proud of themselves when they succeed in these difficult tasks.

ADAPTATIONS

Consider using a gait trainer or mobile prone stander for children who rely on mobility support such as a walker. This equipment allows the child's hands to be free to manipulate the tire while in an upright position. For children unable to independently handle a tire, tie a rope to the tire for them to pull; use an inner tube; or use a small, inflatable plastic ring. During activities that involve climbing in the tires, place children who are nonambulatory in the tire and let them feel the movement as other children climb about them. Children able to crawl can easily participate in this activity. Use verbal cues or physical guidance to help orient children with visual impairments.

VARIATIONS

- Provide a simple activity for the children to do at each designation. For example, ask them to drag their tires to the posted picture of a favorite children's character and touch its head, nose, or feet.
- Ask the children to form a line, then give their tires one big push at the same time. Have fun seeing where the tires end up.

IN SMALL SPACES

Use a few tires with small groups of children at one time.

Children can roll, stack, push, pull, and swing old tires, and you can get them free!

Tricycle Course

- **Use of recreational equipment**
- **Muscular strength and endurance**

Children love to ride tricycles! Riding a tricycle is a precursor skill to riding a bicycle. We have filled Tricycle Course with suggestions for keeping the children pedaling by using obstacles and tasks to sharpen their skills and keep their imaginations involved.

OVERVIEW

As the children pedal through the course, they have the liberty of stopping for gas, stopping at the post office to pick up mail, or stopping at the mailbox to drop off a letter.

GOALS FOR CHILDREN

- Develop the preschool skill of riding a tricycle.
- Develop muscular strength and endurance.

EQUIPMENT

- Tricycles.
- Bicycles with training wheels.
- Adapted tricycles as needed.
- A pretend gas station.
- A pretend post office.
- A mailbox to mail letters.
- Tires, laundry baskets, or cones to use as obstacles.

PREPARATION

Have the course set up before class begins.

DIRECTIONS

Always have the tricycles parked in one particular area. Make it clear to the children that this is where they get on and off the tricycles when they are finished or when they want to switch to another one. This eliminates tricycles getting dumped in the middle of the room. Play energizing and upbeat music!

ADAPTATIONS

Many children with special needs can learn to ride a tricycle independently, using a variety of equipment adaptations. Tricycles and adaptations that are commercially available are presented in chapter 5.

VARIATIONS

Vary the type of mail used each time you use the course.

- Mail cut out hearts on Valentines Day.
- Mail snowflakes in the winter.
- Mail envelopes with numbers or letters on them.
- Mail index cards with a particular sticker on them.
- Mail anything related to a classroom unit. The children will love it!

IN SMALL SPACES

This activity works best when played in a large area.

It requires much effort for Abdul to push the pedals of his adapted tricycle. His teacher makes sure that there is a pretend gas station nearby to help motivate him and provide him with a rest.

Tunnel Course

- **Cardiovascular endurance**
- **Motor planning**

This activity is one to keep in mind when you are planning a high-energy learning experience. It's easy to set up, you can adapt it to any size area, and it will have the children crawling like bugs the entire the class.

OVERVIEW

The children crawl their way through a maze of tunnels, exploring the ins and outs of all the tube-shaped obstacles. Use the suggested equipment list to spark your own ideas. Cover the movement area with as many tunnels as possible. Play upbeat music and let the crawling begin.

GOALS FOR CHILDREN

- Develop the ability to crawl efficiently.
- Develop abilities in motor planning.

EQUIPMENT

- Fabric coiled tunnels. (If you have only one tunnel, borrow more tunnels from other classrooms for a few days.)
- Large boxes with one or both ends opened.
- Folding mats pitched at an angle.
- Tires with mats placed vertically across them.

PREPARATION

Before the children arrive, set up the tunnels in a confined space so they are not tempted to run around the outside of the tunnels instead of crawling through them. Be sure the equipment is stable and will not fall on the children.

DIRECTIONS

Explain and demonstrate crawling through the tunnels. Include any safety statements and provide general supervision for safety.

ADAPTATIONS

This activity easily includes those children who may be unable to walk but can move around by crawling or scooting on the floor. For children who can creep (pulling with their arms and pushing with their legs while moving on their stomachs), put a flat slide or a smooth plank inside tunnels, made from wire coils covered with fabric. The slide or plank provides a flat surface so it is easier to crawl through the tunnel, making the child's journey more enjoyable. You can place children not yet able to creep or crawl on a scooter and an adult can pull them through the course. Children with visual impairments can negotiate their way through the course, aided by physical guidance and verbal cues. Help reluctant children gain the confidence to crawl through tunnels. Using both hands, compress accordion tunnels and allow the reluctant child to crawl through it in its compact form. When the child seems comfortable, forget to compress the tunnel, and watch the child crawl through with ease.

Use stuffed animals and other soft toys to entice reluctant children to crawl through the tunnels. Show the children how the stuffed toy is going into the tunnel, slide the toy through the tunnel, then go around to the exit of the tunnel and pretend the toy is calling to the child to crawl through the tunnel to get the toy.

VARIATIONS

Create a theme for the tunnel course, such as making all tunnels the same color or having the children pretend to be specific animals that crawl.

Hide stuffed animals or picture cards inside tunnels. Have children find and retrieve them.

IN SMALL SPACES

Set up only a few tunnels in small spaces. Use as many tunnels as the room will safely allow.

Dennis is highly distractible, yet his teacher has found that when she sets up the tunnels in a confined space, he stays focused and appropriately active throughout the activity.

Turtle Races

- **Locomotor skills**
- **Spatial relationships**

Children think it's great fun pretending to be a turtle while setting out on their own to explore the world. In Turtle Races, children learn to creep, crawl, go under, move forward, move backward, and share space with others.

OVERVIEW

At this age many children, particularly those with special needs, fear exploring spatial concepts. Here is a silly way to explore the world of "under" in which the key word is fun, not fear. Children crawl across the room on their hands and knees with an upside down swimming pool or laundry basket (turtle shell) on their back. After crossing the room, the children ring a bell by the picture of a turtle, then start their journey back. Provide one shell for every one or two children.

GOALS FOR CHILDREN

- Develop the skill of crawling.
- Develop the spatial concept of under.

EQUIPMENT

- Small, round plastic swimming pools, one pool for each child in a small group or station setting. Green pools are best for turtle shells. If unavailable, cut and tape green paper circles on the bottom of each pool, which becomes the top of the shell. Plastic laundry baskets can substitute as turtle shells.
- Play lively music for motivating slow turtles.

PREPARATION

Hang bells and tape photographs or hand-drawn pictures of turtles on a wall close to the floor at one end of the room. Place the turtle shells on the opposite end of the room.

DIRECTIONS

1. Introduce the turtle theme using a turtle picture or stuffed animal. Explain to the children that they are to pretend they are turtles going for a walk across the room. Point to their destination of the bells and turtle pictures.

2. Encourage the children to get on their hands and knees. Place the shell on their backs or, if the children will allow it, over their whole bodies including their heads. Then start the music and have fun!

ADAPTATIONS

Place children who cannot crawl on scooters or drape the shell over whatever type of mobility equipment best meets their needs. The children are still able to explore the spatial concept of "under" while participating with their peers. Help children with visual impairments orient themselves in the room by placing a speaker along one wall and playing music during the activity as a reference point. Also provide physical guidance and verbal cues as needed. In an activity in which several sighted children have their heads covered by the shells, children with visual impairments are at no special disadvantage.

VARIATIONS

Give the turtles a chance to explore the room, going in any direction, bumping into others' shells, sharing a shell with a friend, or just lying still under a shell.

IN SMALL SPACES

Use only a few swimming pools, and ask two children to share each pool.

A child of any ability level can enjoy pretending to be a turtle. Participation can be as simple as cuddling under the turtle shell or crawling across the floor.

Zip Line

The Zip Line, also called the Flying Fox or Fun Ride, is a strength-enhancing activity the children will love!! This activity is designed for a physical educator to lead in a gymnasium with careful attention to safety.

OVERVIEW

Children grasp the handles of the zip line as they descend the angled wire. Many children love the feeling of being suspended in space as they glide through the air.

GOAL FOR CHILDREN

Develop muscular strength and personal courage.

EQUIPMENT

- Zip Line, called Fun Ride, is available for purchase through Southpaw Enterprises, P.O. Box 1047, Dayton, Ohio 45401-1047. **www.southpawenterprises.com.**
- Helmet, mats, and any other safety equipment necessary.

PREPARATION

The zip line is a piece of equipment that you can purchase through Southpaw Enterprises. You will find the instructions necessary to set up the zip line in the purchasing box.

DIRECTIONS

Please follow the assembly and operating directions provided by Southpaw Enterprises when using the zip line. Be sure it is a safe situation, and require that children using the line wear helmets. Place mats on the floor under where the children will be sliding, and spot the children as needed.

ADAPTATIONS

Provide physical assistance for children with difficulty grasping or with upper-body weakness as they use the zip line. Other children, including those with visual impairments, may also require physical assistance as they become comfortable using the zip line. With children who are blind and have the skill and desire to use the zip line independently, provide a verbal cue to signal when they are approaching the end of the ride so they can prepare to stop.

VARIATIONS

There are no variations.

IN SMALL SPACES

This activity requires a large open space.

Be sure to read and follow the manufacturer's instructions fully and provide supervision by a trained professional to minimize the risk involved in this activity.

Part III
Movement Program Considerations

Part III is written for professionals who are responsible for leading movement programs. It builds on the foundation presented in parts I and II. We begin part III with an explanation of children's motor development. Next, we guide you through the process of developing and implementing a movement curriculum, followed by ideas for teaching movement to toddlers. Finally, we offer successful strategies for promoting your movement program.

Preschool Motor Development

A child's life is like a piece of paper on which each passer-by leaves a mark.

Ancient Chinese Proverb

Mr. Smith completes his brief directions for the learning experience Stop and Go to Music. He starts the music, filling the room with one of the children's favorite tunes. As the children run around the room, he reflects on how great this learning experience is for observing children's motor development. He notes that within this group of preschool children, they show at least three stages of the fundamental movement phase of motor development. He watches Dashiki, with Down's syndrome, break into a fast-paced walk, not yet running (initial stage). Anthony enthusiastically propels himself forward, pushing the wheels on his mobile prone stander (not a phase, but a functional adaptation). Ling darts past him, looking like a miniature sprinter, already demonstrating a mature run (mature stage). David runs behind Ling, holding his arms high and flailing his legs (elementary stage). He now slows his pace to run alongside Anthony. At this point, Mr. Smith stops the music and all the children sit down. He thanks them for sitting down so quickly, then he restarts the music to observe further.

Teachers who understand motor development are well prepared to facilitate mature movements in the children they teach. This chapter explains the four movement phases of motor development. Teachers of preschool movement programs who know these phases have a context for understanding the variety of movements observed in preschool children. These teachers can also appreciate the movements of children who show motor delays.

Motor development is the study of how human movement originates and changes across the life span. This chapter describes the aspects of motor development that are most relevant to preschool children, following the movement development phases as presented by Gallahue (1995). Figure 7.1 presents a progression in which humans develop movement.

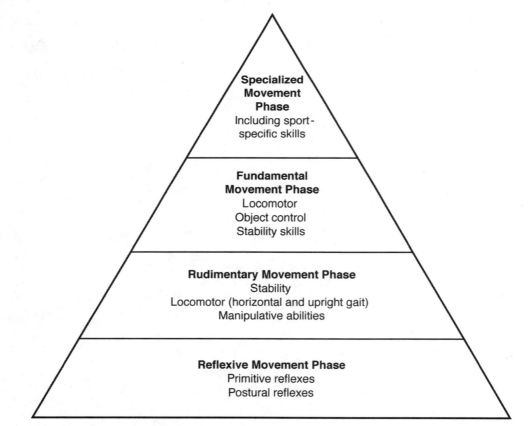

Figure 7.1   Four movement phases (data from Gallahue 1995).

Reflexive Movement Phase

As life begins, it is primarily through the assistance of reflexes that human beings first move. Reflexes help organize our bodies so we can learn a wide repertoire of voluntary, skillful movements.

"Early reflex activity can also be viewed as primary motor patterns. This reflex activity can provide a coordinating structure that initially supports limited interactions with the environment. The infant can use the beginning tonic reflexes, such as the asymmetric tonic neck reflex (ATNR) to turn their head and swipe at a toy. As the infant's voluntary movement repertoire increases motor learning occurs, and the evidence of reflex activity decreases. The persistence of primitive reflex activity is not indicative of difficulties with reflexive movement, but rather due to a problem with the sensory motor system which is preventing more mature movement patterns from developing. This creates a deprivation of voluntary movement options" (Sookie Kayne, personal communication, March 22, 1999).

Please note that some children with special needs who are experiencing motor delays may require additional work in developing voluntary movements. Please consult with a physical therapist for positioning and activity suggestions. These children's IEPs may include goals and objectives fostering their voluntary movement repertoire.

Rudimentary Movement Phase

Even as newborns, when most movements are reflexive, basic voluntary movements such as lifting the head are beginning to develop. Rudimentary movements are basic survival motor behaviors that develop in a predictable sequence (see figure 7.2 on the next page). Typically developing children, for example, first learn to lift their heads; then lift their heads and chests; followed by learning to roll over, sit, stand, and eventually walk. Gallahue (1995) notes that the predictable sequence in which children learn these rudimentary movements is the result of maturation, heavily influenced by heredity. Infants vary somewhat in the rate at which they learn these behaviors, with most developing rudimentary movements by two years of age. Some infants walk at an earlier age than others, but nearly everyone learns to sit and stand before learning to walk.

Children who experience delays in the rudimentary movement phase may benefit from extra assistance in learning to reach, grasp, and release as well as sit, stand, and walk. Some children with restricted physical capabilities may need to find their own movement forms, which may differ from the typical mature skill stage as presented in chapter 4, figures 4.1 through 4.7. Movements may need to be modified to become more functional. A child with spina bifida, for example, may be unable to creep, crawl, or walk independently, but may develop an unconventional but functional technique of scooting across the floor independently. Some children who are experiencing difficulties with rudimentary movements may need to use specialized mobility equipment to move independently. Examples of such mobility equipment include walkers, mobile prone standers, gait trainers, and wheelchairs, as discussed in chapter 5.

Fundamental Movement Phase

Walking, first learned in the rudimentary movement phase, provides the foundation for running, jumping, throwing, catching, and other basic movement skills that form the fundamental movement phase. The fundamental movement phase is a wonderful time of exploration and experimenting with movements. Many preschool children's movements are examples of the fundamental movement phase.

Between two and seven years of age, typically developing children go from their initial attempts to learn these basic movement skills to mastering the mature stage of the skill. According to Gallahue (1996), children move through three stages in learning basic movement skills, such as throwing and catching: initial stage (around two to three years of age), elementary stage (around four to five years of age), and mature stage (around six to seven years of age). A toddler will often throw facing the target and move only the throwing arm, whereas a seven-year-old child with a mature throw will begin with the side to the target and step forward with the foot opposite the throwing arm while forcefully releasing the ball toward the target. Refer to figures 4.1 through 4.7 in chapter 4 for sketches of seven fundamental movement skills.

> **Only when children have many opportunities to practice and learn fundamental movement skills will the mature skills develop!**

Prone with head extension

Prone on elbows

Rocking side to side

Rolling from prone to supine

Rolling over

Prone extended arm support

Crossing midline

Crawling (on belly)

Four-point or all-fours stance

Creeping

Kneeling

Half-kneeling

Cruising

Standing

Walking

Figure 7.2   Rudimentary Movement Phases (reprinted from Kasser 1995).

Reflexive Movement Phase

This movement phase includes primitive reflexes and postural reflexes.

Children with special needs that include neurological involvement may require activities designed to normalize reflexes. Consult a physical therapist for activity and positioning suggestions.

Rudimentary Movement Phase

Stability Abilities

Control of head and neck
Control of trunk
Sitting
Standing

Manipulative Abilities

Reaching
Grasping
Releasing

Locomotor Abilities

Horizontal
    Scooting
    Crawling
    Creeping
    Walking on all fours

Upright Gait
    Walks with support
    Walks with handholds
    Walks with lead
    Walks alone (hands high)
    Walks alone (hands low)

Toddlers, and those preschool children with motor delays, may need learning experiences that provide practice in rudimentary movements.

Fundamental Movement Phase

Locomotor Skills

Walk	Jump—vertical and horizontal
Run	Hop
Gallop	Skip
Leap	Stair climbing
Slide	Ladder climbing

Object Control Skills

Grasp	Catch
Release	Kick
Rolling	Two-hand strike
Underhand throw	Bounce
Overhand throw	

Stability Movements

Static balance	Landing
Dynamic balance	Stopping
Twisting	Dodging
Turning	

The objective is to achieve the most mature movement pattern possible for each child. Some children who are still working at the reflexive or rudimentary phase of motor development also need the opportunity to develop these fundamental movement skills. The movement pattern most successful for these children may be a functional adaptation of the typical mature pattern.

For more information on the Rudimentary Movement Phase, please see Gallahue, 1995.

The rate at which children master these fundamental movement stages depends on opportunities for practice. Children are constantly using and refining movements they learn at each stage as they experience more challenging skills. This is why it is so important to provide preschool children with quality movement programs. Only when children have many opportunities to practice and learn fundamental movement skills will the mature skills develop!

Children who have not fully mastered the earlier movement phases in a timely manner will find learning the later phases increasingly challenging. Sometimes the most functional way for a child with special needs to run, kick, or throw is different than the typical mature patterns illustrated in figures 4.1 through 4.7. A child with neurological impairments, for example, who has motor control when she moves slowly may be able to participate with other children in stationary activities without falling. However, when the activities require fast-paced running, as in the activity Musical Hoops, she may not be able to keep up with other children and might fall while trying. When she uses a walker or other mobility equipment to provide stability, she once again becomes an active participant in the game.

There are several approaches to organizing the fundamental movement phase. The organization presented here is slightly modified from Gallahue's (1996) components of stability, locomotion, and manipulation. We organized fundamental movements into three categories: locomotion, object control, and stability. Locomotor skills are the various ways of moving through space, including walking, running, jumping, galloping, hopping, skipping, and leaping. Object control skills involve maintaining control of an object using hands, feet, or any other body part and include throwing, catching, kicking, striking, and bouncing. Stability includes both static and dynamic balance. Static balance is keeping your balance while staying in one place. Dynamic balance is keeping your balance while moving through space.

Specialized Movement Phase

The specialized movement phase is the most advanced phase of motor development. As children refine the earlier movement phases, they have the foundation to learn specialized movements that they can apply to specific sports and activities. In this phase, they now combine and use locomotor, object control, and stability skills in new sport-specific skills (Gallahue 1996). The game of softball, for example, combines the fundamental movement skills of striking (object control skill) and running (locomotor skill) to swing the bat, hit a pitched ball, and run to first base.

Typically developing children enter the specialized movement phase around seven years of age and continue to develop highly refined movement skills for the remainder of their lives. Mastering the specialized movement skills opens a lifetime of enjoyment of physical activity—skiing, skating, swimming, hiking, dancing, riding, playing tennis, golf, basketball, and so much more. The work of the preschool teacher is crucial in providing the opportunities for young children to move and thereby providing opportunities for a lifetime of movement!

The next chapter builds on a knowledge of motor development in designing a preschool movement program curriculum.

> **The work of the preschool teacher is crucial in providing the opportunities for young children to move and thereby providing opportunities for a lifetime of movement!**

Developing a Movement Curriculum

Instruction, not students, must be adaptable to individualized differences.

**Janet Wessel
and Luke Kelly,**
*Achievement-Based
Curriculum Development in
Physical Education*

Chapter 3 on the child-centered teaching approach introduced a scenario in which both Mr. Jacob and Mrs. Baker teach movement to preschool children in two different settings in the same community. We noted their contrasting approaches to teaching. We will now consider their varying attitudes toward curriculum as our scenario continues.

The goal in Mr. Jacob's movement program for preschool children is to keep the preschool children busy, happy, and good. He selects activities he has found can achieve this goal. Each morning, while driving to school, he decides what he will teach that day. He recalls what the children have enjoyed doing in the past and plans to repeat the popular activities, but today he is stumped. As he waits for the traffic light to change, he searches to recall an activity that he has not done recently, but as the light changes, he still has not thought of a new activity. So he decides he will do tricycle riding again. This activity is always a favorite with the children.

Mrs. Baker's preschool movement program focuses on selecting activities that will help the children learn. Last week, when she planned her lesson for today, she selected the goal for children of jumping vertically with a mature pattern. Her instructional objective is for the children to crouch first, then jump up by extending their legs as they forcefully swing their arms forward and up. For today's lesson, she will set up four jumping stations. She plans to help the children jump and to make notes as to which children already have a mature jump and which children are still at the initial or elementary stages of learning to jump.

As Mr. Jacob arrives at work, his center's director hurriedly explains to him that she needs a copy of his written movement program curriculum for the Board of Director's meeting the next day. There are budget cuts proposed and she needs to show how the movement program helps achieve the mission of the entire preschool program. However, Mr. Jacob is not sure what a curriculum is. He figures he doesn't need one if he has gotten along all these years without one. So he plans instead to give the director a list of the activities he does with the children throughout the year.

Last month, when Mrs. Baker's director made a similar request for her movement program curriculum, Mrs. Baker went immediately to her files and pulled written copies of her curriculum for distribution at the Board meeting.

Mr. Jacob has a successful day, and the children are, as usual, busy, happy, and good. The next evening, when he presents his curriculum to the Board of Directors, Mr. Jacob hands them a neatly typed list of the varied games and activities he typically teaches the children each year. When a Board member asks him to show how his program helps meet the mission of the preschool program, Mr. Jacob's response is that the children have fun in the movement program he teaches, they get to move around a lot, and they have an opportunity to blow off some steam. The Board member responds that central to the preschool program's mission is the goal of helping children learn. Can Mr. Jacob demonstrate what the children have learned in his movement program? Caught unprepared, Mr. Jacob rambles on about the children learning discipline, having fun, and cooperating in group activities. He then falls silent. When called upon to justify his program, to explain why he is doing these activities and games, he can't, because Mr. Jacob's preschool movement program lacks a well-designed, well-written curriculum.

When Mrs. Baker presented the curriculum of her preschool movement program to the Board of Directors, she distributed her list of curricular goals for the program, along with the learning activities she conducted that helped the children achieve the curricular goals. She explained to the Board that learning is the focus of her program, but she also tries to teach in a fun way. Using the lesson of jumping as an example, she explained the jumping goal for children listed in her curriculum and told how the interesting activities she chose helped her students achieve this goal. She then shared a chart that indicated the number of children in each age level that had mastered jumping instructional objectives, showing their progress in learning over time. It was obvious to the Board members that Mrs. Baker had a sound educational reason for what she teaches and that she explained it well to others. She also demonstrated that her program is effective, based on records that show what the children have learned. Mrs. Baker was successful in showing the Board how her movement program contributed to the overall mission of the center, because she had a well-designed, written curriculum with assessment data to document its effectiveness.

This chapter introduces the concept of the curriculum and explains why having one is beneficial to preschool movement programs. It expands upon the concepts introduced in chapter 2. After an illustrative scenario, the chapter takes you through the necessary steps to develop your own curriculum. Finally, it links lesson planning to the sample 40-week curriculum found in the appendix.

Definition of a Curriculum

A curriculum is everything that you teach in the preschool movement program. The written curriculum is the document that lists what you teach and provides a rationale for why you teach these things. The written curriculum includes the learning experiences (games and activities) that the children learn, along with the goals for what the children are to achieve through participation in these learning experiences.

The process of deciding what the children will learn is called curriculum development. The steps in curriculum development in this chapter closely follow the curricular process Gallahue (1996) presents, except that we omit the conceptual framework and curricular objectives from this discussion. Begin curriculum development by examining the values and mission statement of the preschool program. Consider how children learn and what knowledge and skills preschool children are ready to learn. Knowing the normal developmental progression of any targeted skill is critical, as is knowing normal child development. Identify curricular goals that children are to achieve throughout the year. Organize these goals to assure a curriculum designed for balance, scope, and sequence. Assess the children's abilities to determine which curricular goals they have achieved and which goals they still need to achieve. Then develop yearly, weekly, and daily plans. Finally, teach lessons to implement the curriculum, using the learning experiences to help the children achieve the curricular goals.

Benefits of a Curriculum

A well-designed, well-written curriculum is a tool that enables a movement program to achieve its mission in the preschool program. The curriculum structures a movement program and gives direction to developing lesson plans. The curriculum also allows teachers and program decision makers to tell others about what you are teaching in a movement program and why. It identifies program goals and explains how to achieve these goals. The curriculum ultimately validates a movement program, showing precisely how teachers are helping children learn.

Developing a Curriculum

Writing a curriculum is similar to planning a trip. Before going on a trip, a traveler may gather many different materials to compile the information needed to decide where to go, how to get there, and what experiences to have along the way. The traveler will use maps and guidebooks. When finished, the traveler has planned a trip that is unique to his or her situation and interests. We have developed the sample preschool movement program curriculum presented in the appendix in a similar fashion. It is a curriculum that works well for the preschool children for whom we designed it. For you, it is a sample of what you can accomplish following the proper steps of curriculum development. For developing your unique curriculum, follow the same curricular development procedure presented here, inserting your values, mission statement, goals, and objectives. The result will be a curriculum you have developed that is tailored to the interests and situation of your preschool movement program. Figure 8.1 illustrates the relationship of a 40-week curricular plan (see the sample in the appendix) to weekly plans and a daily lesson plan.

Continual refinement is a sign of a healthy curriculum.

One final thought about curricular development: A curriculum must be flexible to be effective. As the needs of children change and the mission of a program evolves, the curriculum is best modified to keep pace. You will need to continually revise your preschool curriculum to meet emerging needs. Continual refinement is a sign of a healthy curriculum.

Write a Mission Statement

The mission statement of a preschool movement program is the foundation for the curriculum (Gallahue, 1996). You may base it on an institution's mission statement or develop it alone as a written expression of the teacher's responsibility to provide the learning experiences preschool students need to grow. We particularly encourage physical education teachers whose responsibility it is to provide the movement program for an entire school or center to develop a mission statement for the movement program. The sample mission statement provided here served as the catalyst for developing the sample preschool curriculum presented in the appendix. Inherent in this mission statement is the value we, the authors, place on child-centered teaching and on using a holistic approach to help children develop in all areas.

The Preschool Movement Program Mission Statement is as follows: "Preschool children need to move—to be happy, to express themselves, develop their bodies, their intellects, and their motor skills. At this critical phase of human development, learning to move and learning through movement is a vital part of every child's developmental process. The Preschool Movement Program seeks to enhance each child's development through offering an inclusive, child-centered learning environment that encourages social interaction and self-direction. It also strives to develop functional skills to be used through life, especially for those children with restricted abilities. The program is designed to help children develop their fitness and motor planning, and to enable them to master the fundamental movements of locomotor skills, object control skills, and stability. The Preschool Movement Program will, addi-

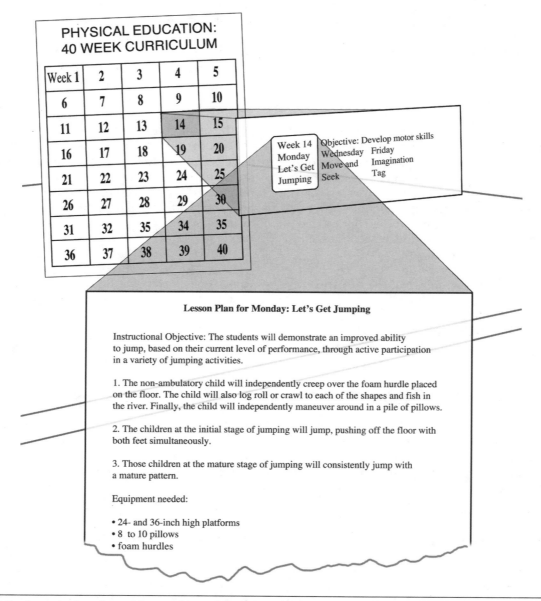

Figure 8.1 A curricular plan guides weekly and daily lesson planning.

tionally, continually adapt and create equipment to enable children with limited mobility to function more independently. It fosters active participation for all students through the use of skill stations, multiple option activities, and group games. The content of each lesson throughout the year is planned to guide students toward improving their affective, cognitive, and motor development."

Prepare Curricular Goals

The next step in curriculum development is to identify a movement program's curricular goals (Gallahue, 1996). Motor development does not occur in a vacuum. Children need prerequisite abilities in many areas for them to learn to hold up their heads, grasp toys, walk, run, or kick balls. Children need cognitive abilities to understand the task, self-confidence to try to learn the task, and fitness and motor planning capabilities to accomplish the task. We present three domains—affective, cognitive, and motor—in the following curricular goals for a preschool movement program. The following Preschool Movement Curricular Goals were first presented in box 2.1 in chapter 2 and are reprinted here in box 8.1 to illustrate how these goals fit within the process of curriculum development.

Individual children learn at different rates. Knowing the child's age does not tell us enough about the child to plan adequately for his or her particular needs.

Build in Scope, Balance, and Sequence

Gallahue (1996) offers the concept of curricular scope, sequence, and balance. Once you choose the curricular goals, organize them to create a written curriculum that is broad based, varied, and ordered. These organizing considerations are called the curriculum's scope, balance, and sequence.

Curricular Scope

Our sample curriculum in the appendix is broad based in its scope. It has breadth of program content across the year. It does not focus exclusively on developing cardiovascular endurance, for example, with the children playing the same few tag games day after day. The curriculum, rather, addresses the three domains—affective, cognitive, and motor—and various aspects within each domain. The children also work on object control, balance, motor planning, and all the curricular goals listed previously, in addition to car-diovascular endurance.

Curricular Balance

The curriculum is balanced to maintain the children's continuing interest in the learning experiences. There is variety in the learning experiences. We do not repeat the same few favorite games and activities, but add new activities and games to the curriculum to address different curricular goals and keep the children's interest level high. In the 40-week curriculum plan presented in the appendix, we repeat each of the more than 50 learning experiences in chapter 6 only a few times throughout the year. This balance adds to a sense of excitement for both teacher and children!

Curricular Sequence

We designed the curriculum to reflect the sequence in which children tend to learn. Children practice rudimentary movements before we teach fundamental movements. They learn fundamental movements before combining them into specialized movements. We present a clear progression of skills from year to year. The skills, rules, and turn taking presented to three-year-old children are simpler, for example, than those presented to four- or five-year-old children.

Plan to spiral goals throughout the curriculum so you revisit each goal repeatedly. This spiraling of goals enables constant repetition and refinement of the skills taught. The curriculum continually spirals back to these goals, providing new and exciting learning experiences through which to achieve the curricular goals. Individual children learn at different rates. Knowing the child's age does not tell us enough about the child to plan adequately for his or her particular needs. This spiraling of curricular goals enables teachers to address the varying needs of children adequately and constantly repeats the skills taught. Children practice jumping, for example, several times each year and across the years, enabling them to first learn jumping, then refine and reinforce their jumping skill. Notice how Mrs. Baker facilitates each child's learning within the jumping lesson in the following lesson plan scenario. Mrs. Baker knows which children need to develop the initial skill of jumping and which children are ready to refine jumping and combine it with other skills.

Box 8.1 — The Preschool Movement Curricular Goals

Preschool Movement Program Goals in the Affective Domain:

☑ **Strengthen the way children feel about themselves:**

Develop positive self-images and self-esteem.

Develop self-motivation to become independent learners who confidently choose to be active.

☑ **Develop social skills:**

Learn to share and cooperate and take turns.

Learn to play safely and talk kindly.

☑ **Develop joyful and purposeful play.**

Preschool Movement Program Goals in the Cognitive Domain:

☑ **Learn how to communicate.**

☑ **Learn basic rules and game play.**

☑ **Learn to follow directions.**

☑ **Learn to recognize objects, colors, and shapes.**

☑ **Learn about body awareness.**

Identify body parts.

Identify movement concepts:

Effort (time, force, flow)

Space (self-space, general space, levels—high, low)

Relationships (of body parts, to objects—over, under, in front, behind)

Preschool Movement Program Goals in the Motor Domain:

☑ **Learn rudimentary movement skills, if not already mastered.**

☑ **Learn fundamental movement skills.**

Learn locomotor skills (walk, run, jump, gallop, hop, skip, leap).

Learn object control (throw, catch, kick, strike, bounce).

Learn stability (static and dynamic balance).

☑ **Develop health-related physical fitness.**

Develop cardiovascular endurance.

Develop muscular strength and endurance.

☑ **Develop motor planning (sequencing movements based on sensory input).**

☑ **Develop functional and generalizable adaptations of motor skills, as needed.**

☑ **Learn to use recreational equipment—tricycles, roller racers, scooters, swings, adapted as needed to increase mobility.**

She knows each child's needs because she is continually assessing their skills.

Assess

Once you select curricular goals, determine which of the goals the children are ready to learn by assessing their skills. Assessment, as discussed in chapter 4, is the cornerstone of teaching because it helps teachers determine what to teach. So before implementing the curriculum, assess the current skills of the children. Chapter 4 includes further information on techniques for informal assessment and using anecdotal notes.

Combine this information with the curriculum objectives, once you assess children's skills. Develop the curriculum, keeping in mind the need for scope, sequence, and balance. Derive weekly plans and daily lesson plans from the curriculum.

Implementing the Curriculum

Curriculum development concludes with planning specific lessons that will deliver the curriculum (Gallahue, 1996). It is through the learning experiences in daily lessons that the children achieve the curricular goals and thus achieve the mission of the program. Write weekly plans that give direction for planning each day's lesson. Finally, use the lesson plan to guide your teaching of children. In this way, curriculum planning culminates with what you do when teaching the lesson.

We provide a sample 40-week curriculum plan, with goals and activities identified for each unit or week, in the appendix. In the lesson plan scenario, notice that Mrs. Baker derives her lesson plan from her weekly curricular plan, which is based on her 40-week curriculum plan. Notice how she uses her curriculum, combined with assessment of individual children's needs, to guide her daily lesson planning and teaching.

With a well-developed, well-written curriculum in place, the preschool movement program is in a strong position to help children move effectively. The following chapter examines the unique considerations in helping toddlers become skillful movers.

Lesson Plan Scenario: Let's Get Jumping

Last week, Mrs. Baker's preschool children played on an obstacle course that encouraged lots of jumping. She observed the children jumping and recorded each child's current level of performance on a daily observation sheet. She placed the sheets in a three-ring binder for future reference when planning the next jumping activity. This week, Mrs. Baker will be setting up stations that promote learning to jump. She refers to her binder of progress notes and sees there are children currently performing at the initial, elementary, and mature stage of jumping. Three children in the class also have special needs. She consults the IEP goals for each of these three children. Two of them have the goal of learning the initial level of jumping. The third child is nonambulatory. One of his IEP goals is to learn functional skills that will allow him to actively participate with the other children in the class. Mrs. Baker considers all this information as she plans this week's lesson on jumping. Here is the lesson plan she develops.

Instructional Goal

The students will demonstrate an improved ability to jump, based on their current level of performance, through active participation in a variety of jumping activities.

1. Instructional objective for the child who is nonambulatory: during the lesson, to independently creep over the foam hurdle placed on the floor, to logroll or crawl to each shape and fish in the river, and to independently maneuver in the pile of pillows at least once.

2. Instructional objective for children at the initial stage of jumping: during the lesson, to jump, pushing off the floor with both feet simultaneously, as least four out of the five times attempted.

3. Instructional objective for children at the elementary stage of jumping: during the lesson, to jump, bending their knees and thrusting their arms forward on the takeoff, then land on both feet simultaneously four out of the five times attempted.

(continued)

4. Instructional objective for children at the mature stage of jumping: during the lesson, to jump with a mature pattern consistently.

Equipment

Platforms 24 and 36 inches high.

Eight to 10 pillows.

An imaginary river created using ropes or mats, with fish cut out of paper placed in the river.

Five hurdles, including foam hurdles, ranging from 2 to 10 inches high.

Brightly colored shapes, either taped or painted on the floor.

Stations

1. Children jump into a pile of pillows from platforms 24 to 36 inches high. In this closely supervised activity, one child jumps at a time. Hold the hand of the children who need assistance.

   Look for the following: Use a two-foot takeoff and landing.

2. Children freely jump over a pretend river with fish in it.

   Look for the following: Children unable to jump will start by stepping (or crawling) over the river. Those able to jump will focus on bending knees and arm thrust and extension.

3. Children freely jump or step over a line of hurdles ranging from 2 to 10 inches off the floor.

   Look for the following: Same as in previous steps. The nonambulatory child practices creeping over the foam hurdles.

4. Children freely jump over a variety of brightly colored shapes on the floor.

   Look for the following: Same as in previous steps.

Assessment

Document each child's progress on a daily observation sheet. File these sheets in the same three-ring binder, next to the child's other observation sheets, providing easy reference by activity date and progress made.

9

Working With Toddlers

Education at this age is not about imparting facts and imposing strict schedules. It's about listening, guiding, helping individual children to make sense of the real world.

**LynNell Hancock
and Pat Wingert,
"The New Preschool"**

Mrs. Stone has been a preschool teacher with three- and four-year-old children for many years. Recently she accepted a position as a toddler teacher with two-year-old children. She felt the transition would be an easy one. After all, her teaching has a sound education base and the children always loved the activities. Mrs. Stone organized her lessons for the first day, sure it would be successful.

At the end of the day, Mrs. Stone collapsed into a chair, reflecting on information she had learned about child development years ago but had let slip her mind. She was now clearly remembering that you cannot instruct a two-year-old in the same way as a three- or four-year-old child. Mrs. Stone learned that lesson again today when she expected the toddlers to sit quietly during the 15-minute circle time, share the limited number of toys in the gross motor area, and follow a lengthy musical tape requiring the children to imitate specific movements.

The long day had been a disaster, but also a great learning experience. Mrs. Stone would plan the rest of the year's lessons around toddler concepts such as exploration, repetition, and child-initiated activity.

The preceding chapter offered curricular ideas for working with preschool children, ages three to five. This chapter explains concepts fundamental to effectively teaching movement to toddlers—children two years of age. Toddlers typically learn best through repetition in child-initiated play within a safe environment.

Curriculum Content

A toddler curriculum centers on self-care activities; coping with separation; making new attachments with adults and children; and free play in a safe, age-appropriate, stimulating environment. Typical toddlers are mastering the rudimentary movements and beginning to learn fundamental movements discussed in chapters 4 and 7.

Repetition and Exploration

Have you ever watched toddlers at play? Watch them climb the minislide: three steps up then slide down, three steps up then slide down, three steps up then slide down. There is pure delight on their faces as they do it again and again.

An important concept in toddler education is to plan movement experiences that offer many opportunities for repetition. Perhaps at no other time in a person's life is such joy found in repetitious play. Repetition is important because it leads to developing routines. Routines, in turn, help a toddler develop a sense of security, which breeds trust.

> A toddler curriculum centers on self-care activities; coping with separation; making new attachments with adults and children; and free play in a safe, age-appropriate, stimulating environment.

Although there will be times when they need to move on to new ideas, permitting repetition is fundamental to toddlers' learning.

Toddlerhood is a distinct stage of development with its own set of tasks and behaviors. Yet it is a common mistake for teachers and parents to treat toddlers as miniature preschoolers, capable of more advanced cognitive, affective, social, and motor behaviors than they have available. Expectations for behaviors and movements are often too high. This can set off a domino effect of failures and frustrations for teacher, parent, and child.

Teachers and parents alike need to strike a balance between demonstrating new ideas and allowing toddlers to work on their own exploration and repetition of activities. When teaching two-year-old children to throw Nerf balls into toddler basketball nets, demonstrate the task then step back, allowing them to experiment on their own. Let children put the ball in forward, backward, and any other way they invent. Their performance does not have to be perfect every time. As children become familiar with a situation through repetition, they are free to experiment and create at a new level, while maintaining familiarity with a task they found satisfying.

Be alert to when it is time for toddlers to go on to another activity. A child's change of behavior can be an obvious cue that the toddler is bored or overstimulated. Watch for signs, and make activity changes immediately.

Child-Initiated Play

Central to a toddler curriculum is the concept that the activities are initiated by the child. Child-initiated play, a good idea with preschoolers, is essential with toddlers. Unlike teacher-directed activities, child-initiated play provides children with the freedom to choose an activity within a framework the teacher creates. Children carry out the activities as they see fit, so except for safety considerations, there is no correct or incorrect way to accomplish the task. Two-year-olds are in the midst of claiming their independence. This child-initiated approach provides a nonconfrontational adult-child environment that allows the child the opportunity to experiment with movements.

Teachers and parents alike need to focus on increasing adult responsiveness and decreasing their directive behaviors when interacting with the toddler-age child. As a child is climbing up a toddler slide, for example, whether on the stomach or back, the responsive teacher enthusiastically describes what the child *is* doing rather than being directive and telling the child what he or she *should* be doing.

Create a safe environment in which toddlers can move and explore. Eliminate hazards from the room such as glass mirrors, floor lamps, uncovered electrical outlets, doors and drawers that can pinch, open stairways, furniture that can topple, heavy toys, sharp edges, and breakable items. When you provide a safe environment, there is no need to hover. Children can continually practice skills without needing constant adult direction and hovering that can inhibit their play. Children can be free to explore.

Toddlers typically participate in parallel play. Parallel play represents the self-centered stage of toddlers development, marked by their unwillingness or inability to share or play with other children. To reach this point of development, children have moved through the stages of play in which they have focused on sensorimotor play (learning to match their senses with their movements, as in hand-eye coordination) and imitation (pretending). However, they may still be a year or more away from attaining the ability to play in a cooperative, interactive way. Wait until the child is older before leading group activities that involve turn taking.

Keep the gross motor movement activities at a level toddlers can handle. A hallmark of the toddler stage is difficulty in taking turns. Don't expect toddlers to go through a tunnel one at a time. Place, instead, a variety of hard plastic tunnels along with soft fabric tunnels in a room during free play. This arrangement allows the toddlers to problem solve and motorically explore which tunnels they can successfully climb over and go through. Toddlers also problem solve as they struggle with the social turmoil that develops when there is more than one toddler in "my" tunnel at a time! Pushing toddlers to perform at a more advanced stage of development robs them of vital time needed at their current stage of development doing something all toddlers love to do—explore.

> **Pushing toddlers to perform at a more advanced stage of development robs them of vital time needed at their current stage of development doing something all toddlers love to do—explore.**

The following learning experiences, found in chapter 6, may be especially appropriate for toddlers.

Let's Balance, using only low heights

Bubble Fun

Let's Get Catching, Throwing, and Kicking with large targets

Garbage Clean Up

Gutter Ball

Mat Maze

Mountains and Valleys

Swings

Tire Play

Tunnel Course

Turtle Races

The following chapter contains ideas for promoting a movement program, whether the program is for toddlers, preschool children, or older children. We wrote it primarily for physical educators, but you can generalize the ideas about program promotion to promoting early childhood education programs as a whole.

10

Promoting a Movement Program: How to Make a Good Program Better

F acts may be facts, but perceptions are reality.

Author unknown

Miss Marchand was jubilant. Several VIP visitors had just left the gymnasium after observing one of her movement program classes with preschool children. As they left, the Board member who had brought them told her how impressed he is with the work she has been doing, adding "Just let me know if there is anything I can do to help your program. I think you are providing such a fine education for these young children."

She recalled her frustration a year earlier when this same Board member knew nothing of the quality movement program she had been offering for three years. Shaken by his ignorance of her program, she vowed to actively promote the program as she continued to offer the quality program she always had.

Over the past year, she invited other teachers in the center to observe in the gymnasium. She also encouraged therapists to use the gymnasium as a setting in which to conduct one of their therapy sessions each week. She arranged to make a presentation explaining the movement program to the center's Board of Directors. At her invitation, the local newspaper ran two stories on special events she organized. Buoyed by the many positive comments she had received about the program from teachers and parents alike, she invited television and radio coverage of various events. As news of her quality program spread, she received an invitation to speak about her teaching at a local college and at a preschool conference. The center's director now proudly invites visitors to observe the movement program, and today it has been selected as the showpiece for the VIP visit to the center. She shook her head in amazement as she thought about how the program had not changed. It has been strong for three years, but now others were noticing it and asking how they could support her work. She now understood how program promotion can make a good program better.

This chapter discusses promoting movement programs within the early childhood educational setting. There are many good reasons why program promotion is important to those who teach movement to preschool children. The chapter focuses on the two-step process of good program promotion: Build an excellent movement program, then tell others about it. We offer many effective tips and techniques for promoting a movement program to three main audiences: decision makers, parents, and the community at large.

The following ideas are for teachers who are employees in center-based or school-based programs with full-time responsibility for providing a movement program. We designed this chapter for teachers who conduct a series of classes in movement throughout the school day. We wrote these suggestions from the perspective of physical educators promoting a movement program to a principal. You could generalize these concepts and just as easily apply them to early childhood educators promoting an early childhood education program to a supervisor.

> **The chief benefit of program promotion is that the more publicity a good program receives, the better the likelihood that the program and teacher will continue to be funded and supported by the community.**

Perception of Movement Programs

In the scenario, Miss Marchand discovered that others didn't necessarily have the same ideas about what was going on in her program as she did. Her successes were unknown outside of the classroom. Her hard work and effectiveness were only obvious to those she taught each day. Facts may be facts, but perception is reality.

The chief benefit of program promotion is that the more publicity a good program receives, the better the likelihood that the program and teacher will continue to be funded and supported by the community. Skillfully teaching movement can contribute substantially to the development of preschool children. The best way for teachers to convey this concept to the general public is by the following:

1. Provide preschool children with an excellent movement program.
2. Create opportunities to let others know about the program.

Promote Your Program

There is no substitute for a movement program that has a clearly defined and relevant purpose, and a thoughtfully designed curriculum based on assessment of the children's needs, that is effectively taught and continually evaluated and refined. Put in the extra effort to make it an excellent movement program. When teachers know they are offering excellent programs, it becomes easier to enthusiastically promote them to others.

There are at least three audiences to whom you can promote programs:

- Decision makers (principals, supervisors, superintendents, directors, board members)
- Parents and guardians of the children in the program
- General community

The following are strategies for developing effective program promotions for each audience. This section begins with ideas for gaining support for programs from decision makers, such as principals and supervisors of early childhood education, and directors of physical education or special education.

Inform Decision Makers

Decision makers need to know about movement programs to support them. Adopt a proactive style. "Proactive means you're not just going to sit back and let things happen. If you have some aspect of the program you want to introduce or continue, you make it more visible to the administration and the public"(Kimiecik, Demas, and Demas, 1994). Begin communicating with decision makers about the program. Don't wait for them to make inquiries. Administrators usually have too many demands on their time to go to teachers. Go to them. Unless teachers initiate communication, business goes on as usual, without concern for the accomplishments or needs of the movement program (Ratliffe, 1986). The following are suggestions for gaining the support of decision makers.

- Give decision makers carefully selected articles on movement for preschool children (such as those found in professional journals) with a note about the information in the article. Use the article to start communication about the movement program with the decision maker.
- Have an open door policy of welcoming parents, staff, and administrators to observe the movement program at any time as an important first step. However, a specific invitation to visit is even better.
- Personally invite decision makers to come visit the movement program. Send a written invitation for a specific date and time. During the visit, provide a copy of the lesson plan with the instructional objectives. Explain what children are learning and why it is important for these children. Follow up with a thank you note for visiting.
- Help decision makers look good. Share any special learning experiences with the decision maker. For example, one teacher developed a short holiday dance with the children. She invited the principal and director of physical education to see the dance. Shortly thereafter, the director of physical education arranged for the children to perform the dance at the next board of education meeting. A few months later the district superintendent was hosting a meeting of superintendents from across the state. As part of their visit to district's schools, the children performed the dance for them at the request of the superintendent.
- Seek to make presentations on the movement program to the board of education or directors. As the movement program continues to improve, highlight innovative aspects of the program every few years.
- Educate new decision makers about the program. Within the first few months on the job, invite the new decision maker to observe the program. As has been wisely observed, the time to make friends is before you need them.
- Dress for success. When teachers dress, speak, and act in a professional manner they are more likely to be regarded as professionals.

Inform Parents

The best promoters of movement programs are the children who participate in them. When these children come home and excitedly talk about what they did and what they learned in the movement program, they are promoting the program in

> **Decision makers need to know about movement programs to support them.**

the best way possible. Preschool children, however, are just learning to use language, so there can be limitations in what they communicate about a program to their parents. Teachers need to take active roles in informing parents about the movement program.

Parents can be powerful and influential supporters of a movement program, but only after they learn about the program. Teachers are employees of the board of education or board of directors. Parents are independent. Parents can advocate for their children directly and forcefully to school and center decision makers and expect immediate results. So the task becomes finding simple, yet effective, ways of informing parents about the movement program.

Typically, parents are eager to learn about their child's day in preschool. Often, though, preschool children don't have the language to describe what they did. This is especially true of the many preschool children with language delays. Prepare information about the movement program and send it home to bridge this communication gap. Here are some ideas for informing parents about the movement program.

- Have an open door policy throughout the year, welcoming parents to observe the program at any time. However, this may not be enough to entice some to visit.

- Invite parents and other family adults to observe the movement program during the regular school day. Send home invitations in advance and post invitations around the school, inviting them to attend on a specific day or during a specific week.

- Host a movement program demonstration once or twice a year. Invite preschool children and parents to participate for about half an hour. Many parents are eager for opportunities to play with their children. Hold it at a time that will maximize attendance. Use this event to educate the family about the purpose, curriculum, and benefits of the program

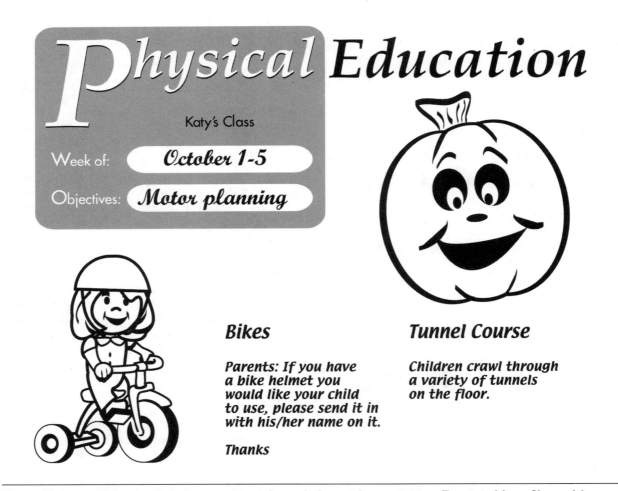

Figure 10.1   Unit notes help keep parents informed of your class activities. (Reprinted from Chermak.)

and the importance of regular physical activity to health. Select typical activities from the movement program curriculum that adults and children can do together. Activity ideas include Big on Balloons, Mat Maze, Musical Hoops, movement activity tapes, Roller Skating, Stop and Go to Music, Tricycle Course, Tunnel Course, and Tag games.

- Become the focal point of an open house. Make a video about the program, along with a poster that explains the movement program's purpose and curriculum. Then set up the video and poster in a central location so everyone who enters the building will see it. Even if you conduct the movement program in the far corner of the building, bring the presentation to the center of the event.

- Invite parents and other family adults to volunteer in the movement program. Some parents may be available and willing to participate. Avoid asking only for room mothers and thereby indicating that fathers are not welcome. Be sure to invite men as well as women.

- Write a one-page description of the movement program and distribute this information to parents and decision makers. Include brief statements about the mission of the movement program. This movement program description can be invaluable to decision makers helping to advocate for the movement program. An example of a mission statement is found in chapter 8.

- At the beginning of each unit, send home a one-page description of the unit and what the children will learn. Parents will know what their children are doing and can ask, "Did you . . . today?" An example of a completed unit note is found in figure 10.1.

- Send home brief notes, certificates, or awards that recognize something the child has done well (figure 10.2). These could be in the form

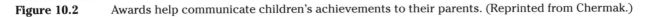

Figure 10.2   Awards help communicate children's achievements to their parents. (Reprinted from Chermak.)

of a "Good News Scroll," or "Physical Education Award," or "Participation Certificate." Teachers who have done this report a positive response from parents as well as from the classroom teachers who see the notes when packing them for home. These notes give parents and other teachers an opportunity to observe first hand the caring, supportive atmosphere in your movement program.

- Hold special events in the movement program. ACES (All Children Exercising Simultaneously) and Ride for Life are excellent examples of international and national events in which preschool children can participate (see photo). We present ideas for organizing an ACES event in box 10.1. Remember to invite the media.

- Seek to make presentations on the movement program before parent groups, such as the Parent Teacher Organization or parent support groups. To maximize attendance and interest, include preschool children demonstrating motor activities learned in the program, or at least show a videotape of children participating in the program. Make a presentation on the movement program every few years. The repetition is especially important for a preschool program in which there is a complete turnover of children and parents every three years.

Box 10.1 ACES

ACES is an international program designed to get as many children in the world as possible exercising at the same time. To date over 40 countries and over 20 million children participate annually. It was started in 1989 by Len Saunders, a physical educator at Valley View School, Montville, New Jersey. The program takes place from 10:00 to 10:15 A.M. on the first Wednesday in May. Each school organizes its own event with children doing any form or combination of exercise, including walking, running, dancing, calisthenics, and aerobics. Exercises and aerobic movements to music work well with preschool children and include children who require adapted mobility equipment. Here is a list of suggestions to make preschool children's participation in ACES a success:

In Advance

- Send home fliers promoting the event, inviting friends and family to participate.
- Decorate bulletin boards around the building promoting the event.
- Invite local media to cover the event.
- Invite local personalities to participate.
- Arrange for an adult personality at the school or center to dress as a cartoon character or as the school mascot.
- Select theme music for each year. Plan musical movement songs and decorations that reflect each year's theme.

During the Event

- Have energizing music playing as the children enter the large room for the event.
- Play the national anthem just before 10:00 A.M.
- Hold up large numbered cards to lead children in the countdown to begin exercising.
- Play high-energy music throughout the 15 minutes. Five songs will typically fill the 15 minutes. Invite a variety of staff or students to lead the audience in musical movement activities.
- Use visual cue cards, especially with a large audience, to tell the audience and performers what to do. Hold up the cue card stating, "Touch your toes," for example, as the exercise calls for toe touches.

Children have fun participating in the ACES program.

- Designate a master of ceremonies to keep the event running smoothly and the audience aware of what is happening next.
- Distribute certificates to participants at the end of the event.

This can be a great event. Get involved and participate!

Inform the Community

Informing the community about your program garners local support and funding, as well as respect for the service your program offers.

- Invite the local newspaper to cover a special event in the movement program. Newspaper reporters and photographers are often eager for positive stories that feature adorable preschool children. Provide a brief written description of the program, for the reporter's reference. Box 10.2 provides all of the information you would want to include in a press release for the Ride for Life program. It also includes suggestions for holding the event.

- Celebrate National Physical Education Week, held the first week of March. This is an excellent time to showcase the movement program.

All these suggestions can help make a good program better. In the final section of the book, we shift our focus to offering a good movement program for those preschool children who have special needs. The following chapter provides an introduction to special education.

Box 10.2 **The American Heart Association Ride for Life**

Ride for Life is a preschool tricycle-riding event to promote the importance of cardiovascular fitness for preschool children of all ability levels. The tricycle riding includes adapted mobility equipment of all types. The event was developed as a joint effort with the Upstate New York Chapter of the American Heart Association (AHA) and the North Syracuse Early Education Program. Ride for Life gives preschool children a chance to participate in an AHA fund-raising event while doing something successfully that they all love. It is also a great way to promote the AHA preschool curriculum Heart Power.

Hold the event over one or two days, either indoors or outdoors. Decorate the event area like a race track with banners, balloons, and such. Group children and select time limits within the children's capabilities. Have the regular tricycles, adapted tricycles, and any other necessary mobility equipment, ready and waiting so every child is actively participating from the start! Children ride their tricycles or other mobility equipment during the 25-minute event.

The fund-raising is accomplished through friends and family donating $1 or more in support of the children who pedal during the designated time. All children receive certificates of participation for their efforts. Ride for Life can be a rewarding experience for children, staff, and families. It is a developmentally appropriate way to successfully and actively involve preschool children in a fund-raising event for the AHA and a way to promote cardiovascular fitness. Contact the local AHA for further information, or contact the North Syracuse Early Education Program Adapted Physical Education Department, North Syracuse, New York, 315-452-3024 for assistance in getting started.

Part IV
Including Children With Special Needs

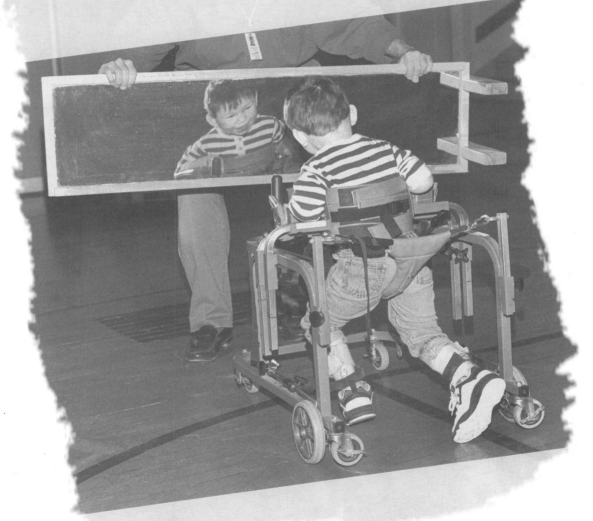

Part IV is written for all those responsible for teaching movement programs to children with special needs. We begin with an overview of special education law and an explanation of the special education process. We then share ideas for writing the gross motor component of an IEP. Next, we address the important role each professional plays as a member of the educational team of a child with special needs. This part concludes with a crucial aspect of educating any child: parents and teachers working together as partners. We urge parents and teachers alike to read this final chapter.

Introduction to Special Education

Controversy may be swirling over the role of public schools in preschool education, but in one area—special education—federal law has settled the issue. Preschool children [with disabilities] (ages 3 to 5) will receive a free, appropriate public education in the least restrictive environment in the same manner that a student [with a disability] in the K-12 program benefits from federal law.

**David E. Greenburg,
"Preschool special
education: New
responsibility for schools"**

Mr. Smith just attended an in-service workshop titled State and Federal Special Education Regulations. He anticipated the workshop would be useful only as a review, but as the workshop progressed, he realized there is plenty of new information about special education law that he could use in teaching preschool children with special needs.

This chapter introduces what special education is and which children are eligible for it. It also explains some major provisions of the Individuals With Disabilities Education Act (IDEA) and its Amendments of 1997, a law that specifically addresses preschool special education. Although in this chapter we refer to a child who receives special education as having a disability, elsewhere in the book we refer to such a child as having special needs.

One Family's Story

We begin this section with a heartwarming story written by a special dad. Mary and Dale King have adopted eight children with special needs over the years. In this story we hear about their adoptive son Steven, an adorable child who was born a healthy boy but days later was severely shaken. Their story picks up when Steven is a three-week-old infant, critically injured, in the hospital with little hope from the doctors that he will survive. The feeling is that even if he does survive, he will have severe mental and physical disabilities. At that same moment, Dale King is opening his newspaper about to read a news article that hits too close to home to ignore. Their story, found in box 11.1, is called A Time of Reflection.

Definition of Special Education

A special education means specifically designed instruction to meet the unique needs of a child with a disability. Many, but not all, children who have special needs may qualify under IDEA as having a disability. An example of a special education is a three-year-old child with a severe intellectual delay who is not yet walking and needs a specialized education to help him learn to walk. Federal laws have been passed that give structure to the education to which these children with disabilities are entitled. The most important of these laws is the federally enacted IDEA, portions of which are quoted in box 11.2.

Eligibility for Special Education Services

In general, individuals between birth and 21 years of age who need special education due to disabilities are eligible under IDEA. A child aged three to nine years may be considered disabled under IDEA if the child is experiencing developmental delays in one or more of the following areas:

Physical development

Cognitive development

Communication development

Social or emotional development

Adaptive development that requires special education or related services

This provision allows children who are too young to have identifiable disabilities, but who are at risk of developing disabilities, to receive special education services. However, in some cases, it is possible to identify children as having one or more of the following disabilities. Please note that these terms may differ slightly from state to state.

Autism

Hearing impairments including deafness

Mental retardation

Orthopedic impairment

Other health impairments

Serious emotional disturbance

Specific learning disabilities

Speech or language impairments

Traumatic brain injury

Visual impairments including blindness

IDEA guarantees the right of every child with a disability to a free, appropriate, public education.

Box 11.1 A Time of Reflection

It's 9:30 in the evening and the last of the eight children are in bed. My wife and I have our chance to reflect on the day. What a day it has been!

The day began with our second oldest son missing his bus and his aunt having to take him to school. The eldest son had made the bus with the project in hand that Dad had helped him with the night before. Mom was busy dressing the three younger children. Two needed to be ready for their bus at 8:15, and the third was leaving on a bus at 8:30. The two older girls are arguing in the family room over who is the best country singer on CMT. They have not even thought about their bus due in 20 minutes. The middle son is upstairs taking his shower, 10 minutes before bus time. All in all, it is a typical morning at our house. I have headed for work at the height of the turmoil. Finally all five buses have left and the kids are off to five different schools.

The day continues with my wife heading out right after the buses departed. Medicine was needed at one of the schools for our children with ADHD (attention deficit with hyperactivity disorder). Four of the kids have been diagnosed with this problem. After that, it's off to a third school to meet with the physical therapist for our son. His foot orthotics had become too small and his legs have to be cast again for new ones.

After that, it was back home to meet a bus for the younger two children. A little housework, lunch for everybody, and it's off again. This time she stops at another school to pick up our little boy with Down's syndrome and is off to the pediatrician. The three younger children are there often with ear infections, asthma, and other ailments. Finally, after the visit to the physician, it's home for good.

Bus after bus arrives home and soon, so does Dad. Everyone is home for the rest of the day and evening. Dad and Mom help each other get the dinner prepared while most of the kids are working on their homework. Both Dad and Mom have to help here and there with homework. Somehow they serve dinner. All 10 of us sit down to eat together and share a little of everyone's day. Many nights, singing breaks out, and we have a hearty round of the Wheels on the Bus, Three Little Monkeys, or a similar song. A while later, the staggered bedtimes begin. Dad and Mom share duties of stories, prayers, and goodnights.

As I said earlier, we come to a time in the day to reflect. I begin to read the paper, and once again I read about another child who was shaken by its father. Thoughts rush back over the years. You see, we are former foster parents who have adopted the eight children that give us such a busy schedule and many joys. I think we are regarded as the people who couldn't say no to a child with special needs.

This story brings our thoughts back to the day when, like today, we read an article in the newspaper about a young child who had been hurt and hospitalized. The difference then was that we recognized the name of the child in the article. The infant was the brother of our son, Mark, who has Down's syndrome. We were aware that only three weeks earlier Mark's mother had given birth to another baby boy. The story told how the baby was crying and fussing, so the boyfriend bounced the baby on the bed and watched the baby's eyes bug out. He admitted that he had thrown the infant in his crib. The report went on to say that the baby was in critical condition. Upon reading the article, both Mary and I had begun to cry to think of a child three weeks of age being abused in such a manner. We decided to see if we could help, even though at the time we already had six children. The next day I contacted the county social services to offer our help. They said that if the baby survived they would welcome him joining us. I was warned at the time to not hold any hope of a normal child. We were told that if he survived he could possibly be in a vegetative state. (Human beings are not vegetables!) The caseworkers suggested that we visit with him in the hospital before we made up our minds.

The following day we got up all our courage and went to visit the infant, Steven. His physician told us that we should not expect much, that the baby was unconscious most of the time and in poor shape. As we approached the hospital bed where he lay, my first thought was how small he

(continued)

Box 11.1 **A Time of Reflection** *(continued)*

looked compared to that huge bed. Then I took a better look. He was bandaged all around his head with only a few spaces open for his mouth and nose. He had tubes running from every inch of his little frame, or so it seemed. Even in this condition, when my wife reached down to the baby's right hand, he cupped his hand over her finger. It was then that we thought he would be all right.

Over the next three weeks we visited him daily in the hospital. When we brought that little guy home, he was still bandaged, but better than when we first saw him. Those first few days at home we were still unsure of how to handle him. The doctors at the hospital had warned us of the many problems that he may face. They told us that he might not have eyesight. His eating may not be sufficient to sustain him. X-rays had shown that he had received twisting fractures of both his legs. They were not sure that he had any hearing, and they doubted that he would ever be ambulatory in any way. He was on phenobarbital for possible seizures. We would need to keep a close eye on his sleeping. Needless to say, the doctors would have scared many people away, but not us. We are always up for a challenge.

We were lucky that when Steven came home we were already receiving early intervention services through North Syracuse Schools. Steven was evaluated and services provided, beginning at about 12 weeks of age. Early triumphs occurred regarding his eyesight and hearing. We started collecting toys that were black and white with a little red. We had been told that these colors can stimulate eyesight. By use of these stimuli, Steven began to show that indeed he was seeing and would follow objects. Later, he began to respond to the sight of us—Mom, Dad, and his other siblings. Steven also showed us early that he was hearing. He had a propensity for keeping the beat to music. As mentioned earlier, our family sings around the dinner table many times. Steven seemed to catch on to this and would move his functional arm and his legs to the beat. The therapists followed up with this by singing during therapy and found it helped them get further with him.

Our household has adopted the use of music as a therapy. We truly believe that many should study this as an important strategy. In Steven's case music has proven invaluable. He has come to a point that he can initiate a song by humming the melody. He hums so clearly that we understand and will sing with him. From an early age he liked the Jeopardy theme song. Any time he heard it, he would come to watch the show. He also loves the music and images in Walt Disney's *Fantasia*. Because of his love for music, the early education program used this to teach Steven to make choices. They use a voice simulator with symbols of his favorite songs pictured on it. Steven must choose a song to sing by touching the buttons.

Steven has had slow progress in movement. He has tight musculature and little flexion. This high tone prevented him from moving by himself for over a year. The therapists working with him finally got him to the point of pushing himself up into a sitting position. From that point, Steven started to make progress. He could not walk, but that was not going to stop him from moving around. He decided to move by using his one functional hand and scooting along on his bottom. There were those who thought we should not let him move like that. We ignored their well-intentioned concern. We felt that at least he was being a little independent, and he was happy in that independence.

On our youngest daughter's first birthday we gave her a ride on a push car. When two-and-a-half-year-old Steven saw the riding toy, he scooted over to it and touched it. We lifted him onto it, and immediately he began to use his legs to move the car. At first the movement was only backward, but soon he found that he could ride forward too. That small riding toy was his companion from then on. He wanted to get on it the minute he saw it. It must have given him such a feeling of accomplishment. He could now move between rooms on the first floor with ease.

Steven has had many physical problems as a result of his injuries. He gets frequent ear infections and does not usually have a fever when he is ill. The part of the brain that regulates temperature is affected by the damage caused during the shaking. The only way to know when he is ill is to know him as well as we do, so we can tell the signs of illness. He will start refusing food, coughing becomes more frequent, and he has a greenish discharge from his tear ducts. Steven is also afflicted with reflux and will choke at times. We need to keep him near us, especially while sleeping. For that reason, we have a crib for him in our bedroom at night. He also has asthma, which requires nebulizer treatments regularly.

Steven, now five, has attended the early intervention program for the past three years. In the time he has been there we have seen a great change in that little baby who was shaken and for whom there was little hope. He now can stand at the sensory table for long periods at a time. He has been fitted with ankle/foot orthotics (AFOs) to assist in standing. He is learning to walk with the assistance of a walker and can now walk the full length of the halls at the school.

He has been lucky to have another professional in his corner, his pediatrician. She was a physician teacher in the hospital when Steven was admitted after his traumatic episode. Since then she has become the pediatrician at the pediatrics clinic at the hospital and agreed to take on Mark and Steven's case under private insurance. The relationship with this doctor has been wonderful.

Steven has made remarkable progress, surpassing all expectations of the doctors. He has an outgoing personality, and everyone who works with him falls in love with his character. Cognitively, Steven appears to be bright. He understands many things and expresses himself in many ways, even though he is not yet verbal. Getting to know the individual child is so important. Through our work with the North Syracuse Early Education Program we have seen Steven blossom and grow. There is no doubt in our minds that without this early intervention Steven would not be where he is today.

One of our good friends gave us a poem, early on, when we were unsure as to whether we could give Steven what he needed. It went something like this:

A Special Child

The child still in the mother's womb
Spoke to the heavenly Father,
"How will I make it in this world?
I am not like other children.
My speech may not be understandable.
I may look different than others.
I may not be able to walk and
May need to use a wheelchair.
What is to become of me?"
Our Lord replied to the child,
"My child have no fear.
I will give you special parents.
They will love you because you are special,
Not in spite of it.
Your path through life will be difficult,
Your rewards will be great,
And your accomplishments fulfilling.
You have been blessed with
A special capability to love,
And those whose lives you touch
Will be rewarded
Because you are special."

This poem has been a source of strength and hope as we journey along the path with our special son Steven. The words fit his life perfectly. We share this poem with anyone we meet who has a special child. In all of this we have learned that if you set achievable goals you will be able to realize them.

Box 11.2 Individuals With Disabilities Education Act (IDEA) Definitions

"The term 'special education' means specially designed instruction, at no cost to parents, to meet the unique needs of a child with a disability, including

(A) instruction conducted in the classroom, in the home, in hospitals and institutions, and in other settings; and

(B) instruction in physical education" (IDEA, 1999, U.S. Code Service Title 20, sec. 1401 [25]).

"The term 'child with a disability' means a child

(i) with mental retardation, hearing impairments (including deafness), speech or language impairments, visual impairments (including blindness), serious emotional disturbance (hereinafter referred to as 'emotional disturbance'), orthopedic impairments, autism, traumatic brain injury, other health impairments, or specific learning disabilities; and

(ii) who, by reason thereof, needs special education and related services" (IDEA, 1999, U.S. Code Service Title 20, sec. 1401 [3]).

Preschool children with disabilities are eligible under IDEA. "The term 'child with a disability' for a child aged three through nine may, at the discretion of the State and the local educational agency, include a child

(i) experiencing developmental delays, as defined by the State and as measured by appropriate diagnostic instruments and procedures, in one or more of the following areas: physical development, cognitive development, communication development, social or emotional development, or adaptive development; and

(ii) who, by reason thereof, needs special education and related services" (IDEA, 1999, U.S. Code Service Title 20, sec. 1401 [3][B]). This provision allows children who do not have known disabilities but who are at risk of developing disabilities to receive special education services.

With regard to the least restrictive environment, IDEA states:

(1) "That to the maximum extent appropriate, children [with disabilities] including children in public or private institutions are educated with children who are not disabled, and

(2) That special classes, separate schooling, or other removal of children [with disabilities] from the regular educational environment occurs only when the nature or severity of the [disability] is such that education in regular classes with the use of supplementary aids and services cannot be achieved satisfactorily" (IDEA, 1977, U.S. Code Service, Title 45, sec. 1401 [121a.550]).

Physical Education is defined in IDEA as "(I) ...the development of:

(A) physical and motor fitness;

(B) fundamental motor skills and patterns; and

(C) skills in aquatics, dance, individual and group games, and sports (including intramural and lifetime sports).

(ii) The term includes special physical education, adapted physical education, movement education, and motor development" (IDEA, 1977, U.S. Code Service, Title 45, sec. 1401 [121a.14]).

IDEA defines the IEP as a written statement for each child with a disability that includes:

(i) "a statement of the child's present level of educational performance;

   (I) how the child's disability affects the child's involvement and progress in the general curriculum; or

   (II) for preschool children, as appropriate, how the disability affects the child's participation in appropriate activities;

(ii) a statement of measurable annual goals, including benchmarks or short-term objectives, related to—

   (I) meeting the child's needs that result from the child's disability to enable the child to be involved in and progress in the general curriculum; and

   (II) meeting each of the child's other educational needs that result from the child's disability;

(iii) a statement of the special education and related services and supplementary aids and services to be provided to the child, or on behalf of the child, and a statement of the program modifications or supports for school personnel that will be provided for the child—

   (I) to advance appropriately toward attaining the annual goals;

   (II) to be involved and progress in the general curriculum...and to participate in extracurricular and other nonacademic activities; and

   (III) to be educated and participate with other children with disabilities and nondisabled children in the activities described in this paragraph;

(iv) an explanation of the extent, if any, to which the child will not participate with nondisabled children in the regular class and in the activities described in clause (iii)

(v) (I) a statement of any individual modifications in the administration of State or district-wide assessments of student achievement that are needed in order for the child to participate in such assessment...

(vi) the projected date for the beginning of services and modifications described in clause (iii), and the anticipated frequency, location, and duration of those services and modifications;

(vii) (I) beginning at age 14, and updated annually, a statement of the transition service needs of the child...

(viii) a statement of—

   (I) how the child's progress toward the annual goal ...will be measured, and

   (II) how the child's parents will be regularly informed (by such means as periodic report cards), at least as often as parents are informed of their nondisabled children's progress, of—

      (aa) their child's progress toward the annual goals described in clause (ii); and

      (bb) the extent to which that progress is sufficient to enable the child to achieve the goals by the end of the year" (IDEA, 1999, U.S. Code Service Title 20, sec. 1414 [d]).

IDEA testing requirements include that

"tests are not discriminatory on a racial or cultural basis and are provided and administered in the child's native language or other mode of communication unless it is clearly not feasible to do so; and have been validated for the specific purpose for which they are used; and are administered by trained personnel [following the test instructions] provided by their producer. The child is assessed in all areas related to the suspected disability" (IDEA, 1999, U.S. Code Service Title 20, sec. 1414 [b]).

Six Major Provisions of IDEA

The following provisions of IDEA have particular relevance to providing movement programs to children with special needs.

IEP

The IEP is the document that defines the individualized program developed to meet the specific needs of each student with a disability. IDEA requires that writing the IEP be a joint effort between parents or legal guardians and professionals. Refer to chapter 13 for further discussion of the IEP.

Least Restrictive Environment

Children are to be educated in the least restrictive environment. This encourages preschoolers with disabilities to be educated in regular settings with their typical peers, rather than in segregated special education classes or schools.

Parent Participation

IDEA also says that parents or legal guardians participate in the major educational decisions regarding their child. Should parents and school personnel be unable to agree on an appropriate educational approach for the child, the parents have the right of due process (legal recourse) to appeal the committee decision to an impartial judge who can make the decision regarding the child's educational program.

Testing

Nondiscriminatory testing and objective criteria for placement are required when testing to determine if the child is eligible for special education services. Testing children in their native languages, using standardized measures or clinical observation, and using more than a single test to determine eligibility are examples of IDEA testing requirements.

> **Every child with a disability is required to receive instruction in physical education, even if all other students in the preschool do not receive such instruction.**

> **Physical therapy or occupational therapy can not be substitutes for physical education.**

Physical Education

Direct services must be provided for every child eligible for special education services. Physical education is a direct service required under IDEA.

Every child with a disability is required to receive instruction in physical education, even if all other students in the preschool do not receive such instruction. Physical education is much more than free play or recess. At its best, it is instruction in developing fitness as well as learning to move skillfully in a wide variety of physical activities and sport. *Therefore, recess time, free time on the playground equipment, running around the gross motor room, or sitting and watching others play is not physical education.*

Related Services

Related services means transportation, and such development, corrective, and other supportive services (including speech-language pathology and audiology services, psychological services, physical and occupational therapy, recreation, including therapeutic recreation, social work services, counseling services, including rehabilitation counseling, orientation and mobility services, and medical services, except that such medical services shall be for diagnostic and evaluation purposes only) as may be required to assist a child with a disability to benefit from special education, and includes the early identification and assessment of disabling conditions in children (IDEA, 1999, U.S. Code Service, Title 20, sec. 1401 [22]).

Physical education is a direct service, not a related service. Physical therapy or occupational therapy can not be substitutes for physical education.

With this introduction to IDEA, we now turn the attention to the special education process—the explanation of how to determine if a child has a disability and thus is eligible for special education services.

The Special Education Process

 mong the principles for which any great society stands is the equal opportunity for a quality education. Simply stated, education in accordance with potential is the inalienable right of all society members.

Judy Werder and Leonard Kalakian,
Assessment in Adapted Physical Education

This chapter explains the process through which a child may become eligible for special services. Teachers who have the advantage of understanding special education regulations and the implementation process can use their knowledge to obtain needed services for the children they teach.

An Overview of the Process

The following equation developed at the University of the State of New York by the State Education Department in the Office for Special Education Services (1997) shows the special education process, as required in IDEA.

Referral

▼

Evaluation

▼

Recommendation

▼

Implementation

▼

Annual Review

The process begins when there is a referral of a child, usually by a parent or teacher, for evaluation to determine if the child is eligible for special education services. Then, the child is evaluated to determine whether he or she has one or more disability or developmental delay listed in chapter 11. If the recommendation is that the child is eligible for special education services, the process continues with developing an IEP and placing the child in a program that is specifically designed to meet his or her unique needs as delineated in the IEP. The special education process continues with implementing the recommended services for the child. The process includes an annual review of the child's progress and modification of the IEP, as needed. We will explain each step of this special education process here, preceded by a scenario illustrating the step.

Scene One—Referral

It is Friday afternoon and the parents have picked up the last child. Jason's teacher is sitting in her classroom, reflecting on all that she has learned about Jason during his first week in preschool. Even though Jason is three years old, he is unable to do many things other three-year-old children in her class are doing. In a conversation with Jason's mother earlier in the day, the teacher learned that ever since his birth, Jason has

not responded the same as his older siblings. He seldom smiled or fussed as a baby. He was an undemanding infant who would lay quietly in his crib for hours. He was nearly two years old before he began to walk and talk.

At age three, he had not yet learned to run and still used only three- and four-word sentences. Jason's mother commented that she and her husband had talked often about the delays Jason shows in his development but were unsure what action to take.

As she rises to head home, the teacher decides that next week she will make plans to refer Jason to the committee on special education (CSE) for a formal evaluation. As a courtesy, she will also discuss her plans to refer Jason with his mother on Monday.

As she leaves the school building, she thinks again about why she wants to make this referral. She reassures herself that the process will help determine if Jason has developmental delays that would qualify him for special education services, beyond what she normally offers in her preschool class. She thinks these services would help Jason learn.

Referral

The special education referral process is defined and mandated by law (IDEA). The responsibility for implementing IDEA lies at the school district level. Each school district's board of education puts IDEA into action by appointing a committee on special education. Depending on the size of the school district, this committee may appoint a subcommittee responsible for handling special education referrals within each school. Typically, a subcommittee includes, but is not limited to, the child's teacher, a qualified representative of the school district, and a school psychologist. It is this committee that handles the special education student referral, evaluation, recommendation (including the IEP development), implementation, and annual review (see figure 12.1).

Who can make a referral? The student's parents, teacher, judge, or physician, among others, can make a referral. Preschool teachers who provide movement programs can refer children they suspect have disabilities. You would give a written referral of a student you suspect of having a developmental delay or disability to the chairperson of the committee on special education. (Contact the school building administrator or the state department of education to request a specific listing of the state's special education referral procedures.)

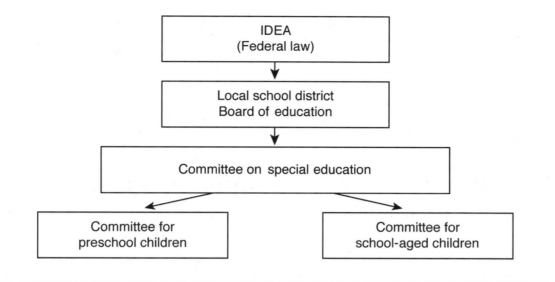

Figure 12.1   Special education committee structure.

Once the committee on special education receives a referral, the committee chair contacts the child's parents, asking for permission to evaluate their child. The request for parent permission to evaluate includes a brief description of each evaluation tool that will be used to evaluate the child's status. After the committee obtains parental permission to evaluate the child, the school conducts an evaluation of the child at no cost to the parents. The evaluation typically includes a medical examination, a psychological evaluation, a social history, an interview with the parents, and any other appropriate evaluations necessary to determine the physical, mental, and emotional factors that contribute to suspected disabilities or developmental delays. If there are suspected gross motor delays, the committee will also ask a physical therapist, an (adapted) physical education teacher, or both to evaluate the student at this time.

Scene Two—Evaluation

It is two weeks after Jason's teacher made the initial referral to the CSE for evaluation. The committee has received parental consent to evaluate Jason's gross motor performance and forwarded this information to the adapted physical educator. Today, Jason and the adapted physical educator are in the gymnasium. She has selected a suitable standardized test for evaluating Jason's gross motor skills through a series of stimulating activities in which are embedded the assessment test items.

Evaluation

Adapted physical education has an important role in the referral process. When considering a child with a suspected motor delay or impairment for an evaluation, it is essential to notify the adapted physical education teacher, either working alone or with a physical therapist (if available). The adapted physical education teacher must become involved in the special education process to assure that appropriate gross motor evaluations are conducted if the child has gross motor needs.

Scene Three— Recommendations

Jason's gross motor evaluation has been completed. The psychologist, speech therapist, adapted physical educator, and Jason's classroom teacher may have spoken informally about Jason's performance. Now the committee on special education is meeting. Jason's parents have been invited and are present.

As the meeting begins, the committee chair explains that the purpose of today's meeting is to discuss the test results and make recommendations regarding possible special education placement and the development of an IEP for Jason. The specialists make their reports. They explicitly ask the parents for input as they present the results of their evaluations. The specialists are keenly interested in whether the test results are consistent with what the parents have observed at home. There is consensus that Jason is showing significant delays in his language, motor, and social development and is therefore eligible for special education services. The meeting continues with the parents and school staff discussing the development of an IEP for Jason that includes his special education services. As the meeting ends, the committee chair thanks everyone for their contribution and explains she will begin working toward implementing the IEP recommendations promptly.

Recommendations

After all parties involved in assessing the child with the suspected disability have completed their respective evaluations, they make recommendations to the committee on special education and to the parents. The recommendations determine whether the child is eligible for special education services. These recommendations are based on test scores, current performance levels, and any individual needs of the student brought to the committee's attention. We provide further information on writing an IEP in chapter 13.

If those assessing a child find him or her ineligible, the recommendations will indicate why. If they find the child eligible for special education services, the next step will determine how to provide the services. The committee and parents now make several decisions together. They decide the most appropriate placement for the child. Will the child receive special education services at a center-based program, in the child's home, through an itinerant teacher who comes to the child's day care setting or neighborhood preschool, or perhaps through a therapist working in any of these settings?

The committee recommends how much of each service the child will receive every week. Based on the evaluation of the child, these services may include classroom special education, adapted physical education, or any therapy deemed necessary to meet a child's special education needs. They also determine the duration of each session, the group size, and any adapted equipment needs. They develop annual goals with measurable short-term instructional objectives for the child.

It is highly desirable that the adapted physical educator attend the IEP meeting for children who have special motor needs and that he or she take an active part in the discussions. If attending in person is not feasible, the adapted physical educator should send a written report of the results of the gross motor evaluation and recommendations for physical education services to the committee on special education to share at the meeting.

Scene Four— Implementation

During the recent committee on special education meeting about Jason, the adapted physical education teacher recommended that Jason continue to receive physical education with his regular preschool class. She also recommended that Jason receive adapted physical education twice each week. This supplemental instruction is intended to give Jason extra help in developing his motor skills, an area in which he shows delays.

Today the physical education teacher is working with Jason and three other children. She has planned a variety of learning experiences to give Jason the practice he needs to learn to run. All four children are laughing with delight as they play the games that teach them to run. Jason's classroom teacher pauses as she walks by the open gym door. Even though it was extra work for all involved, she is glad that she referred Jason for special education services. Now he is getting the extra physical education instruction that he so needs.

Implementation

The student must begin receiving special education services within 30 days of developing the IEP. The school district is responsible for providing all the services stipulated on the IEP. "During implementation, the committee on special education coordinates scheduling, transportation, assignments for staff, and any special arrangements for the child's program" (University of the State of New York, State Education Department, Office for Special Education Services 1997, 24). Any proposed modifications to the services provided require a full committee on special education meeting with the parents and a revision of the IEP.

> The IEP is reviewed annually by the committee on special education and parents to determine whether the services provided continue to be appropriate for the child.

Scene Five— Annual Review

It is now one year since Jason began receiving special education services. Today the committee on special education and Jason's parents meet again to review Jason's progress to date and make any recommended changes to his IEP. As the physical education teacher describes what Jason has learned over the past year, it becomes clear that Jason has made substantial gains in learning motor skills. All agree that Jason will continue to receive both regular physical education and supplemental adapted physical education instruction as required on his IEP.

Annual Review

The IEP is reviewed annually by the committee on special education and parents to determine whether the services provided continue to be appropriate for the child. Every three years there is a complete evaluation required to provide up-to-date assessment information on the child. This triennial evaluation for preschool children usually occurs when children leave preschool and enter an elementary school program.

Potential Problems

We wrote the following section for certified teachers of physical education. The special education process can work well to meet the needs of children with disabilities. Yet, after speaking with several teachers who have children with special needs, and after teaching children with special needs for many years, we are aware that physical educators may encounter frustrations with the special education process. First, there are two aspects of the process that are vital to its success—obtaining appropriate evaluations and including physical educators.

IDEA requires that every child with a disability, ages 3 through 21, receive physical education. As physical educators, it is our opinion that to appropriately teach physical education, the child must first be at least briefly evaluated to determine his or her physical education needs. If there appear to be needs, a more extensive physical education evaluation can be conducted. This evaluation is best performed by a physical educator or an adapted physical educator because of their preparation in assessing the physical education needs of children in the affective, cognitive, and motor domains.

Based on this physical education evaluation, appropriate services can be recommended at the committee on special education meeting and recorded on the child's IEP. As an example, either regular physical education or adapted physical education or a combination of both may be provided.

However, it is sometimes the case that the committee on special education does not involve the physical educator in the special education process. This may happen for several reasons. A common reason is that the special education referral came from an academic area other than physical education. As a result, the committee on special education may not be focused on determining whether this child has unique physical education needs.

We strongly recommend that physical educators who have been excluded from the special education process inform the committee on special education that they have something to offer. They are skilled in evaluating the physical education needs of children and can perform that task to meet the requirements of the law. At every opportunity, ask to be included in the special education process for every child with a disability, even if it is just to sign off that you do not think this child has any special needs in physical education. As physical educators become involved, you can better meet the needs of children with disabilities.

> **At every opportunity, ask to be included in the special education process for every child with a disability.**

Now we will examine some actual physical education experiences with the special education process that resulted in problems. We identify the following in each case: (1) the cause of the problem, (2) a way to correct the problem, and (3) a plan to prevent similar problems from arising in the future.

Excluding the Adapted Physical Educator

What happened: An administrator called a team meeting of teachers and therapists to address a child's gross motor concerns and the possible need for a gross motor evaluation. The adapted physical educator was not invited to the meeting. There is a potential problem here if those at the meeting who have not observed the child's gross motor performance provide inaccurate or incomplete information. They could make inappropriate recommendations if they are using inaccurate information.

How to fix it: Determine, in a professional and courteous way, why the adapted physical education teacher was not invited to participate. This usually means a quick telephone call to the administrator who called the meeting. Explain the desire to be included and that physical educators have the education to make a valuable contribution to the team and child.

How to prevent it: At the beginning of the school year, let the school administrator, secretary, and other staff know that physical educators wish to participate in any team meetings that involve children with known or suspected gross motor needs. These include children who are currently served or may be served in the future. You may need to repeat this request on several occasions until physical educators are automatically included.

Inaccurate Information

What happened: The adapted physical education teacher was requested to evaluate a new student for gross motor development. After writing her report, she found that another team member (who does not have preparation in gross motor assessment and is not a physical therapist) had independently included a gross motor section in the other report. Unfortunately, that gross motor information was inaccurate and conflicted with the findings of the adapted physical education teacher's report.

How to fix it: Promptly and politely speak directly to the person who wrote the report. Work together to correct any inaccuracies in the report, and suggest that next time the physical educator would like to be responsible for the gross motor section of the report.

How to prevent it: Early in the school year, meet with therapists and teachers to clarify role definitions. Decide who is responsible for writing various sections of a child's report. For instance, the occupational therapist typically addresses fine motor performance and the adapted physical educator addresses the gross motor skills.

Premature Evaluation

What happened: The adapted physical education teacher had the impression, through the grapevine,

that the district committee had generated a requirement to evaluate a particular student. The adapted physical educator proceeded with the student's evaluation, only to discover that the school administration was still waiting for district consent. This could be a problem if the parents or school district oppose an evaluation. Doing an evaluation without consent violates the referral process in IDEA.

How to fix it: Make a phone call to the parents, apologizing for the mistake. Explain that once you have received parent and district written consent, the referral process can continue.

How to prevent it: Only proceed with an evaluation when you have received written approval.

Child Not Receiving Physical Education

What happened: A physical educator learns of a child with a disability who is not receiving physical education. The physical educator brings this situation to the attention of the chair of the committee on special education who tells the teacher that the child is not required to receive physical education. This reply is often based on one of two common misconceptions: (1) physical therapy is a substitute for physical education, and (2) physical education is a related service and is optional. Both statements are inaccurate, as discussed in chapter 11 on special education law.

How to fix it: Please consult the definition of special education found box 11.2. Better yet, find the quote directly in a copy of the federal law. Politely inform the chair of the committee on special education that IDEA specifically states that physical education is part of a special education and is therefore required for all children, 3 through 21 years of age, who are receiving special education services. Occasionally, people charged with implementing IDEA are under the misconception that physical education is not required for children with disabilities. Even some state directors of special education have been confused on this point.

How to prevent it: Be proactive and inform school decision makers that physical education is required for children with disabilities.

Again, seek to become involved in the special education process. Physical educators can make a valuable contribution. The next chapter describes writing an IEP and how to use an IEP as a tool to get the needed physical education services for children with disabilities.

Writing an Individualized Education Program

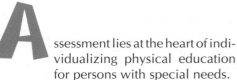
ssessment lies at the heart of individualizing physical education for persons with special needs.

Judy Werder and Leonard Kalakian, *Assessment in Adapted Physical Education*

Mr. Smith, a physical educator, sets up an area of the gymnasium in preparation for four-year-old Katchi to come down for a gross motor evaluation. Mr. Smith includes all the equipment that he will need to assess Katchi's skills. He will then record Katchi's current level of gross motor performance using an assessment format he feels will most appropriately reflect Katchi's current needs. To help Katchi feel comfortable, Mr. Smith has arranged for three of his classmates to join him in doing gross motor activities today. When Katchi arrives with his classmates, Mr. Smith gives him the option of choosing which piece of equipment he would like to try first. Mr. Smith has allowed Katchi to feel in control of the situation, and within no time Katchi is comfortably attempting all the tasks Mr. Smith asks of him. Mr. Smith observes that Katchi is giving each task his best effort, even with the skills that are difficult for him.

When Mr. Smith concludes the assessment, he knows the data collected will be a useful reflection of Katchi's gross motor ability level. From this information he will write a report that includes Katchi's current level of gross motor performance and suggest goals for an IEP.

The IEP is a written plan for providing special education services, including physical education, to children eligible for services under IDEA. This chapter discusses the IEP and focuses on the physical educator's contribution to the gross motor portion of the IEP. We present an example of the written gross motor portion of the IEP.

What Is an IEP?

Each child who is defined as an individual with a disability under the federal law IDEA is eligible for special education services. An IEP is the written document that describes the plan for providing these special education services. The IEP is the mechanism for designing an education that is right for a particular child at this time. There can be tremendous diversity among children with special needs who qualify for services under IDEA. Like snowflakes, no two children are identical, and no two children have identical special education needs. It follows that no two IEPs are identical. There is a unique IEP for each child with a special need. As a child's needs change over time, the IEP for that child will need to be revised. A committee on special education meeting with the parents must be held at least once each year to consider revisions to a child's IEP.

Components of an IEP

The components of an IEP include a description of the child's present performance level, annual goals, and short-term instructional objectives set for the child to achieve; special education and related services to help the child achieve the goals and objectives; the starting dates and duration of these services; a means and time line for evaluating whether the child has, in fact, attained the goals and objectives; and planning for the child's transition into adulthood. The IEP also includes instructional support for staff. For a preschool child, parent education may be part of the IEP. Box 13.1 presents an example of a gross motor portion of an IEP.

The federal regulations specify the components of the IEP, but they do not specify a single national IEP format. The appearance and organization of IEP forms vary considerably from school district to school district across the country. Regardless of IEP form differences, all IEPs must include information pertaining to the following components.

Assessment reports from several different professional areas are typically required to be included in a complete IEP. An early childhood educator; psychologist; physical educator; or physical, occupational, or speech therapist among others may all include a report. This means that one IEP may contain several separate present levels of performance and separate goals and objectives, each suggested by a different professional, describing the child from each professional's unique perspective. The following discussion of the IEP components and the example of an IEP in box 13.1 are written from the perspective of an adapted physical educator assessing the child's gross motor performance.

Present Level of Performance

The present level of performance (PLP) is a narrative describing the child's strengths and needs regarding physical education and gross motor performance. The PLP provides a description of specific behaviors, as well as insights into the interaction of the child with the task and the environment that might be contributing to the

Box 13.1 **Gross Motor Portion of an IEP**

Adapted Physical Education

Student: Katchi Walker

Evaluator: Katie Marchand

Evaluation procedure: Teacher observation, Peabody Developmental Motor Scale

Present Level of Performance

Katchi is an active 44-month-old child who appears to enjoy physical activity. He has a hearing impairment but responds well to sign language. Three of Katchi's peers were present during the gross motor evaluation using the Peabody Developmental Motor Scale. These peers played among the equipment while the evaluator guided Katchi toward specific tasks. Katchi was eager to move and attempted all skills asked of him.

Balance: Katchi can stand on one foot for five seconds independently. He can walk forward across a balance beam and stand on his tiptoes momentarily, both while holding the hand of the evaluator. Katchi can take three steps backward independently but needs an evaluator holding his shoulders to guide him as he continues walking backward.

Locomotor: Katchi can ascend and descend stairs marking time with the use of a handrail. He can jump down from a 12-inch height while holding the hand of the evaluator. He can also jump forward 12 inches using a two-foot takeoff and landing. Katchi can jump over a two-inch hurdle, taking off and landing with two feet. He can hop one or two times in place. He is able to run and gallop, but his gait patterns are inconsistent in both momentum and fluidity. Katchi is just beginning to pedal a tricycle and has difficulty keeping his feet on the pedals.

Object control: Katchi can throw a tennis ball three feet forward, hitting a two-foot-by-two-foot target. He can kick a stationary playground ball forward and can catch the ball thrown from three feet.

In summary, Katchi has a basal score of 24 to 29 months on the Peabody Developmental Motor Scale, indicating he is capable of performing all the skills expected of that age group. He had a ceiling age of 42 to 47 months, indicating he is capable of performing many skills at some level, up to and including this age group. His overall age equivalent was 32 months, which indicates a 14-month delay in motor skills.

Annual Goals and Short-Term Instructional Objectives

Annual goal: Katchi will improve the quality and quantity of his gross motor movement through observation and as measured on the Peabody Developmental Motor Scale.

Short-term instructional objectives and evaluation criteria include the following:

1. Katchi will independently walk across a 10-foot balance beam without stepping off three of five trials.

2. Katchi will ascend and descend stairs, alternating feet with the use of a handrail four of five times attempted.

3. Katchi will jump down from 18 inches and jump forward 18 inches, taking off and landing with both feet together three of five trials.

4. Katchi will independently hop on his preferred foot five times consecutively three of five trials.

5. Katchi will demonstrate an initial skipping pattern over a minimum of 25 feet, four of the five times attempted.

6. Katchi will throw a tennis ball, using an overhand throwing pattern, and consistently hit a two-foot-by-two-foot target five feet away three of five trials.

(continued)

Box 13.1 Gross Motor Portion of an IEP *(continued)*

7. Katchi will catch a playground ball thrown from five feet, using a two-hand catch, three of five trials.

8. Katchi will run and gallop a minimum of 25 feet, maintaining speed and a rhythmical gait pattern, four of five times attempted.

9. Katchi will independently pedal a tricycle freely around the room four of five times attempted.

Criteria for Evaluation

Katchi will be evaluated at least quarterly by the physical educator to determine his progress toward attaining his short-term objectives. He will also be evaluated annually using the Peabody Developmental Motor Scale.

Special Education and Related Services

Physical education: Katchi will receive physical education, modified as needed, with both typical peers and peers with special needs. The physical education is designed to address his overall gross motor development along with his ability to successfully participate and communicate with his peers in a variety of recreational settings.

Program modifications and support: An instructor capable of communicating with Katchi using sign language will accompany him in the physical education program.

---

observed behavior. Parents often appreciate teachers who write in a positive, professional style that clearly and concisely emphasizes all that the child *can* do as well as identifying those skills the child is not yet able to do. The information in the PLP is commonly based on a formal gross motor assessment that may be accompanied by informal teacher observations. We encourage using Linder's (1993) arena assessment as a functional alternative to formal assessment. Regardless of the approach to assessment used, report the test results here, along with a description of the child's behavior during the testing.

> **Parents often appreciate teachers who write in a positive, professional style that clearly and concisely emphasizes all that the child *can* do as well as identifying those skills the child is not yet able to do.**

Annual Goals, Including Short-Term Instructional Objectives

Annual goals and short-term instructional objectives are suggested for the child to work on over the next year. Goals are broad based, measurable, and provide general direction. Instructional objectives are short-term, specific, measurable, and lead to attaining the annual goals. We recommend

that you write goals and instructional objectives to meet the child's current needs and to lay the foundation for the preschool child to have the skills, knowledge, and values to remain physically active throughout adulthood. Wessel and Kelly (1986) and Block (1994) are adapted physical education professionals who promote a top-down approach to curricular planning. A top-down plan looks first to the goals for the child in adulthood, then works backward to determine what the child needs to learn now to attain these goals in adulthood. These goals and objectives guide lesson plan development in the physical education and movement program. Throughout the year, teachers plan lessons that will help a child achieve the instructional objectives on the IEP.

Schools are responsible for providing the special education and related services as specified on the IEP. However, the school and teachers are not held accountable if a child does not meet the goals and objectives of the IEP (IDEA, 1999, U.S. Code Service, Title 20, sec. 1415). The committee on special education determines the components, taking the recommendations of the physical educator and other professionals into consideration. During the committee on special education meeting, be an advocate for the support services you think will benefit the child's education.

Special Education and Related Services

This section contains statements of the specific special education and related services to be provided to the child and the extent that the child will be able to participate in regular educational programs. Here it is noted whether a child will be receiving regular physical education, adapted physical education, or both.

Use this component to suggest any program modifications or supports needed in the child's educational program. A child may need to be in a lower teacher-to-student ratio to get the individual attention needed to learn. List any required specialized equipment or assistive technology devices or services. Include any adaptive equipment, such as a mobile prone stander or gait trainer, necessary for the child to participate successfully in a physical education and movement program. Also discuss whether the services of a teaching assistant would be beneficial for the child to participate in a physical education and movement program.

This section is also used to identify and explain the extent, if any, that the child will *not* participate with typical children in a general education program. IDEA clearly intends for a child with special needs to be educated in the general education setting, with support services brought into this setting as needed. Any recommendation to remove a child from general education to participate in a segregated special education setting, thus limiting the child's time in typical educational settings, must be fully justified.

Starting and Ending Dates for Services

Dates physical education (movement program) services are to begin and the duration of such service are usually listed next to each recommended service noted previously in special education and related services.

Means of Evaluation

The means of evaluating a child's progress toward attaining each goal and instructional objective is usually included in annual goals and instructional objectives described previously. Instructional objectives are written in behavioral terms that you can observe and measure. Each instructional objective describes the situation, task, and criteria for evaluation. Objectives written in this manner contain the means for evaluating whether a child has achieved the instructional objective. The IEP also needs to indicate the way you will report a child's progress to the parents.

Transition Planning

Transition planning, beginning no later than age 14, refers to the need to look ahead to when the child becomes an adult and will no longer attend school, but will instead be expected to assume adult roles. IDEA requires that planning for a child's transition to adulthood begin well before the transition occurs, usually at age 21. Students 14 years of age and older with disabilities must have a section on the IEP that states long-term adult outcomes for transition, reflecting the student's needs, preferences, and interests in adult training, employment, and community living. Clearly, IEPs for preschool children do not need to include a section on transition planning. Nevertheless, we recommend that you give thought to transition planning.

While box 13.1 presented a gross motor portion of an IEP, a typical IEP will also address many other aspects of the child's educational program. We encourage a team approach in teaching children with special needs, yet we include only the gross motor portion here for clarity.

Assessment is the cornerstone of instruction. It is also the basis for writing an IEP. The remainder of the chapter presents ideas on formal and functional assessment of children with special needs.

Formal Assessment for Writing an IEP

IDEA requires that a child with special needs be assessed in all areas related to the suspected disability, including motor abilities. Definitions of IDEA and requirements for testing are listed in box 11.2 on page 184. The law requires that you conduct testing in the child's native language. The tests are to be valid for the purpose for which you are using them. The test administrator needs to be trained in administering the test.

Formal assessment uses tests that involve "the presentation of a standard set of items that require a response" (Horvat and Kalakian, 1996). These are called standardized tests because there is only one standard way to give the test. These standardized instructions are designed to assure that everyone who administers the test is doing so in exactly the same manner. Standardized tests often include norms that enable teachers to compare the performance of an individual child to that of other children of similar age and characteristics. Formal assessment can help determine whether a child has special needs and qualifies for special education services. It can also be useful in determining how the skills of a specific child or group of children compare with their peers at other times and in other countries. There are several formal assessment tests that you can use to assess student learning. Refer to Zittel (1994) for a discussion of instruments available for gross motor assessment of preschool children.

Formal Assessment Limitations

There are many limitations to formal assessment. One critical limitation is that formal assessment tests assume it is possible to hold the task and environment constant to measure the performance of a child. This is often not the case. Yet, there are still strong biases toward formal assessment in many schools and on many committees for special education. A physical educator may find that the school district requires you to conduct a formal assessment. In such cases, consider using the formal assessment setting as an opportunity to observe as much as possible about a child's interaction with the task and environment. Weave these observations throughout the report of the child's present level of performance in the IEP.

> Throughout the year, teachers plan lessons that will help a child achieve the instructional objectives on the IEP.

Functional Assessment

Functional assessment is an alternative to formal assessment. It is a more holistic approach to assessment that encourages studying the interaction among the task, environment, and child to gain a greater understanding about how the child moves and learns. This approach offers the advantage that children feel in control, and thus more at ease. Assessment that you do with children who feel comfortable is likely to produce a more complete and valid measure of their capabilities than formal assessment. We encourage you to study the work of two leaders in this field, Diane Bricker's (1992) activity-based approach and Toni Linder's (1993) transdisciplinary play-based assessment model, to learn more about functional, child-centered approaches to assessment.

The following chapter describes the roles of those on the team providing the special education for preschool children.

Team Approaches

The ultimate success of any program depends on teamwork.

Diane Chermak, teacher

It's Wednesday afternoon and Miss Marchand, a preschool physical educator, is getting ready to attend a team meeting with Billy's teachers and therapists. On the agenda is a discussion of the progress four-year-old Billy is making with his speech. Billy's speech therapist has been joining him in his physical education class twice a week. Both she and Miss Marchand have noticed Billy is most vocal in the preschool program while he is physically active in the gymnasium. His physical education class has become the perfect time to incorporate a speech therapy session. Since he began receiving speech therapy while participating in physical education, Billy is beginning to speak more in the preschool classroom and at home. This is exciting news for everyone!

At the meeting, team members brainstorm to identify new ways to collaborate in serving Billy. Everyone is mindful that coordinating schedules can become complicated. After listening to several concerns and suggestions, the team develops a plan to increase the overlap of Billy's special education services. At the end of the meeting, a team member comments on how much she enjoys working closely with other professionals.

This chapter is about professionals working as a team, cooperating to deliver the best possible educational experience for children of all abilities.

The Team

The teams typically consist of special education and related service providers. A team may consist of two or more of the following service providers: (special education) teacher, (adapted) physical educator, teaching assistant, teacher of the visually impaired, speech and language specialist, physical therapist, occupational therapist, psychologist, social worker, school nurse, and school administrator. The parent, although not necessarily a professional, potentially is the most valuable contributor to the team.

There are several benefits of the team approach. Working as a team allows each professional to draw upon the expertise of others. In this way, professionals view the child they serve as a whole, rather than an arm that can't extend, a body that can't pedal a tricycle, a mouth that says pish instead of fish, a hand that can't grasp, or a mind that is unable to recognize colors. Through working as a team, the physical educator learns how to position the child from the physical therapist; the special educator learns a technique to prompt proper pronunciation from the speech teacher; and the physical therapist learns a new grasping technique from the occupational therapist. Through working and sharing together, each professional benefits from the expertise of other team members, and the child is better served!

Working as a team allows each professional to draw upon the expertise of others.

Three Team Approaches

Three commonly used approaches for providing special education services in educational settings are multidisciplinary, interdisciplinary, and transdisciplinary teams.

Multidisciplinary Team Approach

A multidisciplinary team approach is characterized by professionals with expertise in different disciplines examining and working with a child individually. Each discipline conducts a separate assessment, and service to the child is fragmented rather than coordinated. The multidisciplinary approach lacks close coordination among service providers. The special educators may know little about what is occurring in therapy sessions and the therapists may know little about what is going on in the classroom.

Interdisciplinary Team Approach

An interdisciplinary team approach is also characterized by professionals who assess and serve the child individually, but the team members plan a comprehensive program together. The interdisciplinary approach is the most common practice. Although specific programming is often isolated, the various professionals routinely communicate on a child's progress and share suggestions to enhance programming in other areas. The team looks at the child as a whole being.

Transdisciplinary Team Approach

The transdisciplinary team approach is characterized by a sharing or transferring of information and skills across traditional boundaries. The transdisciplinary approach, potentially the most beneficial because it is the most collaborative, is also the most difficult to implement due to the challenge of scheduling common programming times. Many related service providers have caseloads that take them into different classrooms and even different buildings. With creativity and flexibility, the transdisciplinary approach can work. It just takes time and effort to organize.

Roles of Team Members

An essential part of working with a team is understanding the role each team member plays. Here are some role definitions for each team member.

"*Special education* means specially designed instruction, at no cost to the parent, to meet the unique needs of a child [with a disability], including classroom instruction, instruction in physical education, home instruction, and the instruction in hospitals and institutions" (IDEA, 1999, U. S. Code Service, Title 20, sec. 1401 [25]). *Physical education* includes instruction in adapted physical education. These special education professionals would also be responsible for administering tests, writing an IEP, and establishing the specially designed instruction for the child with special needs.

> An essential part of working with a team is understanding the role each team member plays.

The *teaching assistant,* also referred to as a paraprofessional, assists the teacher in implementing the specialized programs or modifications that have been designated as necessary for a student with special needs. The teaching assistant may be assigned to work one-on-one with a particular child throughout the school day; assist with an entire special education classroom; or assist a physical educator, adapted physical educator, or related service provider.

The *teacher of the visually impaired* implements eye exercises and learning experiences that will improve visual performance or enhance functional capabilities. The teacher will specially design instruction to address problems such as poor depth perception, poor spatial awareness, or dysfunction in tracking.

The *speech pathologist* has the role of identifying children with speech and language disorders, and diagnosing and appraising specific language or speech disorders. They may act as a "referral for medical or other professional attention necessary for the habilitation of speech or language disorders" (IDEA, 1977, U. S. Code Service, Title 45, sec. 1401 [121a.13]) and for the habilitation or prevention of communicative disorders. They may also counsel and guide parents, children, and teachers regarding speech and language disorders.

The *physical therapist* provides services to students who have impairments; functional limitations; disabilities; or changes in physical function and health status resulting from injury, disease, or other causes. The Model Definition of Physical Therapy Acts includes the following: (1) examining individuals with impairments, functional limitation, and disability or other health-related conditions to determine a diagnosis, prognosis, and intervention; (2) alleviating impairment and functional limitation by designing, implementing, and modifying therapeutic interventions; (3) preventing injury, impairment, functional limitation, and disability, including promoting and maintaining fitness, health, and quality of life in all age populations; (4) engaging in consultation, education, and research (American Physical Therapy Association 1995, 1-2).

The *occupational therapist* provides services that include "improving, developing, or restoring functions impaired or lost through illness, injury or deprivation; improving the ability to perform tasks for independent functioning when functions are impaired or lost; and preventing, through early intervention, initial or further impairment or loss of function" (IDEA 1977, U.S. Code Service, Title 45, sec. 1401 [121a.13]). Occupational therapists are concerned with the ability of the child to participate in important and meaningful daily activities or occupations.

The *psychologist* provides services that include "administrating psychological and educational tests and other assessment procedures; interpreting assessment results; and obtaining, integrating, and interpreting information about child behavior and conditions relating to learning." Psychologists also "consult with other staff members in planning school programs to meet the special needs of children as indicated by psychological tests, interviews, and behavioral evaluations" (IDEA, 1977, U.S. Code Service, Title 45, sec. 1401 [121a.13]).

The *social worker* provides services in schools that include "group and individual counseling with the child and family; working with those problems in a child's living situation that affect the child's adjustment in school; mobilizing school and community resources to enable a child to receive the maximum benefit from his or her educational program" (IDEA, 1977, U.S. Code Service, Title 45, sec. 1401 [121a.13]).

The *nurse's* role includes ensuring communication between home and school following a child's absence or physician appointment, maintaining current student health files, and informing other service providers of any medical issues as needed. The nurse promotes programs on good health and hygiene, and may dispense medications and administer treatments such as nebulizer or catheterizing.

Though the *administrator* is not listed as a service provider, this person plays a key role as the facilitator of the team. The administrator provides supervision to assure that professionals are serving children to the best of their ability and consistent with IDEA requirements. The administrator also guides and assists the team in implementing each child's educational programming.

The person with the potential for being the most valuable is the child's *parent*. Though the parents are not officially members of the team, they have a thorough and long-standing knowledge of the child that is valuable to all the team members. The parents do not typically attend most team meetings, but it is important to keep them fully informed so they may offer their valuable contributions. The role of the parents is discussed further in chapter 15.

Movement Program Collaborations

We stated earlier in the chapter that a collaborative approach to teaching a child is potentially the most beneficial way to deliver special education services. Physical educators encourage collaboration when they invite other team members to visit the movement program. The team meeting is a necessary, but static element of the special education process. Working with a team member in the movement program environment offers a dynamic, and therefore relevant, experience providing special education services. Not every colleague may want to spend time in the gymnasium, so start with the professionals who also work in the gross motor area or are the most receptive to collaboration. We can hope the word will spread that the gymnasium is a great place to work on many goals beyond the gross motor domain.

Working with a physical therapist in the movement program environment is most helpful. While working with a child on a gross motor activity, a physical therapist can offer invaluable suggestions regarding body positioning; establishing and maintaining proper gait patterns (particularly when working with children who have severe motor involvement); and the proper use of a large variety of walkers, wheelchairs, and braces. In addition to working side by side as frequently as possible, consider writing the motor portion of a child's IEP jointly. This will ensure that you address goals completely and will reduce redundancy on the IEP.

Children tend to be more verbal in an environment in which they are moving. Though it is not always possible, nor recommended, for speech therapists to commit all their time to the gymnasium, we do suggest inviting the speech therapist to the gross motor environment whenever possible. The physical educator will benefit from learning techniques that you can carry over at other times, and the child will benefit from services received in a motivating, natural environment.

It is important, when collaborating, to understand the terms other team professionals use. We list some terms commonly used to describe communication disorders in box 14.1 and common terms describing motor behaviors in box 14.2.

In the next and final chapter of the book, we offer ideas for ways parents and teachers can work together as partners in the education of each child.

Box 14.1 Communication Disorder Terms

Articulation is the formation of speech sounds, particularly the coordinated movement of the oral structures in producing such sounds (Bloodstein, 1979).

Augmentative communication is any alternative form to the speech mode of communication—such as sign, photographs, or computer—that results in the exchange of information between individuals (Wolery, Ault, and Doyle, 1992).

Disorders of grammar are difficulties with the rules that govern language and contribute to meaning.

Disorders of syntax are difficulties with word order that convey the meaning of a sentence.

Dyspraxia is the discrepancy between what the child seems physically capable of articulating and what is said. The child may be able to imitate words but unable to form them spontaneously (Batshaw, 1992).

Fluency is the smoothness and continuity in the serial execution of speech segments (Bloodstein, 1979).

Fluency disorder is difficulty with the rate and flow of speech.

Language delay or disorder may occur receptively or in terms of auditory comprehension, or expressively involving vocabulary and conceptual development.

Morphemes are the smallest meaningful unit of speech, consisting of a word or part of a word (Bloodstein, 1979).

Phonation is the production of voice through vibration of the vocal folds (Bloodstein, 1979).

Phonology is the study of speech sounds, concerned especially with the rules that govern the way speech sounds are used in a given language (Bloodstein, 1979).

Phonology disorder, also referred to as an *articulation disorder*, is the impaired ability to produce speech sounds accurately or precisely.

Pragmatic disorder is the inability to use language skills for functional or social purposes, such as to make greetings, requests, ask and answer questions, comment, or explain.

Pragmatics of language is the study of how language functions in relation to social contexts (Bloodstein, 1979).

Syntax (grammar) is the arrangement of morphemes (words) into grammatical phrases and sentences (Bloodstein, 1979).

Vocal folds are two shelves of muscular and membranous tissue in the larynx; their vibration produces the voice.

Box 14.2 Motor Behavior Terms

Alignment is the positioning of the body parts in a straight line in relation to gravity.

Apraxia is a loss of the ability to perform voluntary, purposeful movements due to damage to the brain (although there is no actual paralysis). Because of this damage, the brain is unable to make the transfer between the idea of movement to an actual physical response (Coleman, 1999*).

Ataxia is difficulty with coordinating muscles in voluntary movement that may be caused by damage to the brain or spinal cord. Ataxia may be associated with extrapyramidal cerebral palsy and may cause the child to have difficulty with maintaining balance (Coleman, 1993*).

Athetosis is slow, involuntary, writhing movements, particularly of the wrist, fingers, face, and occasionally the feet and toes, caused by injury to the nerves supplying the muscles or by damage to the brain, as in some types of cerebral palsy (Coleman, 1998*).

Base of support is an area bound by the outermost regions of contact between a body and support surface or surfaces (Hall, 1999).

Contracture is the shortening of muscles, tendons, and fascia that causes decreased joint movement so that the joint is bent and does not have the full range of motion (Coleman, 1999*).

Diplegia is a weakness or paralysis in the legs and arms caused by disease or injury to the nerves of the brain or spinal cord that stimulate the muscles, or by disease to the muscles themselves (Coleman, 1999*).

Hemiplegia is the weakness or paralysis of one side of the body caused by disease or injury to the nerves of the brain or spinal cord that stimulate the muscles, or by disease to the muscles themselves (Coleman,1999*).

Hypertonia is increased tone (stiffness) in the muscles (Coleman, 1999*).

Hypotonia is decreased tone, or floppiness, in the muscles, characterized by excessive range of motion of the joints and little muscle resistance when parts of the body are being moved (Coleman, 1999*).

Isometric is a muscle contraction involving no change in muscle length (Hall, 1999).

Isotonic is a contraction against constant resistance (Sharkey, 1997).

Muscle strength is the ability of the muscle to exert force (Sharkey, 1997).

Quadriplegia is a weakness or paralysis in both arms and both legs, and often the head or face and the trunk, caused by disease or injury to the nerves of the brain or spinal cord that stimulate the muscles (Coleman, 1999*).

Range of motion is the angle through which a joint moves from anatomical position to the extreme limit of segment motion in a particular direction (Hall, 1999).

Spastic is having increased muscle tone or stiffness (resulting in difficult movements), and, usually, increased deep tendon reflexes (Coleman, 1999*).

Symmetrical is referring to parts of the body that are equal in size or shape, or are similar in arrangement or movement patterns (Coleman, 1999*).

Tonus is the slight, continuous balanced contraction of muscles. In skeletal muscles, it is involved in the ability to maintain posture and to return blood to the heart (Coleman, 1999*).

---

*Reprinted from Coleman 1999.

Parents as Partners

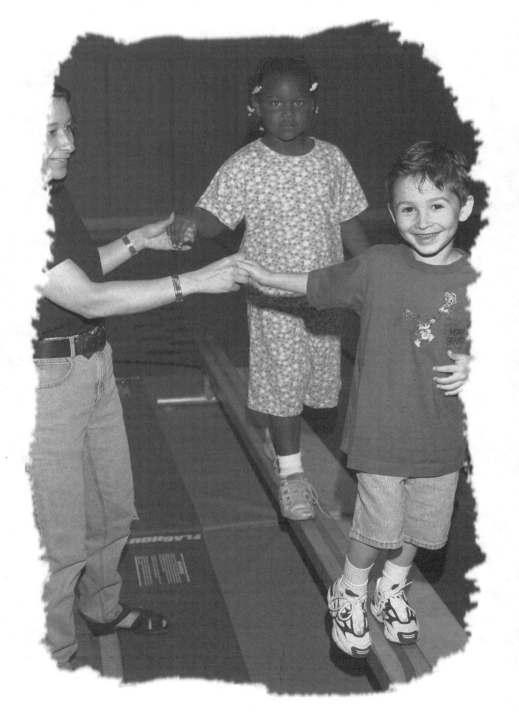

Parents are the single most important resource that children have.

K.A. Ferrell,
Reach Out and Teach

Olivia steps to the lectern and pauses to study the many eager and some uncertain faces of the new parents and teachers in the preschool program she supervises. She begins her welcome to the first parent-teacher meeting of the year saying, "Parents, you sheltered, clothed, and fed your children. You nurtured them. And now you are turning them over to others for the greater part of their waking hours. You know your child well and would like to be a resource for the teacher. The question now may be, 'How do I go about doing that?' There is a special role reserved for you. It is becoming a partner with your child's teacher."

Olivia continues. "Teachers, you've trained and educated yourself for the moment when you assume the important responsibility of educating other people's young children. You're up-to-date on early childhood education theory, and you're motivated to do the best job you can. But you have the children's parents to deal with as well. Just how should the parents fit into the preschool process? Parents are special resources. Work with them as partners in their children's education."

And this is how parent-teacher relationships develop.

What is a partnership? A partnership is a relationship between two or more people who are working together to achieve the same goals. A parent and teacher partnership occurs when both parties are working together, with mutual trust and respect, focused on the joint interest of the child. This chapter presents ideas for promoting such a partnership.

Importance of Parent-Teacher Relationships

An effective parent-teacher relationship is an important factor in determining the child's success during preschool education and therefore has a big impact on a preschooler's development. There are two main reasons. First, though preschoolers yearn to be independent, we should not place them in the position of messenger. When asking a child what she did in the movement program that day, the parent could misunderstand the child as saying "me fall" when she was trying to communicate that she played with a "ball." Simply because of the need for accurate communication, there is likely to be more parent-teacher contact and communication during the preschool years than at any other time in the child's life. This necessity for communication begins the parent-teacher relationship and remains at its core.

Second, as humans, relationships are at the heart of our being. The character of the relationship often determines how children develop within the context of that relationship. When the relationship between families and teachers is positive and mutually supportive, and all work together in a partnership, inevitably trust and respect will develop. Children learning within an environment of trust and respect benefit in many important ways. This environment gives them the necessary sense of security to take risks, try new behaviors, and attempt to acquire new skills. Most important, it gives children the security in which to risk failure, a key element in successful learning.

Communication Between Parents and Teachers

We communicate with so many people so often on a daily basis that we often take this skill for granted. We must understand that communication between humans takes place all the time and in many different manners, whenever we are in the presence of another individual.

Communication is more than what we say and what we write. It is also how we say or write what we say or write, and what we don't say or write. It is what we wear, how we appear to others, and how we interact with them. Because we are communicating so much of our time, it is important to understand some principles underlying the process of communication. For our purposes we will focus on

> A parent and teacher partnership occurs when both parties are working together, with mutual trust and respect, focused on the joint interest of the child.

the process of written and oral communication between parents and teachers. We can create a productive and enjoyable parent-teacher relationship through effective communication.

Basic communication is a two-part process. The process begins with information being exchanged between two or more people. It concludes when those involved understand the thoughts and ideas being exchanged. Basic communication is the knowledgeable speaking (or writing) and attentive listening (or reading) that results in mutual understanding of the issues. In addition, the communication process tends to be goal oriented. That is, we usually have a reason for communicating, and we wish to have something accomplished after we have communicated. Sometimes all we seek is the awareness of others, so our communication centers on transferring information. Many times, however, we use our communication skills to influence the behaviors and attitudes of others to accomplish our goals. A sign of effective communication is seeing participants cooperatively respond to the information they receive. Effective communicators are friendly persuaders!

As parents and teachers with the interests of our children and students at heart, we must strive to develop effective communication skills. Effective communication is the basis for developing trust and mutual respect in new relationships. Poor communication between home and school causes problems, and effective communication avoids or solves problems.

How do we develop effective communication? First, we must be sure of the information we are trying to communicate. We must know our communication goals and write or speak them clearly. Second, we must be persuasive in our communication. We do this by using good basic communication along with a positive attitude that demonstrates interest and concern.

Here are some suggestions for developing effective parent-teacher communications.

Use Honest and Clear Communication

Honest and clear communication is vital to building a trusting relationship.

> Do say, "Please tell me about your child and what your concerns are."

> Don't say, "I've been teaching 10 years and have seen it all. Nothing is new to me."

"Seek first to understand and then to be understood." This quote from the *Seven Habits of Highly Successful People* by Stephen R. Covey, reminds us to listen and seek to understand what the other person is saying, rather than using the time while they are talking to plan our next comments. Listen carefully to what the parents say, giving them full opportunity to complete their thoughts without interruption. The teacher may even wish to use a reflective listening technique, such as "I hear you saying that you wish (identify) for your child and that it is especially important for your child that (identify) be available." The teacher listens fully to the parents before contributing what he or she may wish to say.

Avoid Using Jargon

Avoid using jargon as it can be misunderstood or interpreted incorrectly.

> Do say, "Let me explain what I mean when I use the words 'facilitate movement.'"

> Don't say, "You know what the term 'facilitate movement' means, don't you?"

Jargon can be like a foreign language. When not understanding another's language, many smile and nod in acknowledgment although they have little idea of what you have said. Some may sit silently and nod "yes" rather than admit they do not know what you mean when using an unfamiliar word, abbreviation, or acronym. If it is essential to use a term that might not be understood, work a definition of it into the first sentence in which you use it. Don't put parents on the spot by asking if they know what the word means. Simply define it as you use it, as illustrated in the following example.

"Jason will need you to facilitate his arm movement as he learns to throw a ball. To facilitate, you physically guide him through the motion, as he learns to do it on his own. You can do this by standing behind him, grasping his hand, and guiding him through the throwing motion until he learns to do it on his own."

Treat Parents as Experts on Their Child

Parents know their child best. Respect their knowledge and comments.

Communication is fundamental to all human relationships.

Do say, "I have observed Jason having difficulty doing this task. Have you also observed this? How do you handle it?"

Don't say, "Let me tell you what I think you should do to help Jason with this task."

Teachers should always unequivocally identify the parents as the experts on their child. For this reason, teachers should feel comfortable recognizing the parents as the experts and asking them to share what they have found works with their child. Teachers need to recognize that parents typically spend many more hours each day with their children than the teachers do, and parents are with their children season after season, year after year.

Use Nonjudgmental Language

Use of judgmental language can unwittingly erect barriers to communication.

Do say, "Can you tell me about Jason and how he moves?"

Don't say, "What is wrong with Jason?"

We all appreciate when others accept us, without judging us. Yet, judgmental statements can easily slip into our language without us being aware of it. For example, the teacher who begins a parent-teacher meeting with "Would you please tell me about Jason's problem. Is it apraxia or hypotonia?" is likely to earn little parent respect. In this statement the teacher has identified the motor difficulty as a problem that Jason owns (judgmental), rather than a condition that Jason experiences (nonjudgmental). Questions such as "What's wrong with Jason?", "What's Jason's problem?", "Can he grasp with his bad hand?", and even the term disability all speak to a defect in Jason. To refer to the child as the problem is to blame the child, and indirectly the parents. Focusing on Jason's strengths and needs may be a more positive approach.

Focus on the Positive

Communicate in ways that are positive and sensitive to the feelings of others.

Do say, "Jason seems to enjoy physical activity. He uses his right hand when reaching, and, with physical prompts, he has been using his left hand more and more."

Don't say, "It's too bad Jason can't use his left hand like the other kids."

In describing a child positively, speak in terms of what the child can do. Avoid categorizing the child's skills as good, fair, or poor. Instead describe the skills as those the child has learned (a mastered objective), is now learning (an emerging objective), and has yet to learn (a continuing objective).

Ask Parents Their Goals for Their Child

Parents may share valuable insights about goals that are relevant for their child.

Do say, "Please share with me what goals you have for your child. What would you like your child to be able to do?"

Don't say, "I've decided what goals will be best for your child. Here they are."

Listen carefully when parents respond with goals for their child. Work to always incorporate these goals into teaching.

Avoid Intimidating Parents

Meetings, especially IEP meetings, can intimidate the parents. The purpose of the IEP meeting is for parents, with school administrators, teachers, and other service providers, to design an IEP for the child (see box 15.1 for some tips for teachers). Service providers are those teachers and therapists who work directly with the child. This parent-teacher collaboration has become rare. It is now commonplace that the IEP meeting has become a setting in which service providers tell parents what will be the goals for their child. A service provider may wish to bring a separate list of IEP goals to the IEP meeting. In the interest of parent-teacher collaboration, we urge that service providers refrain from arriving at the IEP meeting with goals already typed on the school's IEP form. In these circumstances, the purpose of the meeting serves only to tell the parent about what the service providers have written for the child and obtain parent approval. This approach may unwittingly intimidate parents and severely reduce the likelihood that parents will add their input. If this does occur, parents need to know that they still have the right to suggest any revisions on goals as they see fit. Only when both parents and service providers agree on its components is the IEP accepted. Parents, remember, you are the expert on your child.

Refer to chapter 13 on the IEP for specific information about the IEP meeting.

Box 15.1 Tips for Teachers

A teacher or therapist who takes the time to do these few items can reduce possible parent intimidation.

1. There are typically several service providers at an IEP meeting. For instance, if a child is receiving physical therapy, occupational therapy, speech therapy, and special education, all of these service providers may be at the table. It would be easy for a parent to feel intimidated and "outnumbered" in this setting. Tell the parent that, if he or she wishes, it is appropriate to bring a friend or relative for moral support to add "balance" at the table.

2. Call the parent at home several days prior to the IEP meeting to seek parent input on IEP goals. Parents feel more comfortable entering the formal IEP meeting when they know what to expect.

3. Begin the meeting by inviting the parents to speak first about their child. Really LISTEN to what the parent says.

4. When it is your turn to speak, make sure to begin with positive statements about the child.

Developing the Parent-Teacher Relationship

The basis for trust and mutual respect between parents and teachers will be established through developing effective, positive communication. Trust and respect—it's hard to think of two words in the English language that are more basic to developing successful relationships. So how can we interact in ways that will promote trust and respect between teachers and parents? Perhaps listening to what one parent has to say about respect and trust will give us some insights:

"For me, respect is earned based on a person's consistent behavior. I see at least two levels of respect. I can respect a person for the knowledge, awareness, and comprehension of issues the person possesses. But there is a second level of respect that focuses on how the person treats others. I respect those who return the respect, who consistently value others and are open to their ideas, are aware of their situations and predicaments. I respect a person who is consistently thoughtful and considerate of others, even when they don't have to act so. When a teacher shows these behaviors, I develop trust in and respect for this person. I know my child's best interests are being served, and the child will benefit from this positive relationship. Demonstrated personal responsibility (ownership) also will lead me to respect and trust an individual. When a person sees a need and follows through to meet that need—

even when it is not that person's job—it builds my respect for that person."

Knowledge, comprehension, consistency, fair treatment of others, awareness of other's situations, demonstrated personal responsibility—these are important attributes and behaviors that can lead to developing trust and respect between individuals. Trust and respect, however, do not automatically develop in a relationship when all these characteristics are present. Effective communication must also be present.

My child has special needs. What then?

Respecting Parents of Children With Special Needs

What do you mean Holland? I signed up for Italy!

A range of emotions can follow hearing the words, "Your child has a disability." Denial, anger, depression, bargaining, acceptance—we each have our unique way of adjusting to these words. Box 15.2 reminds us that it is normal to react in these ways as we find our way toward appreciating the beauty of where we are—the beauty of Holland.

Acceptance

Parents of children with a disability often show a strength and grace in accepting and working with their child's circumstances that is a valuable lesson in character for all. The love and care they display for their child and the patience they show

Box 15.2 Welcome to Holland, by Emily Perl Kingsley

I am often asked to describe the experience of raising a child with a disability—to try to help people who have not shared that unique experience to understand it, to imagine how it would feel. It's like this....

When you're going to have a baby, it's like planning a fabulous vacation trip—to Italy. You buy a bunch of guidebooks and make your wonderful plans. The Coliseum. The Michelangelo David. The gondolas of Venice. You may learn some handy phrases in Italian. It's all very exciting.

After months of eager anticipation, the day finally arrives. You pack your bags and off you go. Several hours later, the plane lands. The stewardess comes in and says, "Welcome to Holland."

"*Holland*?!," you say. "What do you mean, Holland? I signed up for Italy! I'm supposed to be in Italy. All my life I've dreamed of going to Italy."

But there's been a change in the flight plan. They've landed in Holland and there you must stay.

The important thing is that they haven't taken you to a horrible, disgusting, filthy place, full of pestilence, famine, and disease. It's just a different place.

So you must go out and buy new guidebooks. And you must learn a whole new language. And you will meet a whole new group of people you would never have met.

It's just a *different* place. It's slower paced than Italy, less flashy than Italy. But after you've been there for a while and you catch your breath, you look around...and you begin to notice that Holland has windmills...and Holland has tulips. Holland even has Rembrandts.

But everyone you know is busy coming and going from Italy...and they're all bragging about what a wonderful time they had there. And for the rest of your life, you will say, "Yes, that is where I was supposed to go. That's what I had planned."

And the pain of that will never, ever, ever, ever go away because the loss of that dream was a very significant loss.

But...if you spend your life mourning the fact that you didn't get to Italy, you may never be free to enjoy the special, the very lovely things...about Holland.

Reprinted from Kingsley 1987.

toward others who are not so accepting is humbling.

Other times, parents display a whole range of reactions to having a child with a disability. A brief discussion of some of Kubler-Ross' stages of loss follow (1997).

Denial

The teacher is meeting with a parent, reviewing the motor assessment of the child. Upon hearing their child has significant motor delays, the parent says "No, it can't be. There must be some mistake."

Such a statement of denial is a common first reaction to learning that a child has a disability. Why do we deny something that may be obvious? Denial can serve as an important protective function, giving parents time to gather the energy needed to deal with the situation. When a parent is not ready to move beyond denial, it may be difficult to obtain parent permission for testing or special education services for the child. The parent may also react during the denial stage by making the rounds to an endless number of specialists seeking a different diagnosis. Teachers can work successfully with parents in denial by accepting the fact that the parents are in this stage and are likely to move on. Accept the parents' actions as where they are at now, and offer them loving support—guiding them gently through the process toward acceptance.

Anger

"Don't tell me how to be a parent. You have no idea what my day is like." Life is not fair. Anger is a normal response to loss. Parents may be angry at the situation in which they find themselves. It is this anger, however, that can fuel parents' action on behalf of their children, but that does not mean that others need to absorb the anger. Parents who

Box 15.3 Your Rights as Parents

1. The right to feel angry.
2. The right to seek another opinion.
3. The right to privacy.
4. The right to keep trying.
5. The right to stop trying.
6. The right to set limits.
7. The right to be a parent.
8. The right to be unenthusiastic.
9. The right to be annoyed with your child.
10. The right to time off.
11. The right to be the expert in charge.
12. The right to dignity.

Reprinted from Ferrell 1985.

are angry need someone to listen and acknowledge their anger, not dismiss it or explain it away. Listening may be a preferred response to anger. At this point, instead of persisting in a conversation about a child's needs, teachers may want to step aside and let the person who is distressed vent the anger.

Only when you are the target of the anger may you need to change your approach and move beyond simply listening. Typically when there is an issue that has triggered anger, there are more than two people involved. Acknowledge the anger and suggest the conflict could best be resolved a little later. Then offer to arrange a meeting. The brief break between meetings can provide a period in which to cool off. When all involved parties are no longer so angry, often you can clarify the misunderstandings and resolve the issue. Finally, when you are the target of the anger, you may wish to invite a third person to serve as a silent listener. At a later date, this person's recollection can help head off arguments about "I said . . . you said . . . ."

Bargaining

"I'll devote myself fully to helping my child, if only my efforts will make my child's disability go away."

Sometimes we seek to strike a bargain with the universe—if I do this, then please make that happen. Parents can achieve much when spurred to action on behalf of their child with special needs. Many achievements in the field of special education have been as a result of parent advocacy on behalf of their children, but this is not a time for others to take advantage of a parent's devotion. Teachers, especially, need to be careful to not expect parents to run management programs throughout the evening at home. Parents, first and foremost, need to be parents to their children, not just the in-home teacher.

Depression

"I'm just dragging myself through these colorless days filled with endless shades of gray." Losses require change. Things cannot continue as they were before the perceived loss. This means that we cannot continue unchanged. Change can be uncomfortable and draining of energy. At times parents can become depressed after learning that the child has special needs. For a time the parents may need to draw inside and slowly gather energy for the changes they will need to make. Maybe, for the moment, the parents don't follow through with the management plan at home. Maybe the parents do not respond to invitations to attend an IEP meeting. This lack of response does not mean that the parents don't care deeply about their child. Respecting parents' need for this time, and continuing to act in nonjudgmental, supportive, and loving ways, can help the parents pass through this depression and emerge changed and ready for action.

Each parent adjusts in his or her own way to having a child with special needs. Spouses need to remember that the other spouse may deal with the situation in a different way. One may be quiet and not discuss it, and the other may deal with it by discussing it over and over again. The challenge is for each to respect the other's process of grieving and not push but continue to offer the love, support, and patience as each parent finds his or her way through the grieving process.

To provide a balancing perspective on grieving, the following list reasserts parents' rights to be angry, to seek a second opinion, to privacy, and so on. It concludes with the important right to dignity—to be treated with respect and as an equal (see box 15.3). This concept is at the heart of working with parents as partners.

We conclude this chapter with one parent's perspective on her experience, found in box 15.4, titled "Aren't You Lucky."

Box 15.4 Aren't You Lucky

Hi, my name is Lori Davis. I am the mom of six-year-old Louis and nine-year-old Josh. Josh is a typical fourth grader at the Syracuse Hebrew Day School. Louis is now in an inclusive kindergarten at Mott Road School. He just finished four years of intensive early intervention in an early education (total communication) program at Main Street School in North Syracuse.

When people first meet Louis and find out that he is autistic, the conversation usually goes something like this.

I call it, Aren't You Lucky.

"Oh," they say, "Louis is autistic? But he looks like a typical child. Aren't you lucky to have found out at such a young age?"

Yes, we are lucky. My sister happens to be a developmental pediatrician and realized something was not right with Louis when he was 12 months old. My sister insisted (and my pediatrician grudgingly agreed) that we have Louis' hearing tested! We progressed with testing (nothing intensive) until we had a diagnosis of speech delay. We started home-based speech therapy with minimal progress. Louis literally hid under my clothes. We then proceeded to Strong Memorial Hospital in Rochester for more complete testing. Louis was diagnosed with pervasive development disorder, not otherwise specified (PDD-NOS). When we came home, we started looking for a total communication based program. Louis' lack of eye contact and poor communication and socialization skills made him a great candidate for school-based programming. He needed to be away from Mommy and make his own friends. My best friend has a nine-year-old son with fragile X syndrome, so I called her.

"Aren't you lucky," they say, "that your best friend has gone through this before you. I'm sure with her guidance you were able to avoid some bumps along your way."

Oh yes, we were lucky. My girlfriend, Janet, helped us sort through doctors' reports, paperwork, and explained the Onondaga county world of early intervention to us. With Janet's encouragement and her son Chad's progress in mind, my husband and I went to look at Main Street School in North Syracuse. We visited what would be Louis' classroom. The student-teacher interaction we saw was unbelievable! These were loving, caring teachers with only the child's best interest in mind. These children were learning, growing, and having a good time. After we finished our guided tour, all our questions and concerns were thoroughly answered by the vice principal. When we left there, my husband and I were comfortable with our decision. Louis would go to Main Street three days a week for a half day, with three days of speech therapy. We would still keep our home-based speech therapy. We wanted the therapist to help teach Mom and the rest of the family how to communicate with Louis. I would be transporting Louis because the school is 23 miles from home and the bus ride was too long.

"Aren't you lucky," they say, "to have found such a wonderful program, at such a young age, for Louis?"

Yes, Main Street was a wonderful program for Louis. He attended five days a week for three of his four years. He had intensive speech, occupational, and physical therapy along with adapted physical education in both integrated and segregated settings. He also had a private tutor for two or three days a week by a stay-at-home special education teacher with three children of her own. He has also been involved in vitamin therapy, music therapy, and aquatics therapy.

"Wow, aren't you lucky," they say, "to have so much arranged for one little boy. So how did he do?"

Well, it was an extremely hard adjustment for Louis to start at Main Street. He cried and threw up every day for weeks! Can you imagine starting school with no communication skills? After a while he started getting excited when we pulled up to school. He even started to wave good-bye and push me out the door! His eye contact started to improve and his socialization skills started to flourish! He learned how to color, build with blocks, and purposefully play with toys. His speech was slow to progress, but the use of sign communication boards and the patience of his teachers and family helped that along!

"Aren't you lucky," they say, "What do you think has made such a difference for Louis?"

The difference for Louis was early detection and early intervention! Without the dedicated teachers and staff at Main Street School, Louis would still be in his own world. Even though Louis' father and our whole family evolved with Louis, the constant contact with the teachers and staff have taught my family how to help him.

"Aren't you lucky," they say, "How is he doing in kindergarten?"

Wonderfully! He attends a five-day-a-week, half-day program. He now gets speech five days a week, occupational therapy two times a week, and special education services. He can write his name, count to 30, recognize letters, and sight read about 25 words. His social skills are much improved (nothing like learning from a room full of peers). He can keep up with most of what the class is doing. Fine motor skills are still tough for him as well as attending to all his varied activities, but he has assimilated well. He no longer has tantrums and is learning and having fun!! He can't wait to get on the school bus every day!

"Well, aren't you lucky," they say.

Yes, I am!

Adapted from Davis.

Appendix

Forty-Week Curriculum Plan

The following is an example of a 40-week curriculum, broken down into weekly objectives and learning activities. We present this 40-week plan as an illustration only. We encourage you to develop your own plans, based on the unique needs of the children in your movement program. We include some considerations in arranging the weekly objectives and learning experiences in this order. We intend this information to serve as a guide for beginning teachers.

For simplicity, we have chosen not to list all of the curriculum goals for each learning experience under each week of the 40-week curriculum. Only one or two of the four weekly curriculum goals are shown in the appendix. These goals are object control, fitness, motor planning, and locomotor skills. As you use this curriculum and write your own daily lesson plans, you might wish to be more comprehensive in listing the several curriculum goals that can be achieved through each learning experience.

Note how these four goals spiral throughout the curriculum. We revisit each curricular goal throughout the 40 weeks to provide the repetition and refinement children need to achieve the goals. In week 7 the goal is object control, week 8 is fitness and object control, motor planning in week 9, and locomotor skills in week 10. The curriculum then spirals back and revisits the goal of motor planning in week 11, locomotor skills and motor planning in week 12, and so on. In this manner, the goals continually spiral throughout the curriculum. The movement program remains fresh because you are always providing new and exciting learning experiences through which to develop these goals.

Assessment is a primary focus of the first six weeks of the program. Please note that we designed the learning experiences in weeks one through six to enable you to assess the children's skills in all curricular areas. Some of the learning experiences are followed by sentences that describe teaching considerations in arranging the weekly curricular goals and learning experiences.

Week 1

☑ **Curricular goal—Object control (assess body part identification).**

Roll the Ball Name Game

This game helps in learning names and getting acquainted.

Big on Balloons

This game helps you assess and record which children know their body parts.

Bean Bag Activities and Coordination Skills (musical activity tape)

This game also helps assess and teach body parts.

Stickers on the Body Part

Learning body parts is important early in the year so you can use the body part terminology in teaching.

Week 2

☑ **Curricular goals—Fitness and motor planning (assess balance).**

Activities from Let's Balance

Obstacle Course 3, emphasizing balance

Week 3

☑ **Curricular goal—Locomotor skills (assess jumping and climbing).**

Activities from Let's Get Jumping

Assess jumping first because it is more fundamental than hopping or skipping. You may not be ready to have the entire class running. Wait to assess running until week six or later, when the entire class has learned the classroom routines.

Activities from Let's Get Climbing

Assess climbing, especially stair climbing.

Week 4

☑ **Curricular goal—Object control (assess throwing, catching, and kicking).**

Pendulum Bowling

This station keeps the balloons under control, so it is easy to manage, freeing you to assess the children's throw, catch, and kick.

Activities from Let's Get Catching, Throwing, and Kicking

Use the pendulum in catching and kicking skill assessment and adjust the height of the ball off the floor.

Week 5

☑ **Curricular goal—Motor planning (assess motor planning).**

Obstacle Course

Identify which children can move sequentially among pieces of equipment.

Tricycle Course

Assess tricycle riding and begin adapting mobility equipment as needed.

Week 6

☑ **Curricular goal—Fitness and locomotor skills (assess game playing skills and all locomotor skills).**

Stop and Go to Music

Introduce a group game with one simple rule—stop and go with the music.

Musical Hoops

Assess running and other locomotor skills, now that children have learned the classroom routines.

Scooter Play

Assessment is complete. Begin spiraling objectives throughout the curriculum.

Week 7

☑ **Curricular goal—Object control.**

Roll the Pumpkin

Activities from Let's Get Catching, Throwing, and Kicking

Week 8

☑ **Curricular goal—Fitness**

Hand-Over-Hand Pull

Body Bowling

Week 9

☑ **Curricular goal—Motor planning.**

Superstars Challenge

Roller Racer Course

Using the roller racer is a difficult skill to learn, so do not introduce it until now, when the children can better follow verbal cues.

Roller Skating

(continued)

Week 10

☑ **Curricular goal—Fitness and locomotor skills.**

Zip Line

The child needs to develop trust in you before you introduce this activity.

Swings

Activities from Let's Get Climbing using large climbing structures

Week 11

☑ **Curricular goal—Motor planning.**

Tunnel Course

Obstacle Course

Week 12

☑ **Curricular goals—Locomotor skills and motor planning.**

Vegetable Soup

Goldilocks and the Three Bears

Sack Races

Match Tag

Week 13

☑ **Curricular goal—Locomotor skills.**

Obstacle Course

Mat Maze

Swings

Week 14

☑ **Curricular goal—Locomotor skills.**

Activities from Let's Get Jumping

Move and Seek

Imagination Tag

Week 15

☑ **Curricular goal—Object control.**

Activities from Let's Get Catching, Throwing, and Kicking

Basketball With Water Balloons

Week 16

☑ **Curricular goal—Object control.**
      Pendulum Bowling
      Puzzle Pieces
      Activity from Let's Get Catching, Throwing, and Kicking

Week 17

☑ **Curricular goal—Motor planning.**
      Mountains and Valleys
      Zip Line

Week 18

☑ **Curricular goal—Fitness.**
      American Heart Association Heart Power Kit

Week 19

☑ **Curricular goals—Fitness and locomotor skills.**
      Activities from Let's Get Jumping
      Tire Play
      Scooter Pull

Week 20

☑ **Curricular goal—Locomotor skills.**
      I'm the Man From Mars
      Imagination Tag
      Vegetable Soup
      Scrambled Eggs

Week 21

☑ **Curricular goal—Object control.**
      Bubble Fun
      Cage Ball Fun
      Big on Balloons

(continued)

Week 22

☑ **Curricular goal—Motor planning.**
     Obstacle Course
     Tricycle Course

Week 23

☑ **Curricular goal—Locomotor skills.**
     Toothbrush Tag
     Musical Hoops
     Match Tag
     Match the Valentine

Week 24

☑ **Curricular goal—Motor planning.**
     Roller Skating
     Obstacle Course
     Mountains and Valleys

Week 25

☑ **Curricular goal—Motor planning.**
     Activities from Let's Balance

Week 26

☑ **Curricular goals—Locomotor skills and motor planning.**
     Turtle Races
     Activities from Let's Get Jumping
     Obstacle Course

Week 27

☑ **Curricular goal—Motor planning.**
     Tunnel Course
     Tricycle Course

Week 28

✔ **Curricular goals—Fitness and motor planning.**
   Hand-Over-Hand Pull
   Roller Racer Course
   Push and Pull
   Obstacle Course

Week 29

✔ **Curricular goal—Locomotor skills.**
   Stop and Go to Music
   Musical Hoops
   Midnight
   Red Light, Green Light

Week 30

✔ **Curricular goal—Locomotor skills.**
   Activities from Let's Get Jumping

Week 31

✔ **Curricular goals—Object control and fitness.**
   Gutter Ball
   Tire Play

Week 32

✔ **Curricular goal—Object control.**
   Garbage Clean Up
   Big on Balloons
   Puzzle Pieces

Week 33

✔ **Curricular goal—Motor planning.**
   Obstacle Course
   Tricycle Course

(continued)

Week 34

☑ **Curricular goal—Motor planning.**
Tunnel Course
Activities from Let's Balance

Week 35

☑ **Curricular goals—Fitness and object control.**
Push and Pull
Bubble Fun
Basketball With Water Balloons

Week 36

☑ **Curricular goal—Locomotor skills.**
I'm the Man From Mars
Midnight
Red Light, Green Light
Move and Seek
Increase the complexity in the group games to prepare five-year-old children for kindergarten.

Week 37

☑ **Curricular goal—Locomotor skills.**
Activities from Let's Get Climbing
Obstacle Course

Week 38

☑ **Curricular goal—Object control.**
Big on Balloons
Let's Get Catching, Throwing, and Kicking
Frisbee Toss
Gutter Ball

Week 39

☑ **Curricular goal—Locomotor skills.**
Scrambled Eggs
Mat Maze
Goldilocks and the Three Bears
Match Tag

Week 40

☑ **Curricular goal—Motor planning.**
Obstacle Course
Tricycle Course

> The tricycle course is an all-time favorite activity enjoyed once more at the end of the year.

References

American Physical Therapy Association. 1995. *Guide to physical therapy practice.* Alexandria, VA: American Physical Therapy Association.

Avery, M., S. Boos, S. Chepko, C. Gabbard, and S. Sanders. 1994. *Developmentally appropriate practices in movement programs for young children ages 3-5: A position statement of the National Association for Sport and Physical Education (NASPE) developed by the Council on Physical Education for Children (COPEC).* Reston, VA: American Alliance for Health, Physical Education, Recreation, and Dance.

Batshaw, M., and Y. Perret. 1992. *Children with disabilities: A medical primer.* 3rd ed. Baltimore: Paul H. Brookes.

Block, M. 1994. A teacher's guide to including students with disabilities in regular physical education. Baltimore: Paul H. Brookes.

Block, M., and T. Davis. 1996. An activity-based approach to physical education for preschool children with disabilities. *Adapted Physical Activity Quarterly* 13: 230-246.

Bloodstein, O. 1979. *Speech pathology: An introduction.* Boston: Houghton Mifflin.

Bricker, D., and J.J. Cripe. 1992. *An activity-based approach to early intervention.* Baltimore: Brookes.

Charlesworth, R. 1992. *Understanding child development.* 3rd ed. Albany, NY: Delmar.

Coleman, J. 1993. *The early intervention dictionary.* Rockville, MD: Woodbine House.

Covey, S. 1990. The seven habits of highly effective people: Powerful lessons for personal change. Wichita, KS: Fireside.

Davis, W., and A. Burton. 1991. Ecological task analysis: Translating movement behavior theory into practice. *Adapted Physical Activity Quarterly* 8(2): 154-177.

Education for All Handicapped Children Act of 1986, Sec. 121a.550.

Federal Register, Section 300.350 Code of referral regulations 34, Parts 300 to 303 revised as of July 1, 1993.

Ferrell, K.A. 1985. *Reach out and teach.* New York: American Foundation for the Blind.

Gallahue, D.L. 1989. *Motor development: Infants, children, adults.* Dubuque, IA: Brown and Benchmark, 169-175.

Gallahue, D. 1995. Motor development. In *Adapted physical education and sport,* edited by J. Winnick, 253-269. Champaign, IL: Human Kinetics.

Gallahue, D. 1996. *Developmental physical education for today's children.* 3d ed. Dubuque, IA: Brown and Benchmark.

Greenburg, David E. 1989. Preschool special education: New responsibility for schools. *Updating School Board Policies* 201(10): 1-2.

Hall, S. 1999. *Basic biomechanics.* 3d ed. Boston: McGraw-Hill.

Hancock, LynNell, and Pat Wingert. 1997. The new preschool. *Newsweek, special issue* spring/summer, 36-37.

Horvat, M., and L. Kalakian. 1996. *Assessment in adapted physical education and therapeutic recreation.* 2d ed. Dubuque, IA: McGraw-Hill.

IDEA Amendments of 1997, Sec. 602 (22) Definitions.

IDEA, 42 Fed. Reg. No. 163, Aug. 1997, pp. 42479-42480.

Kimiecik, S., K. Demas, and C. Demas. 1994. Establishing credibility: Proactive approaches. *Journal of Physical Education, Recreation, and Dance* 65(7): 38-42.

Krause, W., and H. Richter. 1998. Computer kids: Lack of movement and physical fitness in childhood. In *Paediatric osteology: Proceedings of the conference on prevention of osteoporosis-a paediatric task?* edited by E. Schonau and V. Matkovic. Singapore: Elsevier Science.

Kubler-Ross, E. 1997. *On death and dying.* New York: Simon and Schuster.

Linder, T. 1993. *Transdisciplinary play-based assessment: A functional approach to working with young children.* Baltimore: Paul H. Brookes.

Miles, E. 1997. *Tune your brain: Using music to manage your mind, body, and mood.* New York: Berkley Books.

Mosston, M., and S. Ashworth. 1994. *Teaching physical education.* New York: Macmillan.

Nash, Madeline J. 1997. Fertile Minds. *Time,* February 3.

Pica, R. 1998. Movement and the brain. *Teaching Elementary Physical Education* 9(6): 18-19.

Ratliffe, T. 1986. Influencing the principal: What the physical educator can do. *Journal of Physical Education, Recreation, and Dance* 57(5): 86-87.

Schweinhart, L.J. 1988. How important is child initiated activity? *Principal* 67(5): 6-10.

Sharkey, B. 1997. *Fitness and health.* 4th ed. Champaign, IL: Human Kinetics.

Sherrill, C. 1993. *Adapted physical activity, recreation and sport: Crossdisciplinary and lifespan.* 4th ed. Dubuque, IA: Brown and Benchmark.

Torbert, M., and L. Schneider. 1993. *Follow me too: A handbook of movement activities for three to five year olds.* New York: Addison-Wesley.

University of the State of New York, State Education Department, Office for Special Education Services. 1997. Reprint. *A parent's guide to special education for children ages 5-21: Your child's right to an education in New York State.* Albany: New York, University of the State of New York, State Education Department, Office for Special Education Services.

U.S. Department of Health and Human Services. 1996. *Physical activity and health: A report of the Surgeon General.* Atlanta: U.S. Department of Health and Human Services, Centers for Disease Control and Prevention, National Center for Chronic Disease Prevention and Health Promotion.

Werder, J., and L. Kalakian. 1985. *Assessment in adapted physical education.* Minneapolis: Burgess.

Wessel, J., and L. Kelly. 1986. *Achievement-based curriculum development in physical education.* Philadelphia: Lea and Febiger.

Wolery, M., M. Jones Ault, and P. Munson Doyle. 1992. *Teaching students with moderate to severe disabilities.* White Plains, NY: Longman.

Zittel, L. 1994. Gross motor assessment of preschool children with special needs: Instrument selection considerations. *Adapted Physical Activity Quarterly* 11: 245-260.

Index

About the Authors

Renée M. McCall, MSEd, directs the adapted physical education department for the early education program in the North Syracuse (NY) school district. She works daily with children in an inclusive preschool environment. She has taught preschool adapted physical education for more than 15 years, beginning her career with the United Cerebral Palsy Center of Central New York.

McCall is a stimulating lecturer, workshop leader, and enthusiastic expert on how to conduct a quality preschool movement program. She has written articles on preschool movement for the *Journal of Physical Education, Recreation and Dance (JOPERD)* and *Teaching Elementary Physical Education* journal.

McCall holds a bachelor's degree in physical education from the State University of New York (SUNY) at Brockport and a master's degree with a concentration in adapted physical education from SUNY at Cortland. She is a frequent guest lecturer and college adjunct instructor on the topics of preschool movement and adapted physical education.

Diane H. Craft, PhD, is a professor in the department of physical education at State University of New York (SUNY) at Cortland. She teaches adapted physical education and supervises practica providing physical

education instruction to people with disabilities. She is a frequent lecturer and workshop leader, and a nationally recognized leader in adapted physical education.

Dr. Craft is president of the National Consortium of Physical Education and Recreation for Individuals with Disabilities (NCPERID). She devoted 10 years to directing U.S. Department of Education federal training grants in physical education. She also was a visiting professor at Royal Melbourne Institute of Technology.

Before joining the faculty of SUNY Cortland in 1985, Dr. Craft directed the master's and doctoral programs in adapted physical education at New York University. An experienced elementary and high school physical education teacher, Dr. Craft is a committed advocate of including children with disabilities in regular physical education classes. She has written articles for professional journals on including children with disabilities in regular physical education, and she edited a feature on the subject for *JOPERD*. She also has contributed chapters on learning disabilities and sensory impairments to Joseph Winnick's textbook *Adapted Physical Education and Sport*.

Other Books From Human Kinetics

Physical Activities for Improving Children's Learning and Behavior
A Guide to Sensory Motor Development
Billye Ann Cheatum, PhD, and Allison Hammond, EdD
2000 • Paperback • 360 pp • ISBN 0-88011-874-1
$19.95 ($29.95 Canadian)

Authors Cheatum and Hammond, who together have worked in the special physical education field for more than 40 years, explain the complexities of sensory motor development in easily understood language. And they include more than 130 photos and illustrations of developmental processes and activities to help you understand and implement the information presented.

Movement Activities for Early Childhood
Carol Totsky Hammett, MS
1992 • Paperback • 152 pp • ISBN 0-87322-352-7
$16.00 ($23.95 Canadian)

This collection of 100+ child-tested movement activities makes learning new skills fun for preschoolers. Every activity, from crawling and creeping to jumping and landing, is presented in an easy-to-use format that includes an outline of the skills stressed, objectives, procedures, equipment, teaching hints, variations, and safety considerations. The book also offers numerous resources for equipment and music, as well as resources for further ideas.

YMCA Water Fitness for Health
Mary Sanders (and others)
2000 • Paperback • 368 pp • ISBN 0-7360-3246-0
$35.00 ($52.50 Canadian)

Water fitness is a form of exercise that people of all ages and fitness levels can participate in. *YMCA Water Fitness for Health* is an excellent resource to assist instructors in developing a program that keeps students coming back, class after class. The text integrates water exercise research, fundamental water skills, and training guidelines to assist instructors in helping students reach their individual fitness goals.

Inclusive Games
Susan L. Kasser, MS
1995 • Paperback • 120 pp • ISBN 0-87322-639-9
$14.95 ($21.95 Canadian)

Inclusive Games is an easy-to-follow, hands-on guide that no preschool, elementary, or middle school physical educator or recreation specialist should be without. The book features more than 50 inclusive games, helpful illustrations, and hundreds of game variations. *Inclusive Games* shows you how to adapt games so that children of every ability level can practice, play, and improve their movement skills together.

Movement Skill Assessment
Allen W. Burton, PhD, and Daryl E. Miller
1998 • Hardback • 416 pp • ISBN 0-87322-975-4
$35.00 ($52.50 Canadian)

This unique text focuses exclusively on the assessment of movement skills, offering background information, discussions of six levels of movement skill assessment, and strategies for implementation. Filled with information on more than 150 tests and including more than 650 references, the book emphasizes a top-down, functional approach to the assessment of movement skills.

To request more information or to order, U.S. customers call 1-800-747-4457, e-mail us at **humank@hkusa.com,** or visit our Web site at **www.humankinetics.com.** Persons outside the U.S. can contact us via our Web site or use the appropriate telephone number, postal address, or e-mail address shown in the front of this book.

HUMAN KINETICS
The Information Leader in Physical Activity
P.O. Box 5076, Champaign, IL 61825-5076
2335